Apache Cordova in Action

D0473254

Apache Cordova in action
33305234299935
6an   12/28/15

Apache Cordova in Action

RAYMOND K. CAMDEN

MANNING

SHELTER ISLAND

For online information and ordering of this and other Manning books, please visit
www.manning.com. The publisher offers discounts on this book when ordered in quantity.
For more information, please contact

> Special Sales Department
> Manning Publications Co.
> 20 Baldwin Road
> PO Box 761
> Shelter Island, NY 11964
> Email: orders@manning.com

©2016 by Manning Publications Co. All rights reserved.

No part of this publication may be reproduced, stored in a retrieval system, or transmitted, in
any form or by means electronic, mechanical, photocopying, or otherwise, without prior written
permission of the publisher.

Many of the designations used by manufacturers and sellers to distinguish their products are
claimed as trademarks. Where those designations appear in the book, and Manning
Publications was aware of a trademark claim, the designations have been printed in initial caps
or all caps.

♾ Recognizing the importance of preserving what has been written, it is Manning's policy to have
the books we publish printed on acid-free paper, and we exert our best efforts to that end.
Recognizing also our responsibility to conserve the resources of our planet, Manning books are
printed on paper that is at least 15 percent recycled and processed without elemental chlorine.

 Manning Publications Co.
20 Baldwin Road
PO Box 761
Shelter Island, NY 11964

Development editor:	Helen Stergius
Technical development editor:	Doug Warren
Copyeditor:	Jodie Allen
Proofreader:	Elizabeth Martin
Technical proofreader:	Cody Sand
Typesetter:	Marija Tudor
Cover designer:	Marija Tudor

ISBN: 9781633430068
Printed in the United States of America
1 2 3 4 5 6 7 8 9 10 – EBM – 20 19 18 17 16 15

contents

I've been fortunate to have been a web developer for approximately 20 years. I can remember using NCSA Mosaic to browse the web and picking up HTML books to help me build my first web page. (Yes, I used a rainbow gradient back then.) Things were rough in those days. I can remember playing with LiveScript, the initial release of JavaScript, and having to reboot my entire machine at times to get my browser to work. I spent a good deal of my first decade or so as a developer focused on the server side, first with Perl and then with ColdFusion. I ignored the front-end due to the numerous issues with browsers and, pretty much, just the browsers themselves.

Approximately 10 years ago, I turned my attention back to the client side. I was surprised to find that this Web 2.0/AJAX thing was actually kind of cool, and that, for the most part, it actually worked. I began to spend most of my time learning JavaScript (again) and reacquainting myself with HTML. That may sound like a surprising statement. I certainly *knew* HTML and used it in my server-side applications, but I discovered that when I looked closely, there was quite a bit I didn't know and didn't appreciate.

At the same time, mobile was slowly inching along toward being a big deal. I kept hearing about how big it was in Europe and Asia, but my experience with it was disappointing. I loved my Motorola RAZR, but the first time I sent an SMS message with it was also the last time I sent an SMS message with it. Browsing the web on it was also an exercise in frustration.

And then one day … everything changed. The iPhone was a game changer—it made using the mobile web useful. And when the app market was launched, and folks made millions with fart apps, a whole new breed of developer was born. I began focusing on working on the mobile platform, specifically building mobile-friendly websites. Then one day I discovered PhoneGap (the originator of Apache Cordova—don't worry, we'll discuss the differences in chapter 1). It was rough too—it took me a good 10 minutes or so to get the "Hello World" project set up. But when I first saw my HTML running as an app on my phone, it was incredible. Everything I had learned about web development was now enabling me to create applications on mobile devices—and not just one, but many.

PhoneGap, and Cordova, have come a long way since I began working with them. The platform is simpler to use, but still requires careful consideration and planning, and this is where I think this book will really help. I tried to take information found in multiple sources and bring it together in a concise, easy-to-follow format. I'm not terribly smart. In fact, I struggle a lot. But I've made a career out of taking my struggle and turning that into writing and presentations that will—I hope—help others with their struggles as well.

acknowledgments

This book was a lot of work. No, make that *really a lot* of work! But I believe that this is a great book, and I hope that you will think so as well. There are quite a few people I'd like to thank for helping me along the way.

First and foremost, I want to thank my wife, Jeanne. You've always supported me, always patiently listened while I struggled to get this done, and always made me believe I could finish this. I love you.

Next, I'd like to acknowledge my editor at Manning, Helen Stergius. Thank you for working with me, and thank you more for being patient when things got rough. Your commitment to the quality of this book has made it better for everyone who reads it. Thanks as well to all the other folks at Manning who worked with me on the production and promotion of the book. It was truly a team effort.

I'd also like to thank the reviewers who took the time to read my manuscript at various stages during its development and who provided invaluable feedback: Barry Alexander, Becky Huett, Charlie Gaines, Chris Snow, Chris Wayman, Doug Warren, Greg Murray, Ivo Štimac, Jérôme Baton, Matt Royten, Michael E. Roberts, Natalia Stavisky, Satish Kumar Bairi, and Yogesh Poojari. Special thanks to Cody Sand, technical proofreader, for his careful review of the code one last time, shortly before the book went into production.

Finally, thank you to the entire PhoneGap and Apache Cordova team. You've created something that's incredibly cool and useful for developers around the world. Thank you to Shazron Abdullah, Brian LeRoux, Michael Brooks, and others for answering my questions and helping make this book happen.

about this book

Apache Cordova in Action was written to help you build hybrid mobile applications for the Apache Cordova framework. It begins by focusing on the mechanics of setting up your development environment and then switches its focus to the intangibles of working with hybrid mobile development—things like design, best practices, and what to do when things go wrong.

How the book is organized

The book has three sections that cover 12 chapters.

Part 1 explains what Apache Cordova covers and how to set up your development environment.

- Chapter 1 discusses the Apache Cordova project and what a hybrid mobile application actually is. It also discusses what Cordova does and doesn't provide, even discussing when you would *not* want to use a hybrid mobile application.
- Chapter 2 goes deep into setting up all the necessary parts required to do Cordova development with Android. Because the iOS SDK requires a Mac but Android will work anywhere, the book focuses on explaining Android's requirements, as well as what you need to get the Cordova CLI installed.

Part 2 covers high-level core concepts for working with Apache Cordova.

- Chapter 3 discusses the Cordova CLI and how it's used to create projects. It also discusses what makes up a Cordova project.

- Chapter 4 describes what plugins mean in a Cordova project and how to make use of them. It contains multiple examples of how to use plugins.
- Chapter 5 begins the discussion of how to use a mobile-friendly design for your Cordova applications. Bootstrap is demonstrated and other frameworks are discussed.
- Chapter 6 discusses other considerations for Cordova projects, including things like detecting network status and client-side storage.
- Chapter 7 goes deep into the topic of debugging. Multiple debugging techniques are described.
- Chapter 8 describes the process of creating custom plugins, with a full example of an Android plugin.
- Chapter 9 discusses how to package your applications so they can be released and discusses creating custom icons and splash-screens.
- Chapter 10 demonstrates Adobe PhoneGap Build as an alternative to using a local SDK to build apps.

Part 3 covers the next steps required for a successful application release.

- Chapter 11 describes in deep detail the process of submitting your application to both the Android and Apple stores.
- Chapter 12 ends the book with a demo of a real (if simple) application.

Who should read this book

Apache Cordova in Action is for web developers who are looking to enter the mobile space by building hybrid mobile applications. Both beginner and experienced web developers will be able to learn how to use their skills within the Cordova framework. While plenty of docs and blog posts exist online, this book brings together everything in a very clear, very easy-to-follow format that will benefit anyone wanting to become a mobile developer.

How to use this book

In general, developers should be sure to read the first two chapters so that their development environment is correctly set up. Chapters 3 and 4 provide important information about using Cordova itself. The rest of the book discusses topics like design, best practices, and debugging, and can be read out of order, based on the reader's particular needs.

About the code

All source code in the book is presented in a `monospaced typeface like this`, which sets it off from the surrounding text. In many listings, the code is annotated to point out key concepts, and numbered bullets are sometimes used in the text to provide additional information about the code.

Source code for the examples in this book is available for download from the publisher's website at www.manning.com/books/apache-cordova-in-action.

Online resources

Need additional help?

- The PhoneGap Google Group at groups.google.com/forum/#!forum/phonegap provides a great place to discuss topics related to PhoneGap (and Cordova) development.
- The Cordova tag at StackOverflow (stackoverflow.com/questions/tagged/cordova) is a great place to both ask questions and help others. Helping someone else is a great way to learn!

Author Online

Purchase of *Apache Cordova in Action* includes free access to a private web forum run by Manning Publications where you can make comments about the book, ask technical questions, and receive help from the author and from other users. To access the forum and subscribe to it, point your web browser to www.manning.com/books/apache-cordova-in-action. This page provides information on how to get on the forum once you're registered, what kind of help is available, and the rules of conduct on the forum.

Manning's commitment to our readers is to provide a venue where a meaningful dialog between individual readers and between readers and the author can take place. It is not a commitment to any specific amount of participation on the part of the author, whose contributions to the AO remain voluntary (and unpaid). We suggest you ask the author challenging questions, lest his interest stray.

About the Author

RAYMOND CAMDEN is a web developer with nearly 20 years of experience. He has been a PhoneGap/Cordova user for most of the history of the project and has spoken at multiple conferences around the world on mobile development. He has a passion for web standards and helping explain complex topics to people in a way that is easy to understand as well as inspiring.

about the cover illustration

The figure on the cover of *Apache Cordova in Action* is captioned "A Shepherd from Gonesse, France." The illustration is taken from a collection of traditional French costumes by Nicolas Bonnart (1637-1717). The drawings are hand-colored engravings on paper that depict the various styles of dress popular in Paris and its suburbs in the seventeenth and eighteenth centuries. Gonesse is a small town about 15 kilometers northeast of Paris.

Dress codes and lifestyles have changed over the last 300 years, and the diversity by region, so rich at the time, has faded away. It is now hard to tell apart the inhabitants of different continents, let alone of different hamlets or towns separated by only a few miles. Perhaps we have traded cultural diversity for a more varied personal life—certainly for a more varied and fast-paced technological life.

Manning celebrates the inventiveness and initiative of the computer business with book covers based on the rich diversity of regional life of three centuries ago, brought back to life by illustrations from old books and collections such as this one.

Part 1

Getting started with Apache Cordova

In these first two chapters, you'll learn about hybrid mobile applications and how Apache Cordova fits into their development. We'll look at what Cordova provides and what it doesn't, and when a hybrid app isn't always the best solution. You also will learn how to set up your environment for Cordova development with Android.

In chapter 1, you'll learn how Cordova and PhoneGap relate and what Cordova does and does not provide. Chapter 2 explains how to install the Android SDK and other prerequisites, how to install Cordova, and how to create your first Cordova project.

What is Cordova? 1

This chapter covers

- The history of PhoneGap (and Cordova)
- How Cordova and PhoneGap relate
- What Cordova does and doesn't provide
- When you wouldn't use Cordova

Mobile development is one of the most important skills a developer can learn. The past decade has seen an explosion of mobile devices, from smartphones to tablets, creating an ecosystem of applications covering everything from the silly (remember the fart app?) to the life changing. Learning how to develop for mobile platforms is an important skill to acquire, but it isn't something you can pick up quickly. Wouldn't it be nice if there were a way to reuse the skills you already have as a web developer to create mobile applications? To take those skills and develop not just for one mobile platform but for multiple ones at once?

This is where Cordova enters the picture. Cordova is an open source framework that lets you convert HTML, JavaScript, and Cascading Style Sheets (CSS) into a native application that can run on iOS, Android, and other mobile platforms. Cordova uses a native "wrapper" around a web view (think of it as an embedded

Native application wrapper made with Cordova

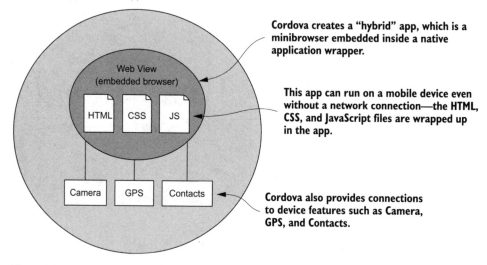

Cordova creates a "hybrid" app, which is a minibrowser embedded inside a native application wrapper.

This app can run on a mobile device even without a network connection—the HTML, CSS, and JavaScript files are wrapped up in the app.

Cordova also provides connections to device features such as Camera, GPS, and Contacts.

Figure 1.1   A simple diagram of how a hybrid app works

browser), commonly called a *hybrid mobile application*. It also provides access to hardware features like the camera and accelerometer. Unlike a simple web page, Cordova applications can be found (and sold!) in app stores just like native-developed applications. Figure 1.1 gives you a visual demonstration of how hybrid mobile applications work. Let's look at how Cordova came about and what it gives developers.

As a concrete example, imagine your web page wants to let a user select a friend from the contact list to receive a free kitten. (Kittens!) Right now, HTML pages running in a mobile browser have no access to contacts on the device, but a native app does. Cordova would let you write JavaScript to work with the user's contacts and do amazing things (with kittens) in a native application.

Other options exist for building mobile applications without native code. Titanium by Appcelerator (www.appcelerator.com/titanium/) is one such example. While it lets you build mobile applications, it doesn't rely on web standards and primarily uses JavaScript. This allows the tool to build straight to native code and skip using a web view like Cordova, but it may not be as friendly, or familiar, to web developers.

1.1   *The history of PhoneGap (and Cordova)*

To talk about Cordova we have to begin with PhoneGap. PhoneGap was created by Nitobi in 2008. Released as an open source and free product, it quickly became popular among developers who wanted to work on mobile platforms but didn't know how to develop using native languages. Developers could use their *existing* skills in client-side development for websites to build mobile apps.

When it launched, PhoneGap provided simple JavaScript APIs to work with native features on the device. At first only a few features were supported. But over time

PhoneGap grew to encompass most of the features native developers had grown accustomed to, including the camera, filesystem, and notifications.

On Oct. 4, 2011, Adobe announced the acquisition of Nitobi. At the same time, the PhoneGap project was submitted to the Apache Software Foundation (ASF). Originally the name Apache Callback was used, but for ease of searching the web, it was changed to Cordova.

1.2 How PhoneGap and Cordova relate

Now we turn to the great naming controversy. Anyone who has spent time working with PhoneGap, or Cordova, has run into the problem of figuring out the difference between the two and which one they should use. Let's try to clear this up now so you can stop worrying about it and start building cool mobile applications quicker.

Cordova, or more officially Apache Cordova, is the open source project managed under the ASF. So what does that make PhoneGap? PhoneGap is Adobe's implementation of the Cordova project. That makes perfect sense, right? Probably not. How about a real example. For a long time, two browsers, Chrome and Safari, made use of an open source project called WebKit (www.webkit.org/). While both were based on the same open source project, they were pretty different browsers. You can think of PhoneGap the same way. PhoneGap is still open source (https://github.com/phonegap), but Adobe has added services around PhoneGap that aren't free.

1.2.1 How are they the same?

Here's the important question. What can you do with Cordova versus PhoneGap? As noted earlier, the project launched with support for a few features. Over time this list grew to cover pretty much everything you could imagine. When it comes to Cordova versus PhoneGap, what you can do is no different using one or the other. Want to make use of the camera? It works in both. Want to access a device's filesystem and manipulate files? Both Cordova and PhoneGap support that. As a practical manner in terms of what you can do, it doesn't matter! When you use either tool to build a mobile application, the end result is precisely the same.

1.2.2 How do they differ?

With that said, there are a few things you want to keep in mind. The command-line tool for PhoneGap versus Cordova is slightly different. They're close enough where you can easily use one or the other, and the general approach will be the same, but the peculiarities of each command-line tool *is* different. As a developer you can use one command line to work on a project and be confident that your core code can be handed to another developer or the client who may be using the other command-line tool. The biggest difference is that the PhoneGap command-line tool integrates with Adobe's commercial PhoneGap Build service. (This will be discussed in chapter 10.) To keep things simple, this book will use the Cordova command-line tool.

Another practical issue to keep in mind is that most folks continue to use "PhoneGap" in their blog posts, their StackOverflow questions, and their resumes. If you were searching for something in particular, like using a camera in your application, you may want to use "PhoneGap camera" as well as "Cordova camera" in your search engine.

1.2.3   *Official websites*

There are two different official websites. For PhoneGap, you'd visit www.phonegap .com, and for Cordova you'd visit http://cordova.apache.org. The PhoneGap site is great for finding sample apps to showcase what the platform can do, as shown in figure 1.2.

The directory contains a large set of apps built with PhoneGap (or Cordova), as well as a set of case studies that go deep into how a particular app was created. If you need to demonstrate to a client that powerful and inspiring apps can be built with the product, then this would be a great resource.

Speaking of clients, if you're reading this book looking to learn more about the platform but expect to hire people to build your application, you can find a list of developers at http://people.phonegap.com, shown in figure 1.3.

As a developer you can use this to find other people to work with, and as a client you can use this to find developers to hire. The site even lets you filter by developers who are actively available for hire.

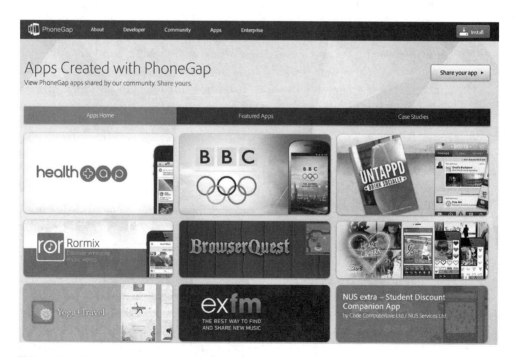

Figure 1.2   The app showcase at the PhoneGap website

Figure 1.3 **Quickly find and connect with PhoneGap/Cordova developers around the world. The number of registered developers is growing daily.**

1.3 *What Cordova provides*

The Cordova project consists of three main features: a command-line tool, access to hardware features, and the ability to support future features.

1.3.1 *Command-line tool*

The command-line tool is used to create projects and compile code to mobile platforms. It takes your source HTML, CSS, and JavaScript and converts them into the native binary required for the platforms supported by Cordova. You'll also use the command-line tool to add support for the features your application uses. The command-line tool can also be used to send your code to either a simulator or a real device. Don't worry if you aren't necessarily a command-line tool ninja. The commands you use day-to-day are relatively simple and you'll quickly become familiar with them.

1.3.2 *Hardware access*

Cordova provides access to various features of the mobile device. For the most part, these are all things that you can't do with "regular" web apps running in the mobile browser. Cordova essentially extends what you can do in JavaScript to give you additional APIs to use in your code. Table 1.1 is a list of these APIs and what they provide.

Table 1.1 Device features Cordova can access

Name	Description	Possible Uses
Battery Status	Reports on battery-level change and low levels	Warning when the battery is low and prompting the user to save
Camera	Provides access to the camera as well as the user's existing pictures	Taking and sharing pictures
Contacts	Searches, creates, edits, and removes contacts	Letting the user find a contact to receive a message from the app
Device	Reports on the device name and OS	Providing options for iOS versus Android
Device Motion and Orientation	Detects device movement and orientation	Detecting a shake to reload data
Dialogs and Vibration	Provides visual, audio, and tactile feedback	Using an alert (visual and audio) to warn a user
File and FileTransfer	Accesses the device's filesystem and upload or download files	Downloading assets to the device for updates
Geolocation	Reports where the device is located	Reporting on the user's location and finding nearby resources
Globalization	Localizes values (dates, numbers, and currencies) to local version	Displaying dates the right way for any country
InAppBrowser	Creates a popup browser	Providing documentation for your app
Media and Media Capture	Records audio and video	Letting users share videos
Network Information	Determines connection status	Warning the user when they go offline
Splashscreen	Provides splash-screen support	Displaying a splash-screen on initial launch and updates
Statusbar	Manages the status bar in Android and iOS	Specifying an overlay or color value
Whitelist	Specifies what remote resources are allowed	Helping prevent security issues from user-created content

1.3.3 *Plugin support*

What about device features not listed here? At the time this chapter was written, the next iPhone hadn't been announced. When it is unveiled, it's possible (but probably not likely) that it will include an attached cowbell. How would you use this new hardware feature from a Cordova application when it isn't supported? Cordova has a plugin API that lets you support *anything* the device supports. It requires that you write custom native code, but once you've done that and paired it with a corresponding JavaScript library, other developers can then easily use the cowbell from the application. Even better, you could then share this code with others so they too can make use of the cowbell in their applications.

This picture came from Cordova's camera support. My code was able to use this API to let me take a picture and then display it within the application itself.

This portion comes from the Color Thief library. It reads the image and determines the most prominent colors.

Figure 1.4 An example of the mashup of the Color Thief library and the camera API.

Of course, there's another huge benefit of using Cordova that isn't listed anywhere in the official docs or marketing material. Because Cordova lets you use client-side technology, you get the benefit of the million or so HTML, CSS, and JavaScript libraries that exist today. Perhaps that's a given, but I really think it bears repeating. As a real (and completely random) example of this, there's a cool little JavaScript library called Color Thief (http://lokeshdhakar.com/projects/color-thief/). It examines a picture and returns the dominant colors. I was able to take this library, mash it with Cordova's camera API, and create an application that lets you take a picture and determine the most important colors. See figure 1.4 for an example. You can find this demo at www.raymondcamden.com/2012/1/13/Demo-of-Color-Palettes-and-PhoneGap.

On top of the million or so existing libraries out there, you can also use the million or so existing APIs available to developers. GitHub, for example, provides an API that lets you do multiple things, including searching for projects. Because you can easily call APIs like this using JavaScript's XHR (AJAX) features, your Cordova projects can also make use of them, and as before, you can combine this with the device-centric features to build incredible apps.

1.4 *What Cordova doesn't provide*

You've already seen that Cordova provides a set of APIs as well as the ability to write your own features not yet supported. But what doesn't Cordova give you out of the box? The

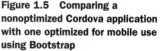

Figure 1.5   Comparing a
nonoptimized Cordova application
with one optimized for mobile use
using Bootstrap

main thing Cordova doesn't do is provide a UI framework for your development. That
means that Cordova will take your HTML, as you code it, and put it on the device. The
HTML (and CSS, of course) you create may not be mobile optimized, and therefore it
may be difficult for people to use on a device. Buttons may be too small to click and text
may be hard to read. Cordova won't "magically" fix these issues for you. Luckily, there
are multiple solutions. As an example, the Bootstrap framework (www.getboot-
strap.com) can be used with your Cordova project to easily make your application more
mobile friendly. In figure 1.5, all that was done was to add one call to the Bootstrap CSS
file and add one class to the button. We'll discuss this in detail in chapter 5.

1.5   When you wouldn't use Cordova

The biggest issue with Cordova and other hybrid solutions is that JavaScript code will
not be as fast as native code written on the device. Gaming is a good example of this.
While a casual game like *Candy Crash* may work well in Cordova, a more graphically
intense game like *Infinity Blade* probably would not. Complex canvas-based animations
aren't going to perform as well as native code would and wouldn't (most likely) be
adequate to give your user a good experience. On the flip slide, a slower puzzle game
could perform perfectly well.

There's no black-and-white guide that will tell you when it is and isn't suitable to
use Cordova. Your best course of action is to research and prototype to see if Cordova
will work for you.

1.6   Web standards and Cordova

In a typical web page, a small HTML mistake may go unnoticed. Most browsers simply
ignore, or silently hide away, a mistake. A small mistake may completely break down a

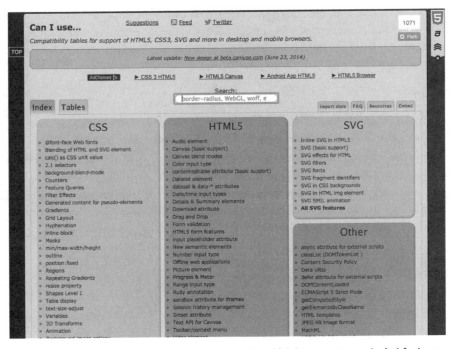

Figure 1.6   www.caniuse.com provides data showing which browsers support what features.

Cordova application. As a developer, you need to be much more cognizant of writing proper code, as well as knowing what your target platforms support. One of the best resources for this is www.caniuse.com, shown in figure 1.6.

This site lets you look up a particular feature and determine what browsers will support it. Because Cordova applications run within a web view on the device, this is important information. While Cordova won't stop you from using a particular feature that isn't supported, it obviously won't make it magically work. Figure 1.7 shows the site's data for SVG filters.

Show all versions	iOS Safari	Android Browser	Blackberry Browser	Chrome for Android	Firefox for Android	IE Mobile
		2.1				
		2.2				
	3.2	2.3				
	4.0-4.1	3.0				
	4.2-4.3	4.0				
	5.0-5.1	4.1				
	6.0-6.1	4.2-4.3	7.0			
Current	7.0-7.1	4.4	10.0	35.0	30.0	10.0
Near future	8.0	4.4.3				

SVG filters - Recommendation

Method of using Photoshop-like effects on SVG objects including blurring and color manipulation.

•Usage stats:	Global
Support:	78.54%
Partial support:	0.05%
Total:	78.59%

Notes   Known issues (1)   Resources (4)   Feedback

Edit on GitHub

No notes

Figure 1.7   Support for SVG filters over mobile browsers

As you can see, scalable vector graphic (SVG) filters are supported in iOS and Android, but only in recent versions. You need to make the determination if that support is sufficient. Android, in particular, suffers from people being stuck in older versions, iOS less so. If iOS is your only target platform, then you're probably pretty safe to use it.

1.7   Summary

Let's review what we covered in this chapter.

- Cordova's biggest strength is letting you reuse your existing skills.
- By a simple-to-use command-line program, you can create projects and send them to mobile devices.
- Cordova provides extensions to web standards to access device-specific features like the camera.

In the next chapter, we'll cover how to install the Cordova command-line tools as well as the mobile software development kits required to start building real projects.

Installing Cordova and the Android SDK

2

This chapter covers

- What mobile SDKs are and why you need them
- How to install the Android SDK and other prerequisites
- How to install Cordova
- How to create your first Cordova project

In chapter 1 you read how wonderful Cordova is because it lets you build mobile applications without having to learn how to develop natively. While that's true, there are a few prerequisites you'll need to set up before Cordova can wield its magic touch. Mobile software development kits (SDKs) are how native developers work with their platform of choice. Apple, Google, Microsoft, and other device manufacturers provide an SDK so that developers can create applications for their platform. Some are free. Some require registration. Some work on one platform but not on others. At the end of the day, the SDK is required to get your creation onto the device (or emulator) of your choice.

Checklist

This chapter walks you through the prerequisites for installing the Android SDK and the Cordova command-line interface (CLI). There's a good chance you may have some, or even all, of them already. Here's a short list that you can check. If you have everything covered, skip down to the "Installing Cordova" section.

Android SDK
Java
Apache Ant
Git
Node.js

At a high level, Cordova has three basic requirements, as shown in figure 2.1. This chapter will detail these requirements and walk you through setting them up.

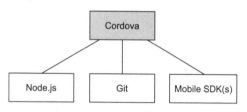

Figure 2.1 Cordova requirements

Cordova works its magic partially by relying on a mobile SDK that you've already installed on your system. It abstracts away the particularities of each individual platform and handles the SDK for you. Essentially, you'll be downloading and installing the "complex" tools of the SDK and letting Cordova handle them for you. There *may* be times when you need to use the SDK directly, and becoming familiar with it will certainly be beneficial, but for your purposes here, we'll have you do the minimal required setup to ensure that the rest of the book goes smoothly for you.

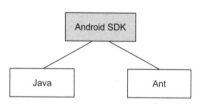

Figure 2.2 Android SDK's requirements

So which SDK will you use here? Android. While the most popular platform is iOS, working with iOS requires a computer running OS X. (In chapter 10 I discuss an alternative using a commercial product, PhoneGap Build.) Android's SDK can be used on Windows, OS X, and Linux. Everything you'll do in this book can be applied to any platform Cordova supports, but to get you up and running from nothing, this chapter will help you set up the Android SDK. After installing the Android SDK I'll walk you through additional prerequisites needed for Android development. Figure 2.2 diagrams Android's requirements.

Run as Administrator

For each of the installations discussed in this chapter, you should probably be an Administrator user on your machine if you're using Windows.

> **Using iOS**
>
> If you're on a Mac and really want to use iOS, you can follow the directions on Apple's website for installing its SDK, as well as Cordova's specific directions at http://cordova.apache.org/docs/en/4.0.0/guide_platforms_ios_index.md.html. Everything described in this book will work for any of the platforms supported by Cordova.

2.1 Installing the Android SDK

To begin working with the Android SDK, point your browser to http://developer.android.com/sdk/index.html. This is the main landing page for the SDK and offers a few options. The default option is a bundled version of the SDK along with Android Studio. While Android Studio is a good editor, you probably already have a favorite editor. Scroll down to Other Download Options to get to the SDK Tools Only section, as shown in figure 2.3.

SDK Tools Only

If you prefer to use a different IDE or run the tools from the command line or with build scripts, you can instead download the standalone Android SDK Tools. These packages provide the basic SDK tools for app development, without an IDE. Also see the SDK tools release notes.

Platform	Package	Size	SHA-1 Checksum
Windows	installer_r24.1.2-windows.exe (Recommended)	111364285 bytes	e0ec864efa0e7449db2d7ed069c03b1f4d36f0cd
	android-sdk_r24.1.2-windows.zip	159778618 bytes	704f6c874373b98e061fe2e7eb34f9fcb907a341
Mac OS X	android-sdk_r24.1.2-macosx.zip	89151287 bytes	00e43ff1557e8cba7da53e4f64f3a34498048256
Linux	android-sdk_r24.1.2-linux.tgz	168121693 bytes	68980e4a26cca0182abb1032abffbb72a1240c51

Figure 2.3 List of options for SDK-only downloads

Based on your current platform, download the option that makes sense for you. For this chapter you'll be using Windows as the platform. Download the recommended .exe installer. Once downloaded, double-click the installer and begin the process shown in figure 2.4.

Figure 2.4 Android SDK Tools Setup Wizard

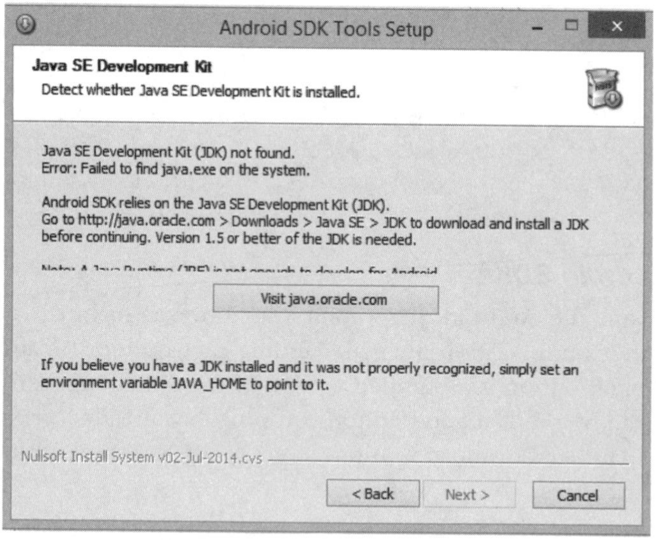

Figure 2.5   Oh no! No Java!

Click Next. For the most part this should be simple, but you may immediately run into a problem if you don't have Java installed, as shown in figure 2.5.

Java is a popular programming language and there's a good chance you already have it installed, but if you don't, follow the directions on the screen shown in figure 2.5 to install the Java Development Kit (JDK). If you've never used Java, don't panic. After installing Java you won't need to worry about it again. Android development uses Java and it's a useful language to pick up in general, but you won't have to think about it once installed. After Java has been detected (or you install it), continue with the wizard, as shown in figure 2.6.

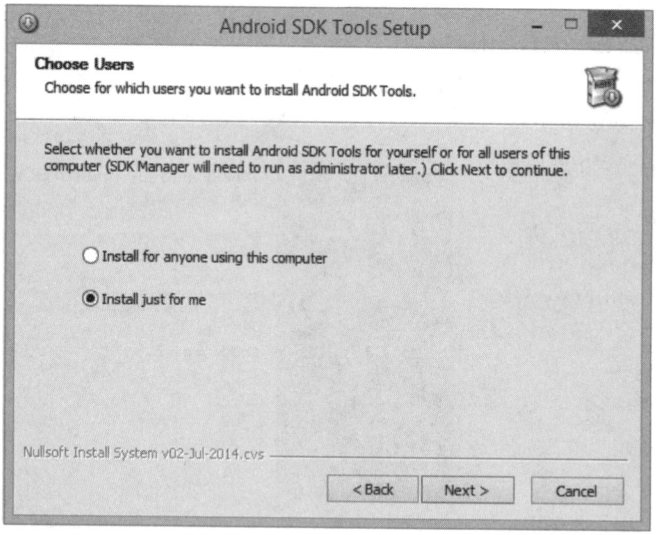

Figure 2.6   Don't even think about it. Click Next.

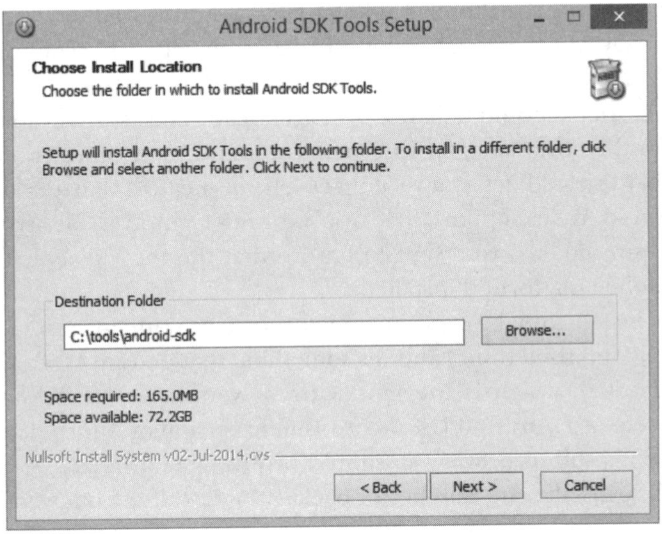

Figure 2.7 Selecting the final installation folder for the SDK

After deciding which users will need access to the SDK (use the default; see figure 2.4), the final step is to specify the installation path. In this case it may be recommended to use a simpler default path. For this book you could use C:\tools as the root directory for the SDK, as shown in figure 2.7.

The last step asks which Start Menu option you want to use. Choose the default and click the final Install button to kick off the process. Once about a thousand or so files have been copied, the installation wizard will prompt you to click Finish and open the SDK Manager, shown in figure 2.8. You want to do this because the SDK Manager is what allows you to work with the emulator.

Figure 2.8 Final screen of the Android SDK installer

The SDK Manager is a simple visual tool that helps keep your Android tools up to date. Running it immediately will give you a way to finalize your setup. I recommend running the SDK Manager every two weeks or so to update the bits.

On your first run, there should be a few options already checked, as shown in figure 2.9. When I run the SDK Manager, I normally accept what it wants to download and let it tell me what I should get. But recent versions of the SDK Manager default to installing only Android Wear support. Because we aren't going to be working on watches (that's a future book!), you want to ensure that the most recent version of Android's default mobile platform is installed.

It's okay if you install things you don't need, but you want to ensure you get Android 4.something or 5.something, and *not* something that ends in W. In figure 2.9 Android 4.4.2 is checked, which is the most current version as of this book, and Android 4.4W isn't selected. Android L is the upcoming version of Android and could be used as well, but it's still in preview so should probably be avoided. After you've made that tweak, click Install. The number of packages may differ from what's shown in figure 2.9.

Again, the idea here is that the SDK Manager is simply completing the process of getting the SDK ready for your system. If this seems a bit complex for now, don't worry. Once you're past this you won't need to worry about it again. This part of the process can take a little while so it may be a great time to grab a cup of coffee. Or two. You can watch the progress bar like that shown in figure 2.10, but note that when the installation

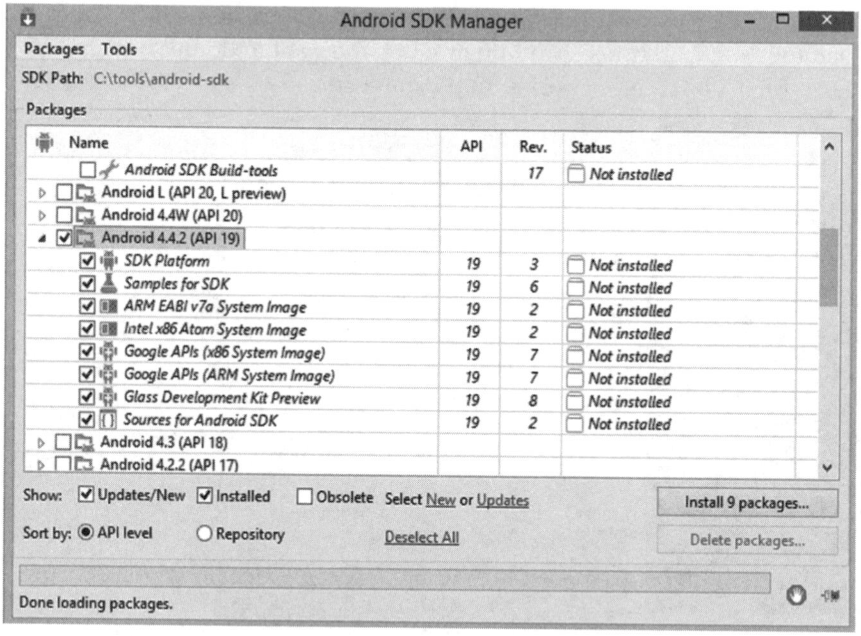

Figure 2.9 The Android SDK Manager

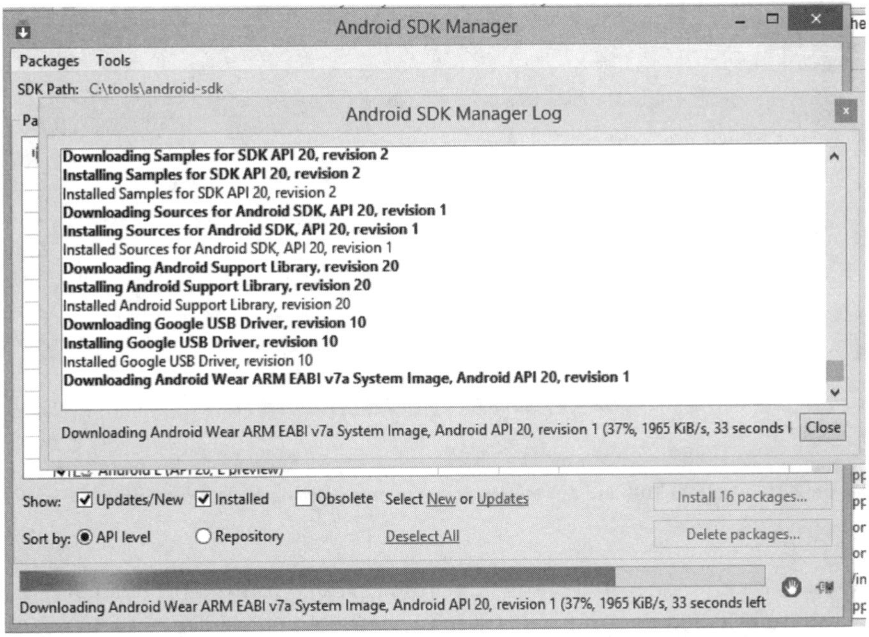

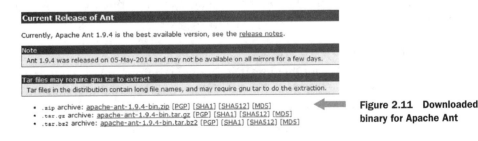

Figure 2.10   The SDK Manager downloading vital assets and tools for the Android SDK

is done, there isn't a good indicator that the process is complete. Basically, if you no longer see the progress bar, you should be good to go.

Once the SDK Manager has finished downloading what it thinks it needs, you can close the program.

2.2   Installing Apache Ant

The next application you'll need is Apache Ant. This is required for Android development. Ant is a platform that has been around for some time and helps developers automate build processes. Essentially, if you've ever found yourself doing a set of steps on your computer multiple times, Ant can help automate that. You've probably heard of Grunt or Gulp, which are similar tools built with JavaScript. You absolutely don't need to know anything about Ant but you do need to install it on your system. Go to http://ant.apache.org, click Binary Distributions, and scroll down to the zip archive, shown in figure 2.11.

Current Release of Ant

Currently, Apache Ant 1.9.4 is the best available version, see the release notes.

Note
Ant 1.9.4 was released on 05-May-2014 and may not be available on all mirrors for a few days.

Tar files may require gnu tar to extract
Tar files in the distribution contain long file names, and may require gnu tar to do the extraction.

* .zip archive: apache-ant-1.9.4-bin.zip [PGP] [SHA1] [SHA512] [MD5]
* .tar.gz archive: apache-ant-1.9.4-bin.tar.gz [PGP] [SHA1] [SHA512] [MD5]
* .tar.bz2 archive: apache-ant-1.9.4-bin.tar.bz2 [PGP] [SHA1] [SHA512] [MD5]

Figure 2.11   Downloaded binary for Apache Ant

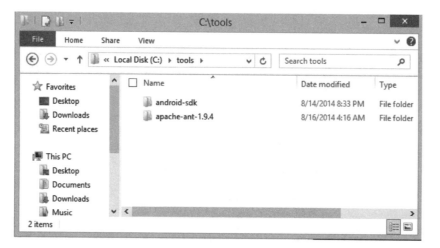

Figure 2.12   Android SDK and Ant installs found in one common tools directory

Ant doesn't have an installer, so extract the zip once you've downloaded it. Earlier you may have installed the Android SDK in C:\tools, so it may make sense to copy the zip to the same root folder. This isn't necessary, but it does make it easier to remember where you've installed these packages and you'll need to know this later. Figure 2.12 demonstrates how your folder may look now.

2.3   Installing Git

The next software package you'll need is Git, a *very* popular source-control tool and there's a strong chance you already have it installed. If you do, skip ahead to the next section. If you aren't using Git, you probably want to start to at some point. An incredible amount of open source software developers make use of Git servers to host their work, and the Git command line will be your main (although not only) way to download those packages. If you aren't using source control at all, then you definitely need to start. That's a topic for another book, of course, but consider this your warning. As with Apache Ant, you don't need to learn Git, it's just another tool used by Cordova. Git's homepage is www.git-scm.com and the Downloads page can be found at http://git-scm.com/downloads, shown in figure 2.13.

As before, choose the version for your OS and begin the download. Git provides a simpler installer and you can accept all the defaults, but ensure that you let Git adjust your PATH environment (this is the default, but just double-check) as shown in figure 2.14.

2.4   Installing Node.js

You're almost there. Yet another tool that Cordova requires, and yet another one highly recommended, is Node.js, Node for short. Node has exploded in popularity over the past few years as a new way to create server-side web applications and command-line

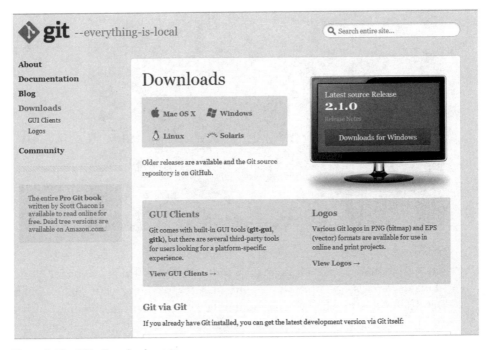

Figure 2.13   Git's Downloads page

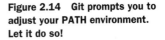

Figure 2.14   Git prompts you to adjust your PATH environment. Let it do so!

tools. Applications in Node are built in JavaScript, so it's very appealing to web developers looking to expand their reach (much like Cordova). Not to sound like a broken record, but you only need to install Node for one particular tool you'll make use of in a minute, but Node is something else worth spending some time on as well.

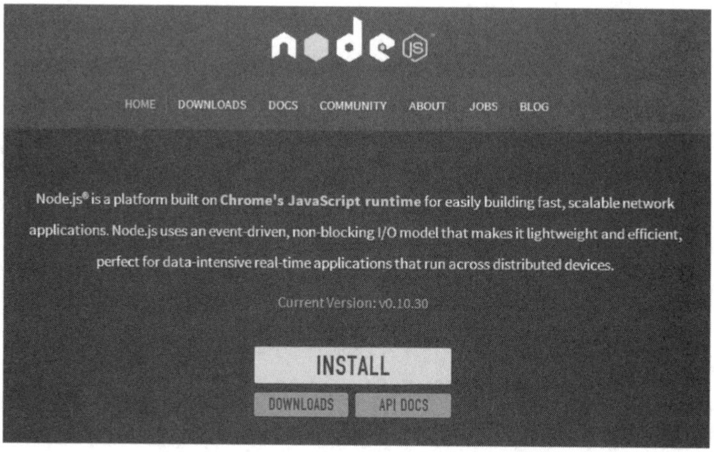

Figure 2.15   The Node homepage provides an easy way to grab the installer.

Node is popular because it includes a tool called npm, which stands for Node Package Manager. npm is a simple way to install software along with all its dependencies. Because of this simplicity, many people have created programs that can be installed via npm, which is exactly how Cordova has done it. Installing Node to get npm will most likely be useful for you going forward as you'll probably encounter other applications asking you to use npm to install them as well. Head over to https://nodejs.org and click the obvious big, green Install button, as shown in figure 2.15. (Node, like other sites, autodetects your OS, so if for some reason you need another platform, simply use the Downloads button.)

As before, you can accept all the defaults. Like the Git installer, Node offers to modify your PATH environment, shown in figure 2.16, and you definitely want to accept that default.

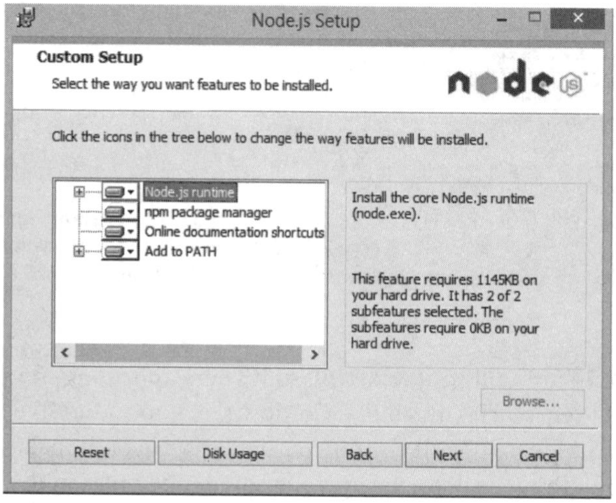

Figure 2.16   During Node's installation process, ensure Add to PATH is enabled.

2.5 *Setting up your PATH*

Congrats, you're almost there! In the last few steps, you were asked to ensure that the installer modified your path. In all OSes, there is a concept of a PATH environment for the command line. When you type in a command, like `foo`, your OS will first see if a command called `foo` exists in the current directory. (Note: In UNIX/OS X-based OSes the current directory isn't checked unless you explicitly specify it.) If it doesn't, it then checks all the folders specified by your PATH environment setting. Folders for tools you use a lot can be added to this setting so that you can run the tools anywhere. For Cordova to make use of the tools you've just downloaded, you need to ensure they are available everywhere. Each OS has its own instructions for how to modify the PATH setting. Because Windows was used earlier, let's demonstrate how it's done there.

Find My Computer (or This PC), right-click, and open the Properties window. From there, choose Advanced System Settings. Click the Environment Variables button.

Most likely the PATH setting in the top portion will be selected already, but you want to work with the System Variables PATH setting instead. Scroll down until you find it, choose it, and click Edit, as shown in figure 2.17.

There are multiple folders that need to be added to the PATH setting:

- Android SDK platform-tools folder
- Android SDK tools folder
- Apache ANT's bin folder
- Java's JDK bin folder

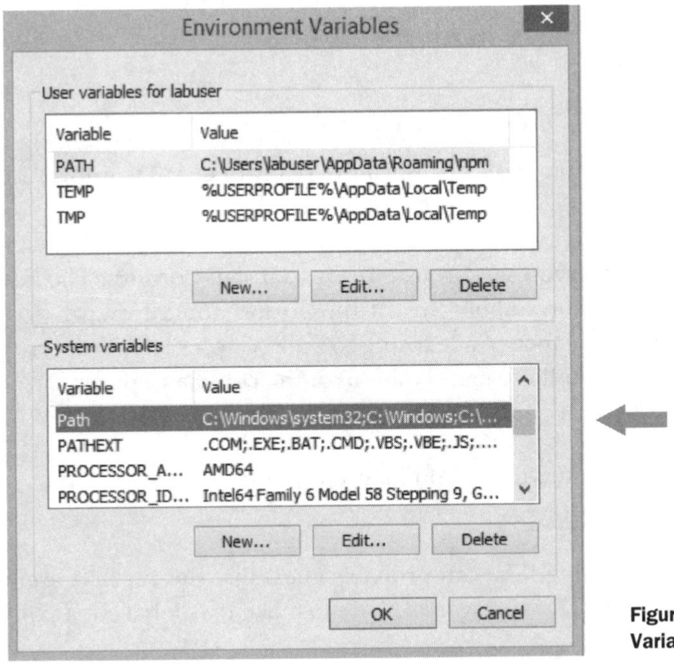

Figure 2.17 Environment Variables values for your computer

- Git's bin folder
- Node's bin folder

If you followed the preceding directions, both Git and Node should be taken care of, but they're listed for completeness' sake. The PATH value is a list of directories separated by semicolons (on Windows at least). Based on the installation described in the chapter so far, these are the directories that need to be added. *Your installation may have been different, so double-check!*

- c:\tools\android-sdk\platform-tools
- c:\tools\android-sdk\tools
- c:\tools\apache-ant-1.9.4\bin
- c:\java\jdk1.8.0_11\bin
- c:\Program Files (x86)\Git\cmd (this should already exist)
- c:\Program Files (x86)\nodejs\ (this should already exist)

Carefully enter each folder path using a semicolon after each one. After saving this setting, open a command prompt. (For those working on a Mac, open a terminal window.) If you already had one open, you need to open a new one to test the updated PATH settings. Type the following commands at the command prompt. (Each one will react a bit differently, and you honestly don't need to care, but if any command returns a "not recognized" error, then double-check your PATH settings.)

- adb
- ant (This command will return something that may look like an error: Buildfile: build.xml doesn't exist. This is the correct response and doesn't mean Ant isn't properly installed.)
- javac
- git
- npm

As long as each of these commands runs, you're ready to install Cordova!

2.6   *Installing Cordova*

At last, after all those prerequisites, you're ready to install Cordova. The good news is that you won't have to worry about any of those tools going forward (for the most part), and you can instead focus on learning to build Cordova applications.

To install Cordova, you'll use npm. Type this at the command prompt:

```
npm install -g cordova
```

For people on OS X, type this at the command prompt:

```
sudo npm install -g cordova
```

What's this command doing? You can probably guess that the install argument tells npm to install a program. The -g flag asks Node to make it a global command. This lets

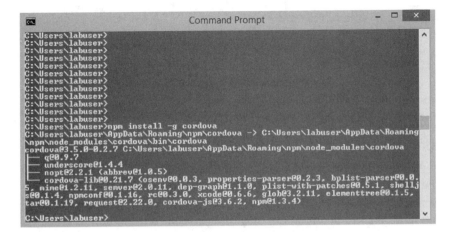

Figure 2.18 Installing Cordova via npm at the command prompt

you skip the PATH modification you had to do for the other programs. You can see the result of running this command in figure 2.18.

To verify that the install worked, type cordova at the command prompt. If everything worked okay, the command line will output use information, as shown in figure 2.19.

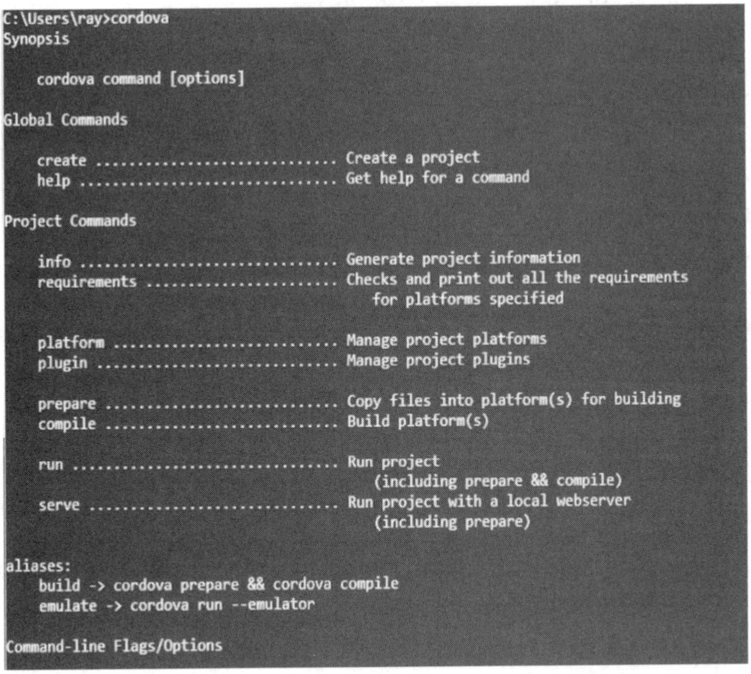

```
C:\Users\ray>cordova
Synopsis

    cordova command [options]

Global Commands

    create ............................. Create a project
    help ............................... Get help for a command

Project Commands

    info ............................... Generate project information
    requirements ....................... Checks and print out all the requirements
                                         for platforms specified

    platform ........................... Manage project platforms
    plugin ............................. Manage project plugins

    prepare ............................ Copy files into platform(s) for building
    compile ............................ Build platform(s)

    run ................................ Run project
                                         (including prepare && compile)
    serve .............................. Run project with a local webserver
                                         (including prepare)

aliases:
    build -> cordova prepare && cordova compile
    emulate -> cordova run --emulator

Command-line Flags/Options
```

Figure 2.19 Successfully running the cordova command. Congratulations!

> **Updating Cordova via npm**
>
> Because you just installed Cordova you don't have to worry about updating it, but down the line, you'll probably want to do so. Updating the program is a matter of changing `install` to `update`. Type `npm update -g cordova` (or `sudo npm update -g cordova`) and `npm` will handle updating Cordova. If Cordova hasn't been updated, this command is completely harmless.

2.7 *Making your first Cordova project*

Now that you've gotten everything ready to go, it's time to make your first project. Begin by changing to a new directory (for example, cordova-tests) that will store all of the examples you work on during the book. The next chapter will cover the process of creating projects in detail, so the only thing you need to do here is create the project and ensure it correctly executes. At the command prompt, type:

```
cordova create myfirstproject
```

If everything worked correctly, you'll see output something like the following:

```
C:\Users\labuser\Desktop\cordova-tests>cordova create myfirstproject
Creating a new cordova.
```

Congratulations! You've created your first Cordova project. Feel free to take a look inside the folder just created. The command you entered set up folders and assets that will be used to power your Cordova application.

2.8 *Summary*

Let's review the major topics covered in this chapter.

- Mobile SDKs allow native developers (and Cordova users) to create applications for their particular platform.
- Android development with Cordova requires:
  - Android SDK
  - Java (the JDK)
  - Apache Ant
  - Cordova requires:
  - Git
  - Node.js, which provides the `npm` tool
- The Cordova command-line program should be used to work with Cordova projects.

In the next chapter we'll dig deeper into what it means to use Cordova and make use of a simulator/emulator to view your project.

Part 2

Core concepts

In the eight chapters of part 2, you'll learn the core concepts of development with Apache Cordova. Chapter 3 discusses Cordova projects and the Cordova command-line interface (CLI). Chapter 4 teaches you how to use plugins in a Cordova project. Chapter 5 begins the discussion of how to use a mobile-friendly design for your Cordova applications, including Bootstrap and other frameworks.

Chapter 6 continues the theme from chapter 5 of building better, more optimized, Cordova applications. While chapter 5 focuses on the UI of an application, chapter 6 discusses architecture, network status, localization, and data storage. Chapter 7 provides debugging techniques. Chapter 8 teaches you how to create custom plugins and walks you through development of an Android plugin.

You'll learn how to package your applications for release and create custom icons and splash-screens in chapter 9. The last chapter in this part of the book, chapter 10, shows you how to build apps using Adobe PhoneGap Build as an alternative to a local SDK.

Creating Cordova projects

This chapter covers
- Creating Cordova projects from the CLI
- Adding platform support
- Working with Android emulators and devices
- Sending your project to an emulator or device

Now that you've got your local environment running, it's time to look closer at what makes up a Cordova project. At the end of chapter 2, you created a project just for testing purposes; let's cover how projects are created with a bit more detail, and then examine what's created in the filesystem. We'll also walk through setting up an Android emulator and detail how to send an application to it or a real device. Finally, you'll build a real (although rather simple) application.

Let's start by looking at the typical process flow of working with Cordova. Figure 3.1 demonstrates the steps you'll follow when working on a Cordova project.

You begin by creating a project and then telling it which platforms you'll be supporting. At that point you begin editing your web files (HTML, JavaScript, CSS) and sending them to an emulator (or a device) so you can see how they look (along with testing functionality, of course). In the next chapter we'll slightly enhance this, but for now this gives you a high-level look at what the typical Cordova project process is like. Now let's dig deeper.

3.1 *Creating projects with the Cordova CLI*

In chapter 2 you used the following command to create a project:

```
cordova create myfirstproject
```

The first thing you typed was the name of the command. The second was the action you wanted to take. The third argument was the location (subdirectory) of the application. The Cordova CLI supports even more arguments. Instead of simply repeating the documentation (and because there's a good chance things may change between the time this book is published and you read it), the easiest thing to do is run cordova at the command line with no arguments. When you do, a full report of possible arguments and their meanings will be printed.

The create action lets you specify additional arguments when creating projects, the most important being the ID and name. (Don't forget you can always use cordova help to get help at the command line for a particular feature.) The ID value is a reverse-domain style package name. If that makes no sense, consider using this as your ID: *com.your-lastname.yourappname*. There's no hard-and-fast rule here, but if you're planning on releasing the application to the public you want a unique ID. Using *com.yourlastname* (or *com.yourcompany*) creates a namespace that (most likely) won't be used by others. When you don't specify one with the CLI, the default value of io.cordova.hellocordova is used. This is perfectly acceptable while you're testing and you don't have to worry about multiple apps using the same ID while you learn. But if you want to ensure that one doesn't overwrite the other, use different IDs. The name value is what appears on the device itself. For a released application you want to make this something sensible, but again, during your learning period, you can use whatever you want. The default value chosen by the CLI is HelloCordova. This is the application name you'll see on your device, or emulator, while you carry on through the book.

The default Cordova application is pretty, but it has a bit of code that I need to rip out every time I start a project. Luckily the CLI provides a --copy-from argument that lets you specify a folder to copy the initial assets (HTML, JavaScript, and CSS) from. Here's an example:

```
cordova create testtwo --copy-from=/Users/ray/Dropbox/blankcordova
```

So, what's created when you make a new project?

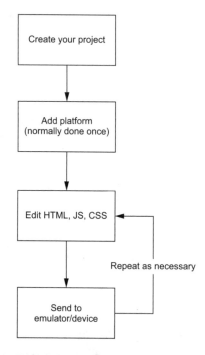

Figure 3.1 **Typical Cordova process**

3.2 *Digging into a Cordova project*

A Cordova project is really nothing more than a folder with a few files and folders in it. The CLI is smart enough to recognize what exists inside a project so you don't want to delete, or rename, any of the existing folders, but you can add your own. Let's look at the folders, shown in figure 3.2, and describe their roles.

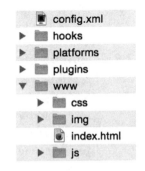

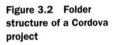

Figure 3.2 Folder structure of a Cordova project

Let's take it top to bottom:

- *The config.xml file*—Used to configure options related to how the project is built. If you open it, you'll see both the ID and name value you specified at the command line, or the defaults. For the most part, you won't need to worry about modifying this, especially in the beginning.
- *The hooks folder*—A way for advanced users to modify how the CLI works. Every action of the CLI, from creating projects to working with platforms to sending your code to a device, can be modified so that something happens before or after a particular action. As an example, you can have code that adds a custom platform-specific style sheet before a project is built. This is also something you won't need to worry about often and will be covered briefly later in this book.
- *The platforms folder*—Where the native bits go for your projects. You don't *need* to know native development, but if you do, there are times when you may want to see how the native projects look and you may want to modify them. In the platforms folder you'll find one subdirectory for every platform your application is supporting. In general, this is also something else you'll rarely touch, especially while learning, but it wouldn't hurt to take a peek in there. Note that the folder will be empty until you add a platform.
- *The plugins folder*—Where, you guessed it, plugins will be stored. Plugins are how Cordova applications do their magic—like accessing the camera. You'll learn more about plugins in chapter 4.
- *The www folder*—Where the heart of your Cordova application lives. This is where you'll write HTML, JavaScript, and CSS to build out the functionality of your application.

What you're seeing is the *default* Cordova structure for web assets. *This is completely arbitrary.* You probably want to avoid renaming index.html, (Cordova projects assume that file by default; you can tweak this, but it's easier to leave it be) but everything else can be changed to whatever you want.

Want to change that css folder to stylesheets? Go ahead. Want to change js to scripts? Go for it. Want to ditch subdirectories and put every single file in the www folder? Don't. You can, but don't. The point is, the structure here is whatever makes sense for you. If you're considering using a popular framework, like AngularJS, you can use its preferred structure when building your Cordova application. It truly is up to you.

3.3   *Adding platforms*

A Cordova project has to—or should—end up on a platform. Luckily the CLI makes it easy to set up a project for working with different platforms. You can list current platforms, add a platform, and remove a platform. This is typically something you'll do once, early in the project, when you know what platforms you're going to support. But you *can* change your mind and add a new platform. Your boss, for example, may say that the application will only be shipping for iOS, but two weeks later lets you know that Android needs to be supported as well. This isn't a problem—just add Android. If your boss comes back in a few weeks and says they changed their mind and only iOS is necessary, you can remove Android support just as easily. The primary command line to work with platforms will be `cordova platforms`. Typing this in the project created earlier shows that you have no current platforms but you have multiple ones that are supported. What you'll see in the supported list depends on what platforms you added in chapter 2 (figure 3.3).

Figure 3.3   Listing of installed and available platforms

If you're curious, the CLI also supports using the singular version, `cordova platform`, which does the same thing. Even though it's a bit more typing, I almost always use the plural version. Adding a platform is as simple as using the `add` command. To add Android support you'd type `cordova platforms add android`. After adding a platform you'll see a success message, as shown in figure 3.4.

```
→  myfirstproject  cordova platforms add android
npm http GET https://registry.npmjs.org/cordova-android
npm http 304 https://registry.npmjs.org/cordova-android
npm http GET https://registry.npmjs.org/cordova-android
npm http 304 https://registry.npmjs.org/cordova-android
Adding android project...
Creating Cordova project for the Android platform:
        Path: platforms/android
        Package: io.cordova.hellocordova
        Name: HelloCordova
        Activity: MainActivity
        Android target: android-22
Copying template files...
Android project created with cordova-android@4.0.2
Discovered plugin "cordova-plugin-whitelist" in config.xml. Installing to the project
Fetching plugin "cordova-plugin-whitelist@1" via npm
npm http GET https://registry.npmjs.org/cordova-plugin-whitelist
npm http 304 https://registry.npmjs.org/cordova-plugin-whitelist
Installing "cordova-plugin-whitelist" for android
→  myfirstproject  
```

Figure 3.4   Installing the Android platform

Figure 3.5 Confirming that Android was installed

Every project can have its own unique list of platforms it will support. Again, this is typically something you'll do once, probably immediately after you create a project. You can run `cordova platforms` again to confirm what is being used, as shown in figure 3.5.

Removing a platform is as simple as using the `remove` command: `cordova platforms remove android` would remove Android support from your project. Go ahead and do so if you want, but be sure to add Android back. Note that you can also use `rm` as a shorter version: `cordova rm android`.

3.4 Working with Android emulators and devices

Even if you have a physical device to test your applications with, it's sometimes easier to use an emulator for testing mobile development. Emulators not only let you test different device characteristics (screen sizes, available RAM, orientation), they also let you test different devices. So, for example, you can see how your application looks on an Android phone and then an iPad. In chapter 2 we walked through the steps of setting up the Android SDK because it's the best one for folks across multiple different OSes. Let's continue along that path and demonstrate how to create an Android emulator for use in testing.

Open the folder where you installed the Android SDK and find the program AVD Manager.exe. Double-click to run it. On OS X, you can instead launch the program from the terminal using `android avd`. This launches the AVD Manager. AVD stands for Android Virtual Device, which for our purposes will mean emulators. Because you just installed the SDK, you won't have any emulators defined and your screen will look like figure 3.6.

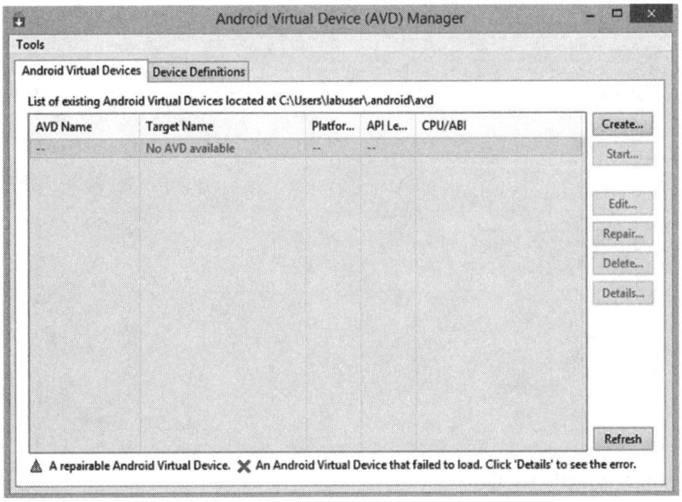

Figure 3.6 AVD Manager

Click Create to begin the process. While there are quite a few options here, let's do the minimal required to create an emulator. Table 3.1 lists each setting we care about and what value you should use.

Table 3.1   Android emulator settings

Setting	Value
Name	Set this to whatever you want. MyEmulator would be fine.
Device	Choose whatever you want here as well. Nexus 5 is a good choice. But make note of the display size. If you're on a laptop with a smaller screen, you may wish to select a device with a smaller resolution.
Target	The target value represents the OS level of the device. Depending on when you read this book and which Android SDK installer is selected, your values here will vary. As warned in chapter 2, avoid the options with W in them as they refer to the wearable version of Android.
CPU/ABI	Choose ARM. This represents how the CPU will be emulated. It's not the fastest option but it's the safest for the most readers.
Skin	Choose Skin with dynamic hardware controls.
Use host GPU	Click the check box as it will speed up the emulator.

You can configure other options, but for now that's the bare minimum and is enough to get you started. See figure 3.7 for what your screen will show.

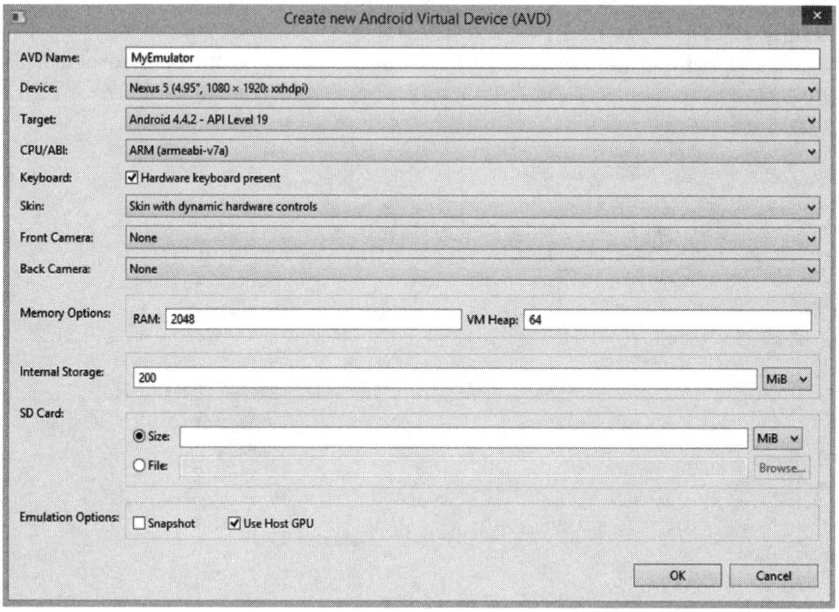

Figure 3.7   Creating a new Android emulator

You can create more emulators with specific features and OSes later on. Click OK to create the emulator. Once the emulator is created, choose it and click Start. This will open the prompt shown in figure 3.8.

Click Launch at this point to finish the emulator launch process. This will take a little while but, once begun, it will act like a real Android device on your computer. You'll see an Android loading screen and a welcome screen once the virtual machine has booted, like that shown in figure 3.9.

Note that this emulator is just like a real device even to the point of offering advice about how to use it. These welcome screens will not be shown in future launches. Get past them (by clicking OK) for now to get them out of the way.

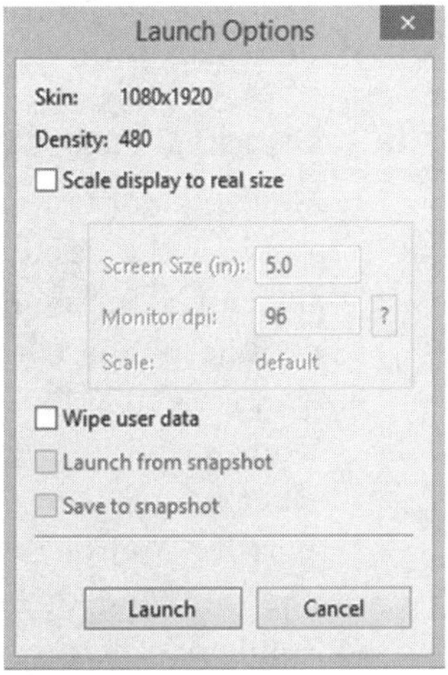

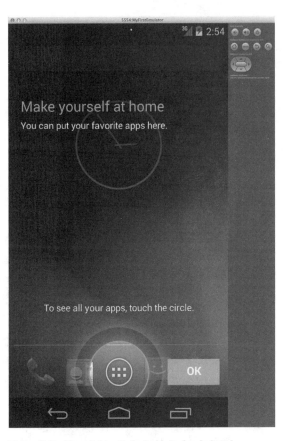

Figure 3.8 Launch options for an Android emulator

3.4.1 *Working with devices*

But what about devices? If you have a real Android device, you can enable it for Cordova testing rather easily. First, connect your Android device to your computer via a USB cable. On the device, open the settings. Every device will have a slightly different UI for the Settings panel, but in general, you need to go to the About Phone menu, find the Build Number value, and click it seven times.

Yes, seriously, I know that sounds like a videogame cheat, but Google, in its infinite wisdom, decided to make it nonobvious how to enable developer options. Once done, you'll now have a Development menu option under Settings and can enable USB Debugging. Luckily you have to do this absurdity only once.

Figure 3.9 Your (virtual) Android device is here!

At this point you now have at least one Android emulator, and possibly an Android device, that you can use for testing your Cordova applications!

3.5   *Sending your Cordova application to the emulator (or device)*

You're almost there. Your desired result is the application running in the emulator, as shown in figure 3.10.

Luckily the last step is incredibly simple. Remember that you have a Cordova project. You also have specifically told it to add platform support for Android. The last step is to get the code onto a device or an emulator. The first step in doing this is to copy the files from the www folder into the appropriate platform folder:

```
cordova prepare
```

You can optionally tell Cordova to prepare one specific platform

```
cordova prepare android
```

but if you leave off the platform, the Cordova CLI will do it for all supported platforms in the project. Next, you need to compile the platform code into the binary that can run on a device:

Figure 3.10   Default Cordova application running in Android emulator

```
cordova compile
```

Like the prepare action, you can optionally include the platform. To make things even easier, you can use the following command:

```
cordova build
```

The build command combines both prepare and compile in one action. This action can be made specific to a platform by adding it at the end. After running the build, you'll see quite a bit of output, but the final result should include a success message.

Okay, finally, you're ready to see this on the emulator! That's one more command:

```
cordova emulate
```

That's it. Like the previous commands, this will work on all platforms in your project. And guess what? You can skip the build command too! Yep—the emulate command is smart enough to do *everything*—it will prepare the platform, compile it, and send it to the emulator. If you're wondering when you'd need the other commands, they're useful for preparing the build for submission to the app stores, as well as working with native code. You don't have to use native code, but Cordova lets you do things with the native code if you choose. Please give your first run a few minutes to complete.

How about sending it to a device? You can probably guess:

```
cordova run
```

Again, this will try to use a connected device on any supported platform.

So how do you test this process? Open the www/index.html file from the project in your favorite editor. Any editor is acceptable as long as it doesn't try to rewrite your code for you. (Older Dreamweavers had a nasty habit of doing that.) Find the <h1> tag:

```
<h1>Apache Cordova</h1>
```

and change it to whatever you want. For example:

```
<h1>Kittens Rule</h1>
```

Save the file (don't worry about backing up the original) and run `cordova emulate` (or `cordova run`) again, and you should see the screen shown in figure 3.11.

That's truly all you need to do now. Continue editing the HTML and send it to your emulator. Figure 3.12 shows the same chart as in figure 3.1, but with the steps replaced by Cordova CLI commands.

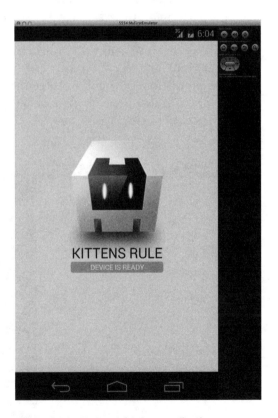

Figure 3.11   Updated Cordova application

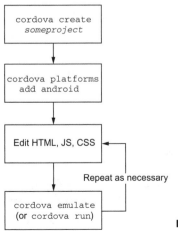

Figure 3.12   The Cordova process

In figure 3.12, you can see a simple flow chart that mimics what you did earlier in the chapter. Remember, technically you can modify platforms later in the process, but typically it's done initially. In general, the project creation and platform setup will be done first, while editing your web assets and sending it to the emulator (or device) will be the steps you do many, many times.

3.6   *Building your first real application*

Now that you have some idea of what a Cordova project is and how to send it to the emulator, it's time to build a real, if rather simple, application. Your application will make use of the GitHub API to search projects. On launching the application, the end user has a simple form, like that shown in figure 3.13.

After your user types in a search term and clicks Search, the app will use GitHub's API to search for projects and return the results, as shown in figure 3.14.

Technically this application doesn't need Cordova. You could run this as a simple web page, but it serves as a good introduction to working with Cordova. Following the flow chart from figure 3.12 you know the first step is to create the project. You can create it in any folder you wish, but I recommend using one core directory for all the samples from this book and creating each application within it. Remember that creating a Cordova project will, by default, give you the sample application you saw earlier. That's perfectly okay for now. But if you want, you can use another option.

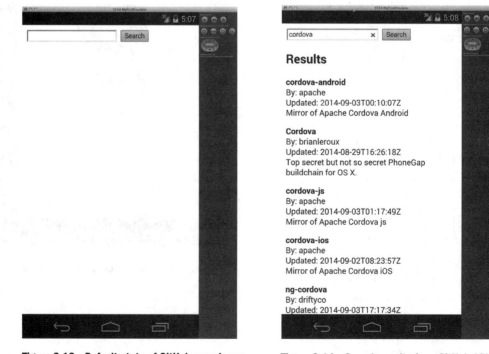

Figure 3.13   Default state of GitHub search app   Figure 3.14   Search results from GitHub API

In the zip file of code samples from the book you'll find the folder c3/searchapp. The Cordova CLI can create a new application and seed it from a folder. This will essentially copy whatever is in the folder to the www folder of the new project. If you extract the zip to /Users/mary/Downloads/cordovabook, you could use the following command to do that:

```
cordova create searchapp --copy-from=/Users/mary/Downloads/cordovabook/c3/
    searchapp
```

Either way is fine, but using the --copy-from option will save you from typing in the code manually.

Again, following the flow chart, you know you need to add support for the Android platform. This is done by using cordova platforms add android, the command you learned earlier in the chapter.

Let's look at the code of the application in the following listing.

Listing 3.1 Application homepage (index.html)

```
<!DOCTYPE html>
<html>
  <head>
  <meta charset="utf-8">
  <title>GitHub Search Demo</title>
  <meta name="description" content="">
  <meta name="viewport" content="width=device-width">
  <script type="text/javascript"
  src="http://ajax.googleapis.com/ajax/libs/jquery/2.1.0/jquery.min.js">
  </script>
  <script type="text/javascript" src="app.js"></script>
  </head>

  <body>
    <input type="search" id="searchField">
    <button id="searchButton">Search</button>

    <div id="results"></div>

  </body>
</html>
```

Loads jQuery

Loads application JavaScript code

Searches field for entering input ❶

Button to do search ❷

❸ Empty div for results

There isn't much here. You can see the basic building blocks of the application UI though: the searchField ❶, the searchButton ❷, and an empty div tag ❸. Most of the work is done in the app.js file that handles recognizing the button click and performing the search. When the results are retrieved, it then writes it out to the DOM, as shown in the following listing.

Listing 3.2 Application JavaScript code (app.js)

```
/* global $,document,console */

$(document).ready(function() {
```

```
$search = $("#searchField");
$results = $("#results");
$searchButton = $("#searchButton");

$searchButton.on("click", function(e) {
  var search = $search.val();
  if(search === "") return;

  $(this).prop("disabled",true);          ◁──┐ Disables button
                                               while searching

  $results.html("<i>Doing a search for "+search+"</i>");

  $.get("https://api.github.com/search/repositories",   ◁──┐ Does an HTTP GET
  {"q":search}, function(res,code) {                         against GitHub API
    if(res.items && res.items.length) {
      var s = "<h2>Results</h2>";
      for(var i=0, len=res.items.length; i<len; i++) {
        var entry = res.items[i];
        s += "<p><strong>"+entry.name+"</strong><br/>";
        s += "By: " + entry.owner.login+"<br/>";
        s += "Updated: " + entry.updated_at+"<br/>";
        s += entry.description;
        s += "</p>";
      }
      $results.html(s);                  ◁──┘ Creates result
    }
    $searchButton.prop("disabled",false);       ◁──┐ Reenable button
  });

});
});
```

This code uses the jQuery library to simplify both DOM access and AJAX calls and it's assumed that most readers are familiar with it. The GitHub API (https://developer.github.com/v3/) offers quite a few different features, but all you need is the simple search mechanism. It returns an array of items that you can iterate over and display as HTML.

Pretty simple, right? But there are a few problems.

- *The application doesn't do anything that a website couldn't do.* While that would be okay for some app markets, Apple will *most likely* reject something as simple as this. In later chapters you'll make use of Cordova plugins to do things web pages can't do. Cordova will provide you access to the filesystem, camera, and other device features that will truly differentiate your application from a simple web page.

- *The application isn't really designed well.* That search field and the button aren't necessarily optimized for use on a mobile device. Even the event you listened to with jQuery (click), is a *mouse* event. It works, but it suffers from a delay in many devices. You should use an event that's more appropriate, such as touchend. Later you'll learn how to apply a good responsive design to your application and make it more mobile friendly.

- *What happens if the device is offline?* Right now a whole lot of nothing. But the users will never know. They aren't provided any sort of feedback about *why* their search didn't do anything. This is also something you can easily correct with Cordova. By using a plugin, you can check the application's online status and respond accordingly.

So is this a "bad" project? Absolutely not! You've created a project, built it for a platform, and seen it running on either an emulator or a device. While it may not yet make use of any cool features, you've practiced the development cycle for Cordova and are now ready to begin adding in all those special features that make a truly powerful mobile application.

3.7   *Summary*

Let's review the major topics covered in this chapter.

- A Cordova project can be created from the CLI and consists of a set of common folders.
- The most important for developers will be the www folder.
- The Cordova CLI provides a simple command to add, list, and remove platforms for a project.
- The Android SDK provides a way to create emulators, and Android devices can also be used for debugging.

In chapter 4, we'll look at Cordova's plugin system and how it provides access to native device features.

Using plugins to access
device features

This chapter covers

- What plugins are and what they provide for Cordova projects
- How to find and evaluate plugins
- How to use the CLI to manage plugins
- How to use the `deviceready` event

So far you've concentrated on using the Cordova CLI to translate web stuff (HTML, JavaScript, and CSS) to native code. You've seen how to create a Cordova project and how to test it as a native application on either an emulator or a real device. The last piece of the puzzle is tapping into the rich set of device features that websites do *not* have access to: the filesystem, the camera, and so on. This was mentioned in chapter 3 as a problem with your simple application. This is where plugins enter the picture.

4.1 What are plugins?

Suppose you want to write a Cordova application to access your phone's camera and take a picture. JavaScript, by itself, doesn't have access to the camera. One of

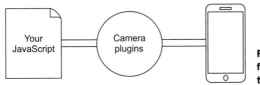

Figure 4.1 Cordova plugins stand between and facilitate communication between JavaScript and the device.

the great features of Cordova is that it provides a mechanism to allow JavaScript to access things it normally wouldn't be able to. This is done via plugins.

Plugins work by providing a way for your JavaScript to communicate to the device. Figure 4.1 illustrates this.

Plugins are code written in native languages (Objective-C, Java, and so forth) that provide a hook that can be called by a JavaScript file loaded by your Cordova application. They allow your JavaScript code to do things it wouldn't normally be able to do. There's no `camera.getPicture()` function available to mobile browsers, but by using plugins, Cordova provides support for doing just such a thing. The Cordova version (and you'll see a full example later in this chapter) looks like so: `navigator.camera.getPicture()`. This only works because the plugin behind the camera support adds this functionality.

For a plugin to work across multiple platforms, multiple versions of the plugin are built. Taking the Camera plugin feature as an example, someone must create native code for Android, Windows Phone, iOS, and other platforms that can access the device camera. Once that's done, one JavaScript API can be used so your code will work the same (or close enough) on all those platforms. Luckily there are quite a few plugins available for you to use in your Cordova projects.

4.2 *Finding (and evaluating) plugins*

Before we get into using plugins in your Cordova project, let's discuss how you find them. While you can write your own plugins (to be discussed in chapter 8), most people find their plugins online. You used the command line npm to install Cordova; as mentioned previously, npm is a tool often used to install other programs. Cordova plugins are now (a *very* recent change) stored at www.npmjs.com so you can search for them there. At the time this chapter was written, there were nearly 150,000 npm packages available, but you can search for Cordova plugins using `ecosystem:cordova` in the search box. Or simply bookmark www.npmjs.com/browse/keyword/ecosystem :cordova. The search results are shown in figure 4.2.

Note that this search returns plugins *and* related Cordova assets. For example, `cordova-app-hello-world` is the source for the www folder in new Cordova projects. Providing a way to search for *only* plugins is something that's currently being worked on.

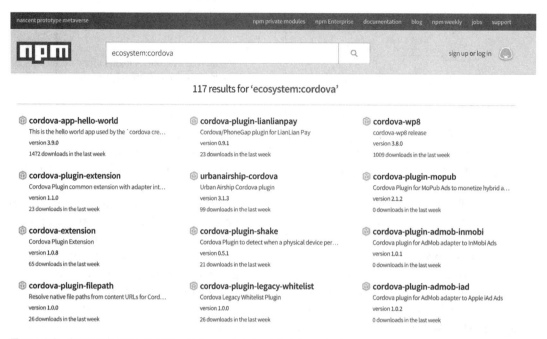

Figure 4.2   Cordova assets at www.npmjs.com/package/cordova-plugins

You probably won't have any trouble finding a plugin for common needs. What's more difficult is evaluating which plugin makes the most sense for your project. Given that you can find a plugin to support some particular need, how do you handle figuring out if the plugin is well written? Or what do you do when *multiple* options exist? In general, the same types of checks you should make for any open source project will apply here as well.

- *How long ago was the plugin updated?*—Typically I look for a plugin updated within three months. I also mentally sort plugins by when they were last updated. Given two plugins that match a particular need, I'll automatically give precedence to the one updated most recently.
- *Is the plugin used by many people?*—While it's impossible to tell exactly how many people are using a plugin, the Cordova Plugins Registry does report on the number of downloads for a particular plugin. As with the date it was last updated, I'll typically check the plugin with the most downloads first.
- *Are there many open issues for the plugin?*—Any project is going to have bugs. The question is, how quickly does the author respond to and try to fix those bugs? If you see a plugin with many open issues, and ones that are quite old, it may be another sign of an abandoned project.

For the most part, we'll be focused on the core plugins that are maintained by the Apache Cordova project. Technically every plugin is just as usable as any other, but there is a set of plugins maintained by the Apache Cordova team that is kept up to date and tested on the platforms supported by Cordova. These plugins once were part of the core Cordova framework itself, but in version 3, every feature was converted into a plugin. This was done so that developers didn't have to ship code for a feature they weren't using. The core plugins are:

- Battery Status (`cordova-plugin-battery-status`)
- Camera (`cordova-plugin-camera`)
- Console (`cordova-plugin-console`)
- Contacts (`cordova-plugin-contacts`)
- Device (`cordova-plugin-device`)
- Device Motion and Orientation (`cordova-plugin-device-motion` and `cordova-plugin-device-orientation`)
- Dialogs and Vibration (`cordova-plugin-dialogs`)
- File System and FileTransfer (`cordova-plugin-file` and `cordova-plugin-file-transfer`)
- Geolocation (`cordova-plugin-geolocation`)
- Globalization (`cordova-plugin-globalization`)
- InAppBrowser (`cordova-plugin-inappbrowser`)
- Media and Media Capture (`cordova-plugin-media` and `cordova-plugin-media-capture`)
- Network Information (`cordova-plugin-network-information`)
- Splashscreen (`cordova-plugin-splashscreen`)
- Vibration (`cordova-plugin-vibration`)
- StatusBar (`cordova-plugin-statusbar`)
- Whitelist (`cordova-plugin-whitelist`)

We'll discuss those `cordova-plugin` values in a bit.

ANOTHER OPTION You can also browse plugins at Telerik's Verified Plugins Marketplace (http://plugins.telerik.com/). Telerik constantly updates this list to ensure the listed plugins actually work and are well maintained.

4.3 *Managing plugins and the Cordova CLI*

Now that you know what plugins do and where to find them, how do you get them into your project? The Cordova CLI provides a method to add new plugins, remove existing plugins, list what's installed, and search against the main registry. The simplest action to take is to list the current plugins for a project. Navigate to any existing project, and simply type `cordova plugin`. This will output a list of plugins that for you will most likely be blank. Note that you can use the alias `plugins` instead of `plugin`. Either works just fine.

Adding a plugin is done via the `cordova plugin add` command. There are a couple of different options you have in terms of from where the plugin will be loaded, but for the purposes of this book you'll use the pluginid value—that is, the cordova-plugin values you saw in the list of core plugins. The command diagram at right demonstrates this.

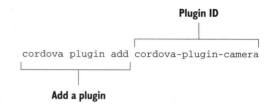

The result of this command can be seen in figure 4.3. In the figure, pay particular attention to the last line. For this project, the only installed platform was for iOS. Basically, the Cordova CLI grabbed the plugin and then prepared it for the platforms your project supports. The CLI is intelligent enough to know that if you decide to add Android, it needs to install the Camera plugin, as demonstrated in figure 4.4.

```
→  apr29  cordova plugin add cordova-plugin-camera
Fetching plugin "cordova-plugin-camera" via npm
npm http GET https://registry.npmjs.org/cordova-plugin-camera
npm http 304 https://registry.npmjs.org/cordova-plugin-camera
Installing "cordova-plugin-camera" for ios
→  apr29
```

Figure 4.3   Response from the Cordova CLI after adding the Camera plugin

Adding the Android platform

```
→  apr29  cordova platform add android
Adding android project...
Creating Cordova project for the Android platform:
        Path: platforms/android
        Package: io.cordova.hellocordova
        Name: HelloCordova
        Activity: MainActivity
        Android target: android-22
Copying template files...
Android project created with cordova-android@4.0.0
Installing "cordova-plugin-camera" for android
Installing "cordova-plugin-whitelist" for android
→  apr29
```

The Cordova CLI automatically handles the existing plugins.

Figure 4.4   After installing Android, the currently installed plugins are copied to the new platform.

Removing a plugin is simply a matter of using cordova remove and the ID of the plugin you want to remove. As before, the CLI is intelligent enough to know what platforms you've installed for a project and will correctly remove the plugin from each, as shown in the command diagram at right.

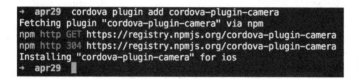

The search option is useful if you can't remember the name of a plugin. The CLI searches

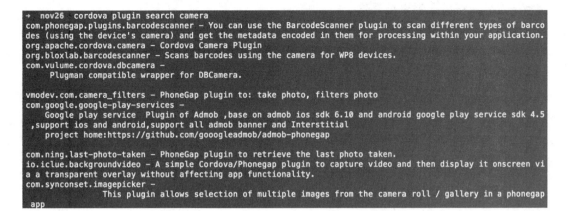

```
→ nov26  cordova plugin search camera
com.phonegap.plugins.barcodescanner - You can use the BarcodeScanner plugin to scan different types of barco
des (using the device's camera) and get the metadata encoded in them for processing within your application.
org.apache.cordova.camera - Cordova Camera Plugin
org.bloxlab.barcodescanner - Scans barcodes using the camera for WP8 devices.
com.vulume.cordova.dbcamera -
     Plugman compatible wrapper for DBCamera.

vmodev.com.camera_filters - PhoneGap plugin to: take photo, filters photo
com.google.google-play-services -
     Google play service  Plugin of Admob ,base on admob ios sdk 6.10 and android google play service sdk 4.5
  ,support ios and android,support all admob banner and Interstitial
     project home:https://github.com/gooogleadmob/admob-phonegap

com.ning.last-photo-taken - PhoneGap plugin to retrieve the last photo taken.
io.iclue.backgroundvideo - A simple Cordova/Phonegap plugin to capture video and then display it onscreen vi
a a transparent overlay without affecting app functionality.
com.synconset.imagepicker -
            This plugin allows selection of multiple images from the camera roll / gallery in a phonegap
 app
```

Figure 4.5   Searching for the Camera plugin

against the website (http://plugins.cordova.io) and returns the results at your command prompt. Figure 4.5 demonstrates the result of searching for "camera."

Once you've installed a plugin, you can begin using it in your code. How you use a plugin will depend on what it does. Each plugin has its own API and documentation. Later in the chapter we'll go over a few example plugins so you can see them in action. Just remember that every plugin is unique. Be sure to *carefully* read its documentation to know how to correctly use it.

4.4   *Plugins and the development cycle*

In chapter 3 we outlined the development cycle for a typical Cordova project. How does working with plugins change this? Not much! Figure 4.6 demonstrates the updated process.

As you can see, we've simply added a new step (add plugins) to the flow. You can add plugins late in the development process (perhaps the client changes the requirements right before release, something that never happens, right?). But typically, much like with platforms, you'll set up your plugins at the beginning of your project.

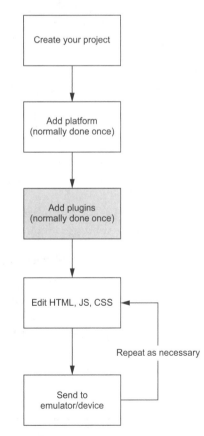

Figure 4.6   Final flow chart of the Cordova development process

4.5   *The deviceready event*

You've seen how to find plugins. You've read about how to perform due diligence and judge the health of a plugin. You've seen how easy it is to use the CLI to install, list, and remove plugins from your project. Most likely you're excited to jump into development and start doing cool things with the camera and other device features.

First, there's a critically important aspect of Cordova development that you need to learn. Before your application can talk to a plugin, Cordova has to set up a line of communication between your code and the device. That sounds complex, but it really isn't. Basically, Cordova knows what it has to do on each supported platform to let plugin code access device hardware. All you have to do is wait for Cordova to finish. So how do you know when this has happened? All Cordova applications will fire an event called `deviceready` which can be listened to in your JavaScript code. So why did the real (but simple) application in chapter 3 work? Because you weren't doing anything special. Listening to events in JavaScript is fairly simple.

At the most simple level, the DOM method `addEventListener()` is what you'd use to create a listener for an event. If you use jQuery, you'd use the on API. The following listing demonstrates this.

> **Listing 4.1   `deviceready` example**

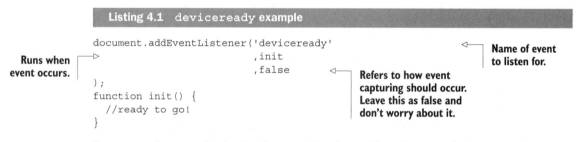

```
document.addEventListener('deviceready'
                          ,init
                          ,false
);
function init() {
  //ready to go!
}
```

Runs when event occurs.

Name of event to listen for.

Refers to how event capturing should occur. Leave this as false and don't worry about it.

Pretty much every single Cordova application will make use of the preceding code block. The name of the function that will be run, `init` in the listing, is completely up to you, but should be named something obvious. If you do any jQuery work you may be familiar with using `$(document).ready` as a way of delaying your code until the DOM is ready. For the most part you can mentally exchange that with the `deviceready` handler and use it in much the same way.

4.6   *Plugin example: Dialogs*

For our first example of a plugin we'll look at the Cordova Dialogs plugin. It provides native dialogs and audio notifications to your Cordova application and is a big improvement over what JavaScript provides by default. After I demonstrate how to use the plugin and why it's better than the default JavaScript method, you'll use it in a sample application.

4.6.1   *Better dialogs with the Cordova Dialogs plugin*

JavaScript has long had a way to create dialog, or modal, windows. While these methods work, they tend to be avoided as they cannot be styled and can be overly obtrusive.

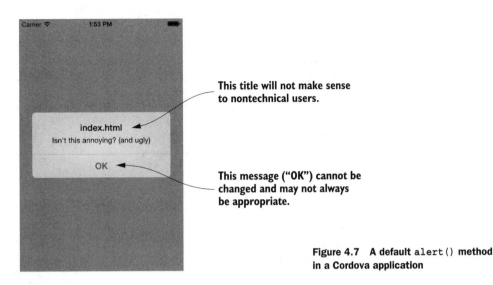

This title will not make sense to nontechnical users.

This message ("OK") cannot be changed and may not always be appropriate.

Figure 4.7 A default `alert()` method in a Cordova application

When used in a mobile browser they can be even more obtrusive. In figure 4.7, a Cordova application is using the `alert()` method to display a message to the user.

Notice that the dialog has a title on top, index.html. This cannot be changed or modified and immediately flags your application as being a web page. The OK button cannot be changed either. Now compare the same (well, a similar) use of the Dialogs plugin's `alert()` method in figure 4.8.

By switching to the Dialogs plugin, you have a much nicer dialog. You can customize the title as well as the button. You cannot control things like color and fonts, but you can still create a much better-looking dialog with minimal effort.

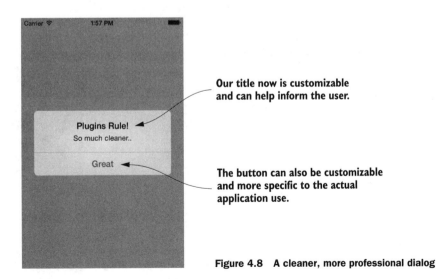

Our title now is customizable and can help inform the user.

The button can also be customizable and more specific to the actual application use.

Figure 4.8 A cleaner, more professional dialog

4.6.2   *Building an application with the Dialogs plugin*

Dialogs are used to alert the user about something important happening in your application. What that important event is doesn't necessarily matter, but the idea is that you want to get the user's attention. For this first example you'll create an application that lets you test all of the methods of the Dialogs plugin:

- *Alerts* are modal dialogs (miniwindows) that float on "top" of the application. Use this when you want to present a message to the user.
- *Prompts* are also modal, but ask the user to type something in. Like alerts, they're modal.
- *Confirmations* ask the user to specifically accept or deny a particular action. Use this when you want to ensure the user really wants to perform some action while also providing the user a quick way to say no.
- *Beeps* make noise. You can use this with the dialogs to *really* get the user's attention.

Beeps are—obviously—not a dialog but an auditory alert; but as they're pretty simple to use we'll demonstrate them as well. Your final application, as shown in figure 4.9, will provide a set of buttons to test each aspect of the plugin.

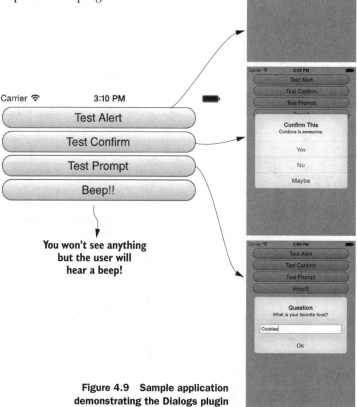

Figure 4.9   Sample application demonstrating the Dialogs plugin

Each of the buttons tests one aspect of the plugin and is labeled appropriately. To create this application, you can follow the same procedure you did in chapter 3. If you extracted the book's zip file to /Users/mary/Downloads/cordovabook, you can create a new Cordova project and seed it with the code for this example like so:

```
cordova create notificationdemo --copy-from=/Users/mary/Downloads/
    cordovabook/c4/dialog_demo
```

Don't forget that before you can make use of a plugin, you need to install it. In the new project you created, run the following command:

```
cordova plugin add cordova-plugin-dialogs
```

You can also create a new project and then modify the code to match the code displayed next. Let's begin by looking at the index.html file shown in the following listing.

Listing 4.2   Dialog demo homepage (index.html)

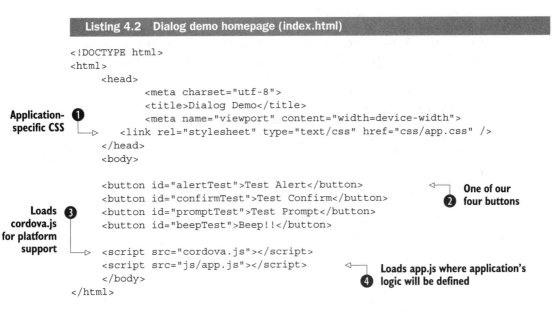

For the most part there isn't much to talk about here. The application is rather simple—four buttons ❷ and nothing more—so the HTML part of the project is only a few lines long. This example calls out to an application-specific CSS file ❶ and a JavaScript file ❹. You may be curious about the line that loads cordova.js ❸. If you look at your project folder, this file doesn't actually exist because this JavaScript file is injected by the Cordova CLI itself when you create a platform-specific build. So when you tell it to create an iOS build, for example, an iOS version of the cordova.js file will be copied along with everything else you write. If you have an Android version, the same thing happens but an Android-specific version is used instead. As a Cordova developer, you don't have to worry about providing the file, but you must include a `<script>` tag loading it so your project can function correctly.

Let's look at the CSS file shown in listing 4.3. Note the use of app.css and app.js in this application just because it makes it obvious that these files are application-specific and not part of some third-party library. There's nothing special about "app" being used in the name. It's nothing more than a convention.

Listing 4.3   Application CSS file (app.css)

```
body {
    margin: 20px;
}

button {
    padding: 10px;
    width: 100%;
    font-size: 1em;
}
```

That's it. Only a few lines to add a margin around the body and make the buttons a bit easier to see on a mobile screen. In later chapters we'll look at how to make this better. Now let's look at the final part of the project, the JavaScript file, shown in the following listing.

Listing 4.4   Application JavaScript file (app.js)

```
document.addEventListener("deviceready", init, false);    ◁─┐ deviceready
function init() {                                              event listener

    //listen for button clicks
    document.querySelector("#alertTest").addEventListener("touchend",
        function() {

                        navigator.notification.alert(
Alert handler └▷            "This is a test...", null,"Alert Test", "OK!");

    }, false);

    document.querySelector("#confirmTest").addEventListener("touchend",
        function() {

                        function youConfirmed(idx) {
                            navigator.notification.alert(
                                "You clicked button "+idx+"!", null);
                        }

                        navigator.notification.confirm(
Confirm handler └▷         "Cordova is awesome.", youConfirmed,
                            "Confirm This", ["Yes","No","Maybe"]);

    }, false);

    document.querySelector("#promptTest").addEventListener("touchend",
        function() {
```

```
                function promptAnswer(answer) {
                    navigator.notification.alert(
                        "You said: "+answer.input1, null);
                }

                navigator.notification.prompt(
                    "What is your favorite food?", promptAnswer,
                    "Question", ["Ok"], "Cookies");
```

Prompt handler ⌐➞

```
            }, false);

    document.querySelector("#beepTest").addEventListener("touchend",
        function() {

                navigator.notification.beep(2);   ⬅⌐ **Beep handler**

        }, false);

    }
```

The more important aspect of this JavaScript file is the initial event listener for deviceready. As noted earlier in the chapter, before you do anything with device features you must listen for this event. Therefore, the majority of the code for this application is nestled inside that function. The Dialogs plugin is documented at www.npmjs.com/package/cordova-plugin-dialogs, and the code simply demonstrates an example of each of the four methods supported by the plugin.

THE ALERT() METHOD

The alert() method allows for customization of the body (first argument) and title (third argument), as well as the button (fourth argument). The second argument, which is specified as null, is a callback function to run after the alert is dismissed. If you wanted your application to do anything at that point you could define it there. Figure 4.10 demonstrates the result.

THE CONFIRM() METHOD

The confirm() method works similarly to the alert() method. Note though that you can actually specify multiple buttons instead of a default set of two. For the confirm() method example you want to display what the user clicked so you use the callback to alert it, as shown in figure 4.11.

Figure 4.10 Demonstrating the alert() method

Figure 4.11   Side-by-side demonstration of the `confirm()` method and the result

THE PROMPT() METHOD

The `prompt()` method is also pretty similar to the last two—you provide a default prompt, a callback, the title of the dialog, a set of buttons, and an optional default. The callback is a bit more complex. It's passed a result object that contains a key for the input (`input1`) and the index of the button selected (`buttonIndex`). For your application you alert back what the user entered, as shown in figure 4.12.

THE BEEP() METHOD

The most simple method of the plugin is `beep()`. You simply pass in the number of beeps to make; the sound will be based on the user's default notification sound. Please use this method with caution and resist the urge to pass an incredibly large number to

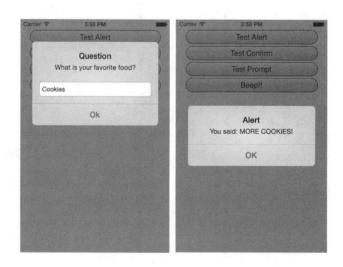

Figure 4.12   On the left is the prompt with the default answer. If the user changed it to say "MORE COOKIES!" then the result on the right would be shown.

it. In case you're curious, you can do both a beep and an alert at the same time to get the user's attention:

```
navigator.notification.beep(2);
navigator.notification.alert(
        "Wake up! ", null, "Alert Test", "OK! ");
```

If you click the buttons and nothing happens, most likely you forgot to *include* the plugin as instructed earlier. Figuring out mistakes like this will be covered in chapter 8 when we cover debugging techniques.

4.7 Plugin example: Camera

Now that you've seen the power of a simple plugin in action, let's kick it up a notch and talk about one of the more popular plugins, Camera. From Instagram to Facebook, users *love* taking pictures. The Camera plugin lets you prompt the user to take a new picture or select from the gallery. It has multiple options for where the image ends up and lets you control the size of the picture returned to your application. At the most simple level you can prompt the user to take a picture and then render that picture in your application. More advanced applications can use these pictures by uploading them to other services and manipulating them.

This demo provides buttons to prompt the user to either take a new picture or select one from the device, as shown in figure 4.13.

Once the user has selected an image, it will be displayed in the application and styled a bit, like figure 4.14.

This button will open up the device's camera, allowing the user to take a new picture.

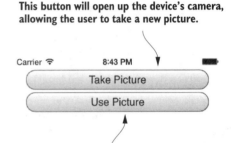

This button will open the "gallery," or existing library of images on the device. The user would click this to use an existing image.

Figure 4.13   Default view of the application

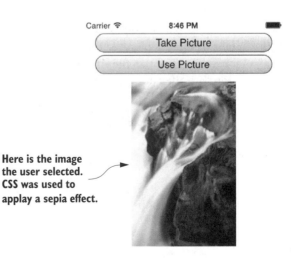

Here is the image the user selected. CSS was used to applay a sepia effect.

Figure 4.14   A selected picture
displayed in the application

Now let's look at the code. Don't forget to actually *create* the new project. As before, you can use the CLI's --copy-from feature to point to the code you downloaded for the book. For this application to work correctly in your emulator, or device, you'll need to install not one but two plugins:

```
cordova plugin add cordova-plugin-camera
cordova plugin add cordova-plugin-dialogs
```

Using multiple plugins is a perfectly normal part of Cordova development and it will not be unusual for your application to use many of them.

Let's begin by looking at the HTML for the application, shown in the following listing.

Listing 4.5   Application HTML page (index.html)

Button that selects existing pictures ❷

Button that takes new pictures ❶

Blank image that displays picture ❸

```html
<!DOCTYPE html>
<html>
    <head>
            <meta charset="utf-8">
            <title>Basic Camera</title>
            <meta name="viewport" content="width=device-width">
        <link rel="stylesheet" type="text/css" href="css/app.css" />
    </head>
    <body>

        <button id="takePicture">Take Picture</button>
        <button id="usePicture">Use Picture</button>

        <img id="myImage">

        <script src="cordova.js"></script>
        <script src="js/app.js"></script>
        </body>
</html>
```

As before, because the application is so simple, the HTML doesn't have much to it. For the most part it comes down to the two buttons (❶, ❷) used to prompt the user to take or select a picture. The empty image ❸ will be used to display what the user takes or selects. The CSS file shown in the following listing is similar to the previous application with the addition of a new style for the image.

Listing 4.6   Application CSS file (app.css)

```css
body {
    margin: 20px;
}

button {
    padding: 10px;
    width: 100%;
    font-size: 1em;
}
```

```css
img {
    margin-top: 10px;
    -webkit-filter: sepia(100%);
    display: block;
    margin-left: auto;
    margin-right: auto;
    max-width: 100%;
    max-height: 250px;
}
```

❶ Sepia filter stylizes image

The sepia filter ❶ is used to colorize the selected image. You can think of it as an Instagram filter done simple. Now review the JavaScript in the following listing.

Listing 4.7 Application JavaScript file (app.js)

```javascript
document.addEventListener("deviceready", init, false);
function init() {
```
❶ deviceready listener

Success handler for camera function
```javascript
    function onSuccess(imageData) {
        console.log('success');
        var image = document.getElementById('myImage');
        image.src = imageData;
    }

    function onFail(message) {
        navigator.notification.alert(
            message, null, "Camera Failure");
    }
```
Error handler for camera function

```javascript
    //Use from Camera
    document.querySelector("#takePicture").addEventListener("touchend", function() {
        navigator.camera.getPicture(onSuccess, onFail, {
            quality: 50,
            sourceType: Camera.PictureSourceType.CAMERA,
            destinationType: Camera.DestinationType.FILE_URI
        });

    });
```
Function to get a new picture ❷

```javascript
    //Use from Library
    document.querySelector("#usePicture").addEventListener("touchend", function() {
        navigator.camera.getPicture(onSuccess, onFail, {
            quality: 50,
            sourceType: Camera.PictureSourceType.PHOTOLIBRARY,
            destinationType: Camera.DestinationType.FILE_URI
        });

    });

}
```
Function to get an existing picture ❸

Once again the code begins with an event listener for deviceready ❶, a consistent technique for your Cordova applications. Both buttons (shown in figures 4.13 and 4.14) make use of touch events to listen for user action. Both make use of the core Camera plugin functionality to get pictures, navigator.camera.getPicture. The only difference in the two calls (❷, ❸) are the options. The first button that's requesting a new picture uses a source of `Camera.PictureSourceType.CAMERA`. This means a new picture driven by the device camera. The second button uses a source of `Camera.PictureSourceType.PHOTOLIBRARY`, which represents an existing picture from the device's photo gallery.

The Camera plugin can send the picture as either Base64 data (a text representation of binary data) or from the location of the picture on the device's filesystem. In general, using the FILE_URI destination as used here is almost always preferred because it uses less memory then the Base64 version. (This is discussed on the plugin's documentation page.) Once the camera action is complete, the success handler is run and, because you're passing in a file URL, you can set that to the blank image created in the HTML page. Note as well the error handler. It's using the nice dialogs described earlier.

4.8 Plugin example: Contacts

For our final example we'll work with the Contacts plugin, which (no surprise here) lets you add, edit, and delete contacts. That's handy. A more typical use for contacts is to *find* a contact to be used in some other action. Imagine you've made use of the Camera plugin. Because you've just taken what is obviously the best picture of a cat *ever*, it would be even cooler if you could share that picture with a friend. The Contacts plugin would make it easy to let you find that friend and fetch their email address, or phone number, so that your friend too can bask in the awesomeness of your cat photo.

While the plugin provides a `find()` method for low-level searching, it has a *better* method of asking the user to select a contact. The plugin can ask the device to use its default Contact Picker UI that's shared among other native applications. This provides a familiar user experience to the person working with your application. By using the `navigator.contacts.pickContact()` method as provided by the plugin, you can display the appropriate UI for the device's OS, as shown in figure 4.15.

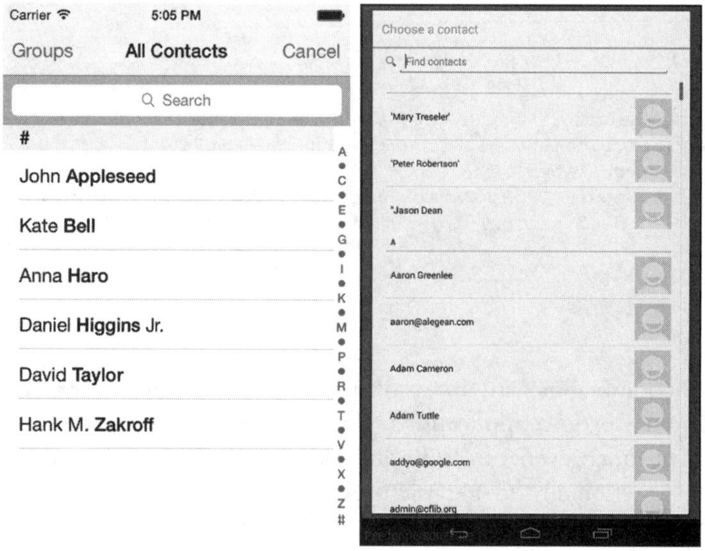

Figure 4.15 How iOS
(left) and Android (right)
handle contact picking

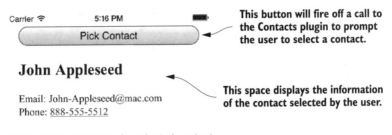

Figure 4.16   Example of a selected contact

The application will make use of this API to simply prompt the user to select a contact. After a contact is selected, information about the contact will be displayed in the application, as shown in figure 4.16.

In doing so though, you'll discover one of the issues you run into from time to time with plugins: platform quirks.

The documentation for the Contacts plugin (www.npmjs.com/package/cordova-plugin-contacts) discusses how the plugin works and points out oddities or quirks for an individual plugin. While all plugins strive to work *exactly* the same across their supported platforms, sometimes this is not possible.

> **TIP** While most developers know it's important to read the documentation, most of us probably don't do a great job of it. I recommend paying attention to the quirks when using any plugin. Many times I've lost time to debugging something that ended up being a quirk that I simply didn't pay attention to.

For the Contacts plugin there's one quirk in particular that's going to impact the sample application. The docs say this:

> **displayName:** *Not supported on iOS, returning* `null` *unless there is no* `ContactName` *specified, in which case it returns the composite name,* **nickname**, *or " ", respectively.*

Interesting. So if the application is going to display a contact, it will need to be prepared to handle running under iOS and not having access to that particular property.

I know you didn't forget to create a new project and add the plugins, right? This project makes use of both the Contacts plugin (`cordova-plugin-contacts`) and Dialogs plugin (`cordova-plugin-dialogs`).

Let's look at the code. The first template is the index.html file for the application shown in the following listing.

Listing 4.8   Contact demo HTML file (index.html)

```
<!DOCTYPE html>
<html>
    <head>
        <meta charset="utf-8">
        <title>Contacts Demo</title>
```

Fires off call to ❶ prompt user to select contact

```
                <meta name="viewport" content="width=device-width">
            <link rel="stylesheet" type="text/css" href="css/app.css" />
        </head>
        <body>

        <button id="pickContact">Pick Contact</button>
        <div id="selectedContact"></div>

        <script src="cordova.js"></script>
        <script src="js/app.js"></script>
        </body>
    </html>
```

Writes out information ❷ about contact

As with the other examples, the HTML is rather simple. You've got one button you'll use to fire off the Contacts plugin ❶ and an empty div that will be filled with details from the selected contact ❷.

Now let's look at the JavaScript code for the application shown in the following listing.

Listing 4.9   Contact demo JavaScript file (app.js)

```
document.addEventListener("deviceready", init, false);
function init() {
    document.querySelector("#pickContact").addEventListener("touchend",
    doContactPicker, false);
}

function doContactPicker() {
    navigator.contacts.pickContact(function(contact){

        //Build a simple string to display the Contact
        var s = "";
        s += "<h2>"+getName(contact)+"</h2>";

        if(contact.emails && contact.emails.length) {
            s+= "Email: "+contact.emails[0].value+"<br/>";
        }

        if(contact.phoneNumbers && contact.phoneNumbers.length) {
            s+= "Phone: "+contact.phoneNumbers[0].value+"<br/>";
        }

        if(contact.photos && contact.photos.length) {
            s+= "<p><img src='"+contact.photos[0].value+"'></p>";
        }

        document.querySelector("#selectedContact").innerHTML=s;
    },function(err){
        navigator.notification.alert(
            err, null, "Failure");
    });
}
/*
Handles iOS not returning displayName or returning null/""
```

Fires off request for native contact ❶ picker UI

Some contact properties are arrays ❷

```
*/
function getName(c) {
    var name = c.displayName;
    if(!name || name === "") {
            if(c.name.formatted) {
                    return c.name.formatted;
            }
            if(c.name.givenName && c.name.familyName) {
                    return c.name.givenName +" "+c.name.familyName;
            }

            return "Nameless";
    }
    return name;
}
```

Helps handle iOS not having a display ❸ name value

As in the previous examples, the code begins with a listener for `deviceready`. By now this should be familiar territory. The plugin API, `navigator.contacts.pickContact` ❶, only takes two arguments: a success callback and a failure callback. The success callback is passed an instance of a `Contact` object, a basic representation of a particular contact. The documentation fully covers all the keys but for the purposes here, only a few are displayed. Note that some properties are arrays ❷ and can be iterated over. Make note of how to handle the iOS issue mentioned earlier. The `getName()` ❸ function will check to see if `displayName()` is null and, if so, try to find an appropriate value elsewhere. If all else fails it will return `Nameless`.

In the previous chapter, we discussed a few problems with the sample application you created. It didn't make use of any native features. In this chapter you've seen how easy it is to make use of those features using plugins. We also demonstrated how the application wasn't necessarily designed well for the mobile environment. The next chapter will cover this.

4.9 Summary

Let's review the major topics covered in this chapter.

- Plugins are what provide real power to Cordova applications.
- Plugins can be fully managed via the command-line tool.
- All code that makes use of plugins must wait for the `deviceready` event to fire.

In the next chapter we'll cover how to design applications for the mobile environment.

Mobile design and user experience

This chapter covers

- What works (and what doesn't) on mobile devices
- How to use Bootstrap for responsive, mobile-optimized design
- An overview of Mobile UI frameworks

So far we've discussed how to install Cordova, how to generate native binaries from HTML, and how to make use of fancy device features with plugins. For the most part, what we've discussed has been fairly straightforward. Install an SDK, install the command-line tool, write some HTML, and whammo!, see it on your device.

5.1 Congratulations—you're a (horrible) mobile developer!

Okay, that may be just a tiny bit over the top, but most likely there's a bit of truth to it as well. What we haven't yet discussed is how to create a *good* mobile application. Taste is subjective. While it's difficult to precisely describe what makes a good mobile application, there are definitely guidelines that help define what a successful mobile application looks like. And notice I'm not saying a successful *hybrid* mobile application. Your users don't care what you used to build your application. They only care about the end result. Therefore, the guidelines for a good hybrid mobile application are going to be the same as a good 100% native-built mobile application.

A good mobile application is readable on a variety of form factors. Whether opened in an iPhone 5 or some enormous Android phablet, text should be readable and buttons easy to click with fat fingers. A good mobile application demonstrates these features:

- It has a simple, easily understandable UI. By using common design idioms (a shopping cart icon, for example) users have a better idea of what to expect when using your application.
- It performs well with little to no noticeable lag.
- It works in a variety of network conditions (offline and online).

5.1.1 A good example of a bad UI

Imagine the most simple application possible—an application that prompts for your name and then tells you hello. Figure 5.1 is a mockup of the UI for the application, both the initial view and what's displayed after entering a name.

Building this application would be rather trivial. You should create a new Cordova application if you want to test this. The source code is available in the zip downloaded from the book's website. You'll find it in the c5/simple folder. The following listing represents the HTML used for the application.

Figure 5.1   A simple little application. Looks pretty now, right?

Listing 5.1   Simple application HTML (simple/www/index.html)

```html
<html>
    <head>
        <title>Simple App</title>
    </head>
    <body>

        <form id="nameForm">
            <label for="name">Enter your name</label>
            <input type="text" id="name" name="name">
            <input type="submit" value="Submit">
        </form>
```

Prompts for your name ⟶ (label/input line)

User enters name ⟵

Submits form ⟵

```
              <div id="result"></div>
```

Empty div that will be
filled with user's name
```
              <script src="cordova.js"></script>
              <script src="js/app.js"></script>
      </body>
</html>
```

There isn't anything particularly interesting about this code, but note the lack of any styling via an embedded or included CSS file. That's totally okay—you *don't* have to style anything, but as you can probably guess, this is going to bite us in the rear in a few moments. Now look at the JavaScript in the next listing.

Listing 5.2   Simple application JavaScript (simple/www/js/app.js)

```
document.addEventListener("deviceready", init, false);
function init() {

    document.querySelector("#nameForm").addEventListener("submit",
        function(e) {
                e.preventDefault();
                var name = document.querySelector("#name").value;
                var msg = "Hello, "+name;
                document.querySelector("#result").innerText = msg;
    }, false);

}
```

So far so good. Because the application has one feature (get the name and display it), the code is trivial to the point of being pointless. To be clear, this is *not* something you want to use Cordova for, but it will be very useful in demonstrating the type of design issues you're going to be running into when building hybrid applications. Fire up the application and send it to an Android device to see how beautiful it looks—similar to figure 5.2.

While readable in this book, that text would be rather small on a real mobile device. The field where users need to enter their name is also somewhat small. Your users have rather large hands, and if there were anything else by that field it would be difficult to

Figure 5.2   The simple application displayed on an Android device

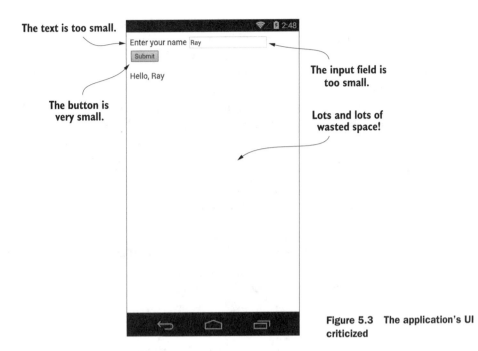

The text is too small.

The input field is too small.

The button is very small.

Lots and lots of wasted space!

Figure 5.3   The application's UI criticized

not touch the wrong thing. Even worse, the button to submit the form is tiny. If your users need to carefully think before they interact with your application then you've probably got a problem. Figure 5.3 calls out these issues, and more.

This is a perfect example of a case where the code works but it isn't optimized for the mobile platform. This is definitely *not* a bug in Cordova. It simply reflects the fact that when building hybrid applications, you need to think differently than you would when building websites for the desktop. Let's fix it up.

5.1.2   *Put some lipstick on the pig: improving the application with CSS*

As mentioned earlier, one of the things missing from the application's HTML code was a CSS style sheet. You can improve the application by adding basic styling to your elements to make better use of the mobile form factor. Figure 5.4 demonstrates the improved application.

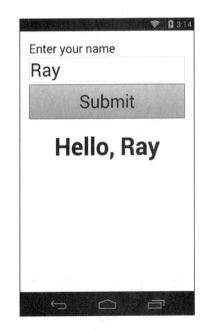

Figure 5.4   A (somewhat) prettier version of the application

Let's be honest. This "improved" application won't be winning any design contests. That's not your goal. What you wanted to do was make this application easier to use and more readable. While there's definitely *more* that could be done, figure 5.4 demonstrates how you can address the concerns identified in figure 5.3. The text is larger. Both the input field and the Submit button are much larger, which will be easier for users to tap with their fingers. The result area (where the user's name is displayed) takes up more space and you don't have a lot of empty whitespace being wasted. Listing 5.3 shows the CSS code used to make this design change. You can find the complete application in the c5/simple2 folder. Also note that the CSS file was included in the HTML via a simple `<link>` tag: `<link rel="stylesheet" type="text/css" href="css/app.css">`. You don't need to create a new Cordova application to test this—you can simply modify the existing one.

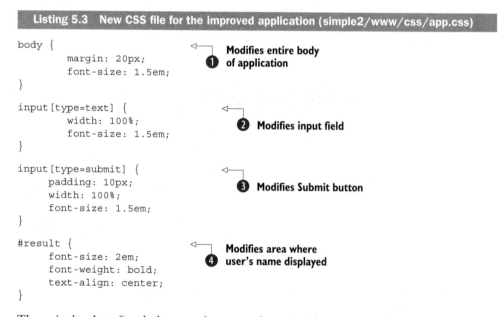

Listing 5.3 New CSS file for the improved application (simple2/www/css/app.css)

```
body {
        margin: 20px;
        font-size: 1.5em;
}

input[type=text] {
        width: 100%;
        font-size: 1.5em;
}

input[type=submit] {
        padding: 10px;
        width: 100%;
        font-size: 1.5em;
}

#result {
        font-size: 2em;
        font-weight: bold;
        text-align: center;
}
```

❶ Modifies entire body of application

❷ Modifies input field

❸ Modifies Submit button

❹ Modifies area where user's name displayed

There isn't a lot of code here and, as stated previously, more could be done, but this gets the job done. Each block in the CSS file in the listing modifies a different part of the application. The body block ❶ updates the application as a whole. Remember that your application is a web page. You've added margins around all the edges and increased the base font size a bit. The next two blocks modify the input field ❷ and Submit button ❸. Changes to the font size specified at the body level don't apply here so they're specified too. The width is increased ❹ to take the full width of a device minus the margins you specified in the body. You've made the `result` div use even bigger text, bold, and centered.

5.1.3 *The meta viewport tag*

If you've done any research in mobile web design, you've probably encountered the suggestion to add a `meta` tag to your page to specify a viewport setting, such as `<meta`

`name="viewport"` `content="width=device-width">`. At the simplest level, this tag tells the mobile device to consider the web page to have the same width as the device, something it will not do by default. So why wasn't it mentioned before?

Cordova applications automatically handle the viewport, and in fact, you have to modify a configuration setting (something we haven't touched on yet) to override this. This means you can, if you choose, skip setting this tag in your HTML. But because many people test in a browser before they work with native builds (something we'll cover in chapter 7), it makes sense to include the tag. If you look at the HTML for the updated simple application (c5/simple2/www/index.html), you'll see the tag is included even though it doesn't do anything for the application when run as a Cordova application. My suggestion? Include it!

5.2   *Enhancing your Cordova UI with Bootstrap*

While one solution would be to write all the CSS required for a well-designed app, maybe you don't want to, or may not have the skills to create a nice design. Many developers struggle with this—it's nothing to be ashamed of. Over the past few years, multiple libraries have been released that aim to make this task easier. They allow developers to include a style sheet (or multiple style sheets) to have a design automatically applied to their application. Some aren't necessarily "automatic" and may require you to add specific classes to your HTML to get the design. While not a magic bullet, these libraries can go a long way toward making your life easier as an application developer. They're especially useful when building proof-of-concept applications. You may be building something for a client who hasn't provided any design guidelines at all. By using one of these libraries you can easily add a professional-looking design to your application that can then be modified, or removed, later. For this chapter we'll be discussing one of the most popular of these libraries, Bootstrap.

5.2.1   *Introducing Bootstrap*

Bootstrap (figure 5.5) is used in multiple websites, from blogs to e-commerce sites, and is fully responsive. *Responsive web design* refers to a web page that can automatically

Figure 5.5   The Bootstrap website

adapt to different size viewports. This means a web page that looks good on a desktop machine will also look good on a mobile device. With Cordova, we aren't worried about the desktop, but mobile devices can also vary quite a bit in their sizes as well, ranging from smallish phones to mid- and large-size tablets.

Bootstrap is free and open source, which means you cannot only use it for free but you can also modify it as you see fit. For your needs here you'll be using it to improve the design of your applications. You can download Bootstrap from www.getbootstrap.com, but there's a copy in the zip file you downloaded from the book's website. The copy included in the zip may not be the most recent version, so I recommend downloading the latest bits from the website just to be sure. Figure 5.6 shows a "Bootstrapped" version of your simple application. It isn't radically different from the second version, but if the application were to continue to grow in scope, the benefits of using Bootstrap would become more and more apparent.

Figure 5.6 "Bootstrapped" version of your simple application

The following listing shows how you implement Bootstrap in the application. Your code base used the initial version of the sample application as a starting point, so we'll focus on the changes from that.

Listing 5.4 Updated and "Bootstrapped" application (simple3/www/index.html)

```html
<html>
  <head>
    <title>Simple App</title>
    <meta name="viewport"
          content="width=device-width, initial-scale=1">
    <link rel="stylesheet " type="text/css"
          href="lib/bootstrap/css/bootstrap.min.css" />        ◁⌐
  </head>                                                    ❶ Includes Bootstrap CSS

  <body>

    <div class="container">                        ◁⌐ Wraps entire content and
                                                    ❷ adds a bit of padding
      <form id="nameForm">
      <h2>Enter your name</h2>
```

Wraps in a form-group block ❸

```
<div class="form-group">
    <input type="text" id="name" name="name"
            class="form-control">
</div>
<div class="form-group">
    <input type="submit" value="Submit"
            class="btn btn-primary btn-block">
</div>
</form>

<h1 id="result" class="text-center"></h1>

</div>

<script src="cordova.js"></script>
<script src="js/app.js"></script>

</body>

</html>
```

❹ Adds automatic formatting

❺ Adds styling to button

Handles centering text

First, you include the Bootstrap CSS file ❶. Note that this replaces the custom CSS you created earlier. Notice all of Bootstrap is included in a subdirectory under www called lib/bootstrap. This is completely arbitrary. It makes sense to keep Bootstrap stuff within its own folder and lib (short for library) is commonly used as a place to store third-party libraries. This helps separate your code from the code you downloaded. Again, this is *not* a requirement, but it helps keep things organized.

Bootstrap works by a combination of automatic updates and creating a set of classes you can add to your code. container ❷, is a class used to wrap all the content of a particular web page. (For a full look at all Bootstrap CSS classes, see the documentation at http://getbootstrap.com/css/.) This is then complemented by additional classes in your form fields (❸, ❹) that add formatting. As you can see in figure 5.6 the form fields are large and full screen.

This is even more apparent in the button change ❺. Three classes—btn, btn-primary, and btr-block—are added to it. btn handles basic improvements to the button to give it a flat, stylish look. btn-primary adds a color (blue) to the button (there are other options). btn-block creates a full-screen block button. This combination was chosen purely for aesthetic reasons. You could decide that a different color, or no color, makes more sense. You could also choose multiple types of sizes. Consult the Bootstrap documentation for more about the types of things you can do with it. The point is with a relative little bit of typing you've got a nice, clean-looking design for your application.

5.2.2 *Another example: the camera app*

Let's look at another simple example. In chapter 4 you built an application that made use of the Camera plugin. Some very basic styling was done to the buttons used in the app as well as the image that was displayed. You can switch to using Bootstrap *only* to

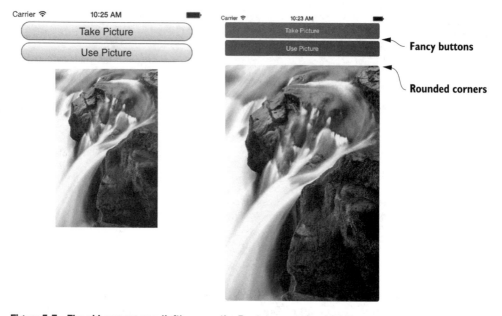

Fancy buttons

Rounded corners

Figure 5.7   The old camera app (left) versus the Bootstrap version (right)

improve the buttons while keeping the fancy sepia look. Figure 5.7 shows the original version of the application next to the updated Bootstrap edition.

Again, this isn't a radical change, but the Bootstrap version does look nicer and overall more professional. Let's look at the changes required to make this happen, shown in the following listing. If you want to try this version, you can either modify the older version (and remember to copy the Bootstrap library), or use the version included with the zip. It can be found at c5/camera_demo_bootstrap.

**Listing 5.5   Updated camera index.html
(c5/camera_demo_bootstrap/www/index.html)**

```
<!DOCTYPE html>
<html>

  <head>
    <meta charset="utf-8">
    <title>Basic Camera</title>
    <meta name="viewport" content="width=device-width">
    <link rel="stylesheet" type="text/css"
    href="lib/bootstrap/css/bootstrap.min.css" />
      <link rel="stylesheet" type="text/css" href="css/app.css" />
  </head>

  <body>

    <div class="container">
```

Application-
specific CSS ❷

❶ Bootstrap CSS

**Updated
button styling** ③

```
              <button id="takePicture"
                      class="btn btn-primary btn-block">Take Picture</button>
              <button id="usePicture"
                      class="btn btn-primary btn-block">Use Picture</button>

              <img id="myImage" class="img-responsive img-rounded">

          </div>

          <script src="cordova.js"></script>
          <script src="js/app.js"></script>
      </body>
  </html>
```

**Updated image
④ styling**

As before, to include Bootstrap you have to include the CSS file ①. But you can also include your own CSS ②. As you'll see in listing 5.6, the CSS is somewhat slimmed down now that Bootstrap is handling more for you. The buttons are updated ③ much like in the previous example. As a final step the Bootstrap image styling ④ is updated. Bootstrap has a responsive image class that handles making the image take up as much real estate as possible. This is important as you want the image to look nice on phones and tablets. The other class, img-rounded, adds rounded corners to the image. (I added this because. Yes, just because.)

Now let's look at the updated CSS.

> **Listing 5.6 Updated camera CSS file
> (c5/camera_demo_bootstrap/www/css/app.css)**

```
body {
  margin-top: 20px;
}

img {
  margin-top: 20px;
  -webkit-filter: sepia(100%);
}
```

The CSS is now much slimmer as you're letting Bootstrap do more for you. Bootstrap doesn't add any padding to the top of the document as you've kept a margin on the body. You also want the image to be a bit below the buttons so a margin is used there as well. Finally, the sepia effect is maintained.

5.2.3 *Bootstrap does more*

We've only scratched the surface of what Bootstrap can add to an application. Along with nice styling for buttons it includes other components, some of which require a JavaScript file as well. I highly encourage you to look over the Bootstrap website to get an idea of what can be easily added to an application.

Bootstrap isn't meant to be a silver bullet. You cannot expect that it will be usable for *every* application. But it can be a great way to get started and a great way to focus your development time on other issues.

If you enjoy using Bootstrap, you can also make it look more unique. Many commercial and free themes exist that integrate well with Bootstrap. For examples, check out https://wrapbootstrap.com.

5.3   Mobile UI frameworks: an overview

Because so many developers need help when it comes to design, there are numerous mobile UI frameworks available. Many are much more than a simple UI framework. They may provide a user interaction (UX), such as pull to refresh, or other related services. This section looks at four such frameworks: Ionic, jQuery Mobile, Ratchet, and Kendo UI. We begin with Ionic, my favorite. My best advice is try each one yourself and find the one that best matches your development style. The best option is the one that makes you, and your app, successful.

5.3.1   *Ionic: UI, UX, and more*

Easily my favorite, Ionic (http://ionicframe work .com/) provides a UI framework (figure 5.8), UX tool (like pull to refresh), and numerous other tools that dramatically enhance the power of hybrid mobile applications, and specifically Cordova. The only reason this book won't cover Ionic is that it requires some other prerequisites that would prevent some readers from being able to use it easily. Ionic relies on AngularJS, a popular JavaScript framework, but also one that's a bit complex for the uninitiated.

Figure 5.8   An example of one of Ionic's UI controls, a Card

Ionic provides a command-line wrapper around Cordova itself. It adds logging and other productivity enhancements on top of what Cordova provides. In my personal opinion, Ionic is the best thing to happen to Cordova. You can read more in *Ionic in Action* (Manning Publications, 2014) by Jeremy Wilkin (www.manning.com/wilken/).

5.3.2   *jQuery Mobile: powerful and simple*

One of the older options, jQuery Mobile (http:// jquerymobile.com/), is one of the easiest UI frameworks to use, and like other frameworks, it provides other features for mobile development. Because of its ease of use (despite the name, you can do a heck of lot without writing any jQuery-related code), jQuery Mobile will be discussed in depth later in the book.

jQuery Mobile does most of its work within HTML, providing simple attributes to enhance controls into mobile-friendly widgets, like those shown in figure 5.9. For example, creating tabs is done by adding `data-role="tabs"` to a `div` block.

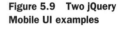

Figure 5.9 Two jQuery Mobile UI examples

5.3.3 Ratchet: Android and iOS friendly

Ratchet (http://goratchet.com/) works a bit like Bootstrap. You include a required CSS file (as well as JavaScript if need be) and then make use of particular classes in your elements to get the desired look. Like Bootstrap, Ratchet has multiple widgets you can use to create your application. Ratchet also includes support for different styling for both iOS and Android, as shown in figure 5.10. (jQuery Mobile, for example, will look the same on both devices.)

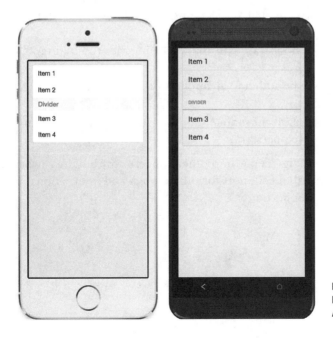

Figure 5.10 Two examples of Ratchet showing iOS versus Android views

5.3.4   *Kendo UI: large and commercially supported*

Kendo UI (www.telerik.com/kendo-ui1), which is part of a much larger set of free and commercial services, provides nearly 80 different UI widgets for use with mobile web pages and hybrid applications (figure 5.11). It can integrate with Bootstrap so an application could make use of both of them at once. Unlike Bootstrap, Kendo UI uses JavaScript to enhance controls as opposed to only adding classes to HTML. Kendo is the product of Telerik, which has an entire platform of services, including testing, server-side data persistence, and even web-based building services, that would be of interest to folks developing hybrid applications.

Figure 5.11   One of the Kendo UI demo applications (not my hand—honest)

5.4   Summary

Let's review the major topics covered in this chapter.

- Creating an application that works well on mobile devices requires planning ahead of time.
- UI frameworks like Bootstrap exist that make it easier to build mobile-friendly applications.
- Bootstrap can easily be added to an application to create a beautiful UI for your Cordova application.
- Because of the popularity of mobile (and hybrid) development, many different options exist for developers.

In the next chapter, we'll dig deeper into other concerns for building hybrid mobile applications. You'll learn about support for offline users and international users, and how to store data in the application.

Considerations when building mobile apps

This chapter covers

- Why you should use single-page applications for Cordova development
- How to make your application work offline
- How to support different countries with internationalization and localization
- How to save data to a device

The previous chapter began—perhaps—a bit roughly. We made it plain that while you now know how to create an application on a device, you don't yet know how to do it well. That's an incredibly important distinction.

6.1 Congratulations—you're a (slightly better) mobile developer!

I hope you agree that—for the most part—Cordova is simple to use. If you have even the tiniest bit of JavaScript knowledge you can easily add support for device features like the camera or accelerometer. But as you saw, making an application that's easy to use on a device is another matter. The last chapter dealt with the UI design of your applications. This chapter covers another side to the equation—the types of functionality that make up a good Cordova application. Let's begin with a look at the concept of the single-page application (SPA).

6.2   *Single-page applications and you*

Let's begin with a quick overview of how traditional websites work for end users.

In figure 6.1 you see a web browser (a happy web browser, why shouldn't the user be happy?) accessing a few web pages. In a typical website, this is done page by page. So a user may first start at the homepage, let's say www.raymondcamden.com. The user sees a link to a fascinating article ("Oh look, Ray's posted more pictures of his cats!"), clicks it, and the browser loads an entirely new page. The user sees yet another link ("Ray's

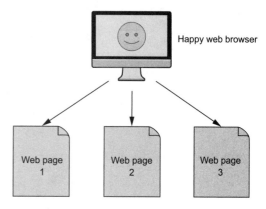

Figure 6.1   A web browser accessing multiple web pages of a website

reviewing another videogame—I *must* read that!"), clicks it, and the process is repeated. On a typical website, the layout remains the same but the actual content changes. The browser has to get the entire page for every unique part of the website. This statelessness of the web is how it's always been. There are ways to get around it (cookies, server-side sessions), but it doesn't change the basic architecture of the website.

You can—if you choose—build a Cordova application the same way. But there's a better way.

In figure 6.2, the website has been rebuilt as a form of SPA. Instead of reloading three unique pages, the user accesses an initial page that then loads other pages via AJAX. The initial page contains the layout of the website (header, footer, advertising banners, etc.) while the requested web pages contain only the data for that particular item. For a blog these might be the text of the articles themselves. To the user, nothing has changed. The user went

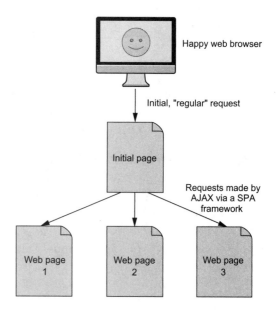

Figure 6.2   A web application being accessed as a SPA

to a website and read three articles. Behind the scenes the browser is being a bit more efficient—loading in pure data for new requests via loading in an entire block of HTML.

> **WHAT IS AJAX?** AJAX stands for Asynchronous JavaScript and XML and is the most common way for a web page to automatically update itself with new content. While XML is rarely used now (JSON is the preferred data format), AJAX in general is heavily used by client-side applications. You used AJAX earlier in the book when doing the GitHub search. The easiest way to think of AJAX is simply using JavaScript to make HTTP requests to resources.

6.2.1   So why should you care?

On first blush, this probably seems like complexity for complexity's sake. The end user gains nothing. As a developer, you have to work more. (We haven't yet discussed how to build a SPA, but as you can imagine, it isn't as simple as old-school websites.) What practical benefits are gained by using the SPA approach?

One of the main benefits of the SPA approach is that client-side data persists. Imagine a web page that uses a JavaScript variable that simply represents when the page was opened:

```
var opened = new Date();
```

The purpose of this variable is to keep track of how long the user stays on the website. In a typical web page, this JavaScript variable would be lost as soon as the user clicks a link to load the next page. That's why server-side solutions using sessions were built— to add state to the statelessness. But a Cordova application doesn't run on a server. It's simply bundled HTML files being loaded from the device filesystem. Switching to a SPA means any data created via JavaScript will persist as the user moves through the application. Because full-page reloads aren't being used, the browser essentially runs, and constantly modifies, the initial web page.

A second benefit relates to the `deviceready` event. As covered in chapter 4, your code cannot make use of any device-specific features via plugins until the `deviceready` event is fired. In a "traditional" web page, every request to a new page (going from page 1 to 2, for example) means waiting again for the event to fire. It isn't difficult, of course, but the more chances you have to mess something up is—well—more chances to mess up. In a SPA, there's one main page load and one wait for the `deviceready` event. You don't have to worry about it again.

One of the biggest benefits of a SPA is organization. An application is inherently different from a blog or other news website. Applications typically have a persistent UI (control bars, for example) and different interactions than a content site. SPAs make this easier to architect as well. To be clear, "single page" does not mean one file. That would become messy as heck.

6.2.2   A SPA for you, a SPA for me, a SPA for everyone!

As you can imagine, because of the usefulness of the SPA concept, there are a number of JavaScript libraries available that help facilitate this (and better development in general). Here is a short, incomplete list—each has its own philosophy and development lifecycle:

- *AngularJS (www.angularjs.org)*—Probably the most popular JavaScript framework. It focuses on properly separating layout from logic and is very extensible.
- *Backbone.js (www.backbonejs.org)*—Also popular and also heavily focused on separating logic and layout.
- *Ember (www.emberjs.com)*—Created by Yehuda Katz, it makes use of the popular Handlebars.js templating language.
- *Knockout (www.knockoutjs.com)*—A lightweight framework with good support for older browsers.
- *jQuery Mobile (www.jquerymobile.com)*—An easy, mostly HTML-based SPA.

Each of these (and the many not listed) would be useful in helping you build a Cordova application (or desktop web application, of course), but there's no way that one framework would work well with everyone reading this book. You're *strongly* encouraged to take time to investigate a number of options and find the one that best fits your (or your team's) development style.

For this book, we'll look at jQuery Mobile, one of the more simple frameworks that supports SPA and handles a UI. In other words, using jQuery Mobile lets you build a SPA and create a mobile-friendly design. Obviously a full description of how to use jQuery Mobile is outside the bounds of this book. (If you want, you can pick up the book I wrote, *jQuery Mobile Web Development Essentials*, Packt Publishing, 2012.) Let's look at a simple example of how jQuery Mobile works, and then we'll follow up with an example that makes use of Cordova plugins and multiple pages.

> **A note for users of Angular, Ember, or other frameworks**
>
> If you're already comfortable with a framework that provides SPA, there's no reason for you to read the jQuery Mobile section (although if you've never seen it, you may find its approach interesting). Knowing that you need to wait for the `deviceready` event is the crucial point for this section, and if you've got your own SPA ready to use, I suggest using it. Cordova is JavaScript framework agnostic; that is, it will work with whatever you're comfortable with.

6.2.3   *jQuery Mobile: the basics*

jQuery Mobile works primarily via automatic enhancement of your code. In other words, your existing HTML code will be made mobile friendly with little to no changes on your own part. By including the library (one JavaScript file and one CSS file) and jQuery itself, jQuery Mobile will start trying to make your HTML nicer on mobile devices. The library scans the DOM (the HTML structure of your web page) for things like buttons and input fields it can enhance with CSS improvements that are mobile friendly. If you supply a few basic HTML attributes, jQuery Mobile can also create different widgets like lists and panels.

The first example demonstrates a basic template. This is *not* a Cordova application. You can open this in your desktop browser. If you want, you can copy this code into a Cordova application to see how it looks on a mobile device, and if you do, consider yourself earning extra credit. Figure 6.3 shows how this simple demo looks in Firefox's responsive design mode.

Figure 6.3 An example of a simple jQuery Mobile page

Now let's look at the code behind this page in the following listing.

Listing 6.1   Basic jQuery Mobile template (c6/jqm1/index.html)

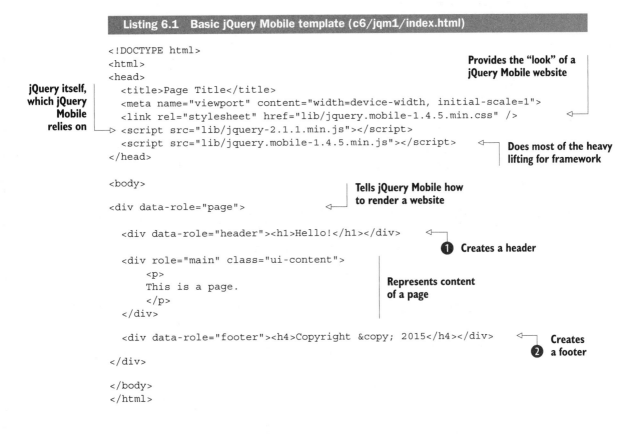

```
<!DOCTYPE html>
<html>
<head>
  <title>Page Title</title>
  <meta name="viewport" content="width=device-width, initial-scale=1">
  <link rel="stylesheet" href="lib/jquery.mobile-1.4.5.min.css" />
  <script src="lib/jquery-2.1.1.min.js"></script>
  <script src="lib/jquery.mobile-1.4.5.min.js"></script>
</head>

<body>

<div data-role="page">

  <div data-role="header"><h1>Hello!</h1></div>

  <div role="main" class="ui-content">
      <p>
      This is a page.
      </p>
  </div>

  <div data-role="footer"><h4>Copyright &copy; 2015</h4></div>

</div>

</body>
</html>
```

Provides the "look" of a jQuery Mobile website

jQuery itself, which jQuery Mobile relies on

Does most of the heavy lifting for framework

Tells jQuery Mobile how to render a website

❶ Creates a header

Represents content of a page

❷ Creates a footer

Like Bootstrap, jQuery Mobile lets you create a UI by modifying your HTML. Unlike Bootstrap, this isn't done primarily through CSS classes (although they're used sometimes), but usually via data attributes. Data attributes are an HTML5 mechanism that lets you add custom attributes to HTML. So, for example, `<b data-ray="awesome">Text</b>` is valid HTML because *anything* is allowed in the data attribute. jQuery Mobile uses these flags to enhance the page, creating headers ❶ and footers ❷, for example.

Okay, this is pretty, but it doesn't address the problem of creating a SPA. Let's enhance the example by adding two more pages. The pages in question don't really matter—you can call them Child page 1 and Child page 2. The homepage will have links to each with the child pages simply linking back to the homepage, as shown in figure 6.4.

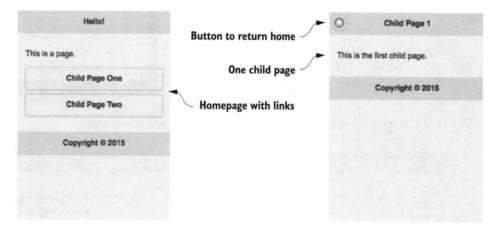

Figure 6.4   jQuery Mobile page with navigation added

Now let's look at the code that modified the homepage with links. Because only a small part changed, the following listing focuses on the central `div` containing the page content.

Listing 6.2   Updated homepage with links (c6/jqm2/index.html)

```
<div role="main" class="ui-content">
    <p>
    This is a page.
    </p>
    <p>
      <a href="child_page1.html" data-role="button">
        Child Page One
      </a>
      <a href="child_page2.html" data-role="button">
        Child Page Two
      </a>
    </p>
</div>
```

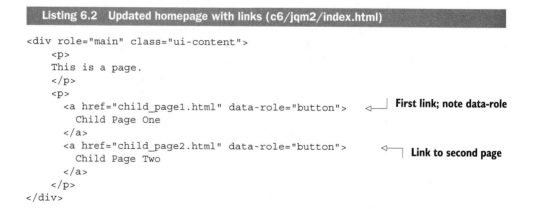

In general, the links are simple <a> tags, but make note of the use of data-role= "button". This tells jQuery Mobile to change the look of the link to a button. The button is nice and large and will work great on a mobile device. Now let's look at one of the child pages. (The second child page is the very same minus replacing 1 with 2. If you aren't using the files from the zip, copy child_page1.html to a new file, child_ page2.html, and change the word "first" to "second" to help make it more clear.)

Listing 6.3   Child page (c6/jqm2/child_page1.html)

```
<!DOCTYPE html>
<html>
<head>
  <title>Child page 1</title>
  <meta name="viewport" content="width=device-width, initial-scale=1">
  <link rel="stylesheet" href="lib/jquery.mobile-1.4.5.min.css" />
  <script src="lib/jquery-2.1.1.min.js"></script>
  <script src="lib/jquery.mobile-1.4.5.min.js"></script>
</head>

<body>

<div data-role="page">

  <div data-role="header">
    <a href="index.html" data-icon="home"            Creates a home button
      data-iconpos="notext">Home</a>             ❶  as shown in figure 6.4
    <h1>Child Page 1</h1>
  </div>

  <div role="main" class="ui-content">
      <p>
      This is the first child page.
      </p>
  </div>

  <div data-role="footer"><h4>Copyright &copy; 2015</h4></div>

</div>

</body>
</html>
```

In general, this is more of the same, but note the link in the header ❶. Another jQuery Mobile feature is the ability to turn links into icon-based buttons—in this case, a simple "home" icon with the text of the link suppressed.

So what's so special about this? Isn't this another example of a website with multiple pages? Not with jQuery Mobile! jQuery Mobile automatically detects links to relative pages (for instance, the link to child_page1.html) and changes them to AJAX-based loads. In other words, without jQuery Mobile the click on the link in the homepage would tell the browser to load the other page. It would be a completely new request. In jQuery Mobile, the framework hijacks the link, uses AJAX to load the other page, and injects it into the view. Poof! Instant SPA with simple HTML.

6.2.4 *Mixing jQuery Mobile and Cordova*

Now that you've gotten an incredibly brief introduction to jQuery Mobile, it's time to put it together with Cordova. Your application will make use of two Cordova plugins you haven't used yet—Device Accelerometer and Device Orientation. The Device Accelerometer plugin reports on any motion that's being exerted on the device. A common use case for this would be noticing when the user has "shaken" the device. The Device Orientation plugin refers to what direction the device is pointing. Both plugins support getting the current values for the accelerometer and compass or getting constant readings. To keep it simple, your app will report the current values. Figure 6.5 demonstrates the three screens for the application.

Begin by creating a new Cordova application at the command line. The application makes use of two plugins that you'll need to add: `cordova-plugin-device-motion` and `cordova-plugin-device-orientation`. Don't forget the handy `--copy-from` option if you want to use the code downloaded from the book's website. (The code can be found in the c6/jqm3/www folder.)

The homepage of the application is very similar to the previous example, but with two small changes. The following listing shows the code.

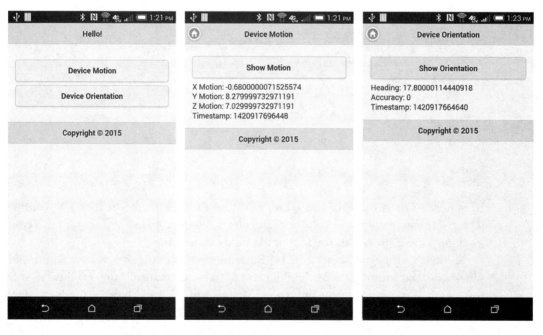

Figure 6.5   A jQuery Mobile–based accelerometer/compass demo

Listing 6.4   jQuery Mobile Cordova application (c6/jqm3/index.html)

```html
<!DOCTYPE html>
<html>
<head>
  <title>Page Title</title>
  <meta name="viewport" content="width=device-width, initial-scale=1">
  <link rel="stylesheet" href="lib/jquery.mobile-1.4.5.min.css" />
  <script src="lib/jquery-2.1.1.min.js"></script>
  <script src="js/app.js"></script>
  <script src="lib/jquery.mobile-1.4.5.min.js"></script>
</head>

<body>

<div data-role="page">

  <div data-role="header"><h1>Hello!</h1></div>

  <div role="main" class="ui-content">
      <p>
        <a href="device_motion.html" data-role="button">
          Device Motion
        </a>
        <a href="device_orientation.html" data-role="button">
          Device Orientation
        </a>
      </p>
  </div>

  <div data-role="footer"><h4>Copyright &copy; 2015</h4></div>

</div>

<script src="cordova.js"></script>
</body>
</html>
```

❶ Handles the app's features

❷ Don't forget to include cordova.js so that Cordova CLI can include platform-specific code

The only things worth mentioning here are the addition of script tags to load first the application's logic in app.js ❶ and cordova.js ❷. Before we get to the JavaScript, let's look at the page that displays motion data, shown in the following listing.

Listing 6.5   Device motion page (c6/jqm3/device_motion.tml)

```html
<!DOCTYPE html>
<html>
<head>
  <title>Motion</title>
  <meta name="viewport" content="width=device-width, initial-scale=1">
  <link rel="stylesheet" href="lib/jquery.mobile-1.4.5.min.css" />
  <script src="lib/jquery-2.1.1.min.js"></script>
  <script src="lib/jquery.mobile-1.4.5.min.js"></script>
</head>
<body>
```

```
<div data-role="page">

  <div data-role="header">
    <a href="index.html" data-icon="home"
       data-iconpos="notext">Home</a>
    <h1>Device Motion</h1>
  </div>

  <div role="main" class="ui-content">
    <button id="showMotion">Show Motion</button>     ←  ❶ Triggers getting
    <div id="motionData"></div>                          motion data
  </div>                                              ←
                                                      ❷ Empty div for results
  <div data-role="footer"><h4>Copyright &copy; 2015</h4></div>

</div>

</body>
</html>
```

This page is relatively simple. It has a button ❶ that you'll use to trigger a call to get motion data and a simple empty `div` ❷ that will be used to render those results. The orientation page is the very same except for the button ID, label, and empty `div id`.

Now let's look at the JavaScript. This is where things get slightly interesting. When working with JavaScript frameworks like jQuery Mobile (and pretty much every other one), they have their own concept of "startup." What does this mean? As stated before, jQuery Mobile does a lot of things automatically. It looks at your HTML and tries to enhance it. It looks for particular attributes and classes as well to add things like headers and footers. This takes time. It should be really darn quick, but it takes time. To help you know when this is done, jQuery Mobile fires an event, `mobileinit`. Okay, so far so good. But don't forget—before you can do anything device-specific, you have to wait for Cordova's event, `deviceready`.

So you have *two* events that you have to listen for before you can get started. This isn't terribly difficult if you make use of a jQuery feature called Promises. A full description of Promises is beyond the scope of this book, but it provides a way to handle complex asynchronous events like this. Specifically, Promises provides support for waiting for a list of asynchronous events to complete. For the application here you're going to use a nice snippet provided by StackOverflow user Octavian in this answer: http://stackoverflow.com/a/12821151/52160.

Listing 6.6   Handling waiting for jQuery Mobile and Cordova

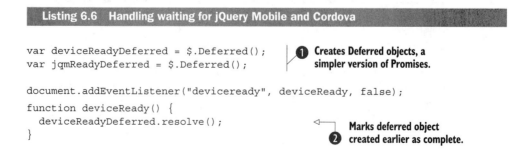

```
var deviceReadyDeferred = $.Deferred();        ❶ Creates Deferred objects, a
var jqmReadyDeferred = $.Deferred();              simpler version of Promises.

document.addEventListener("deviceready", deviceReady, false);
function deviceReady() {
  deviceReadyDeferred.resolve();               ←  Marks deferred object
}                                              ❷ created earlier as complete.
```

```
$(document).on("mobileinit", function () {
  jqmReadyDeferred.resolve();
});

$.when(deviceReadyDeferred, jqmReadyDeferred).then(init);
```

③ By using $.when, you can run something when both async items are done.

If you've never seen Promises in action, this may seem a bit weird. You begin by creating two `Deferred` objects **①**, which are simpler versions of Promises. You can then add a `deviceready` listener as has been done before, but now when it fires you run the `resolve()` **②** method of the object. The same process is repeated for the `mobileinit` event used with jQuery Mobile. The magic happens within `$.when` **③**. The `when()` method lets you wait for a list of asynchronous items to complete. You can have any number of items in here but your code needs only two. The function passed to `then()` is what's run when both Cordova and jQuery Mobile are done.

Promises and `Deferred` objects are a pretty complex topic. You can learn more about them in *jQuery in Action*, 3rd edition (Manning Publications, 2015) by Bear Bibeault, et al. (www.manning.com/derosa/).

While the snippet in listing 6.6 is specific to jQuery Mobile, there are similar ways to handle this in Angular, Backbone, and so forth. The following listing shows the complete app.js file.

Listing 6.7 Application logic (c6/jqm3/www/js/app.js)

```
var deviceReadyDeferred = $.Deferred();
var jqmReadyDeferred = $.Deferred();

document.addEventListener("deviceready", deviceReady, false);

function deviceReady() {
  deviceReadyDeferred.resolve();
}

$(document).on("mobileinit", function () {
  jqmReadyDeferred.resolve();
});

$.when(deviceReadyDeferred, jqmReadyDeferred).then(init);

function init() {

  $(document).on("touchend", "#showMotion", function(e) {
    e.preventDefault();
    navigator.accelerometer.getCurrentAcceleration(
     gotMotion, onMotionError);
  });

  $(document).on("touchend", "#showOrientation", function(e) {
    e.preventDefault();
    navigator.compass.getCurrentHeading(
     gotOrientation, onOrientationError);
  });

}
```

① Listens for touches on motion button

③ Calls device motion plugin to get current motion

② Listens for touches on orientation button

④ Calls device orientation plugin to get current orientation

```
function gotMotion(acc) {
  var s = "";
  s += "X Motion: "+acc.x + "<br/>";
  s += "Y Motion: "+acc.y + "<br/>";
  s += "Z Motion: "+acc.z + "<br/>";
  s += "Timestamp: "+acc.timestamp;

  $("#motionData").html(s);
}
```

⬅ **❺** Renders device's current motion

```
function onMotionError(e) {
  $("#motionData").html("Error! "+e.toString());
}
```

```
function gotOrientation(heading) {
  var s = "";
  s += "Heading: "+heading.magneticHeading + "<br/>";
  s += "Accuracy: "+heading.headingAccuracy + "<br/>";
  s += "Timestamp: "+heading.timestamp;

  $("#orientationData").html(s);
}
```

⬅ **❻** Renders device's current orientation

```
function onOrientationError(e) {
if(e.code === CompassError.COMPASS_INTERNAL_ERR) {
    $("#orientationData").html("Error! An internal error.");
  } else if(e.code === CompassError.COMPASS_NOT_SUPPORTED) {
    $("#orientationData").html("Error! No compass.");
  } else {
    $("#orientationData").html("Error! Unknown error.");
  }
}
```

Outside of the code to handle waiting for deviceready and mobileinit, there are only two things going on here. You have to listen for touch events on both buttons (❶, ❷). For the device motion button you use the API's method ❸ to get the device's motion. This returns an object with X, Y, and Z values for how much the device is moving, as well as a precise timestamp of when the data was fetched. You can simply print this out to the div on the device motion page. Working with orientation follows the same pattern. You ask the plugin for the current value ❹ and then render it ❺. The orientation object ❻ contains a heading value and accuracy, as well as a timestamp like orientation. A fancier version of this application could use CSS to render out an arrow on a compass.

Now that you've seen the basics of creating a multipage application with Cordova, it's time to tackle the next problem—working offline.

6.3   *Building offline-ready Cordova applications*

Most folks don't consider offline when building websites. What's the point of building a website that works offline when you need to be online to hit the website in the first place? But technically, it's possible with an API called AppCache. AppCache lets you define a manifest (a list essentially) of resources for your website/application that the browser can store offline. The idea being that if you try to access the website a *second* time and are offline, the browser can use its cache instead. AppCache exists, but isn't used a lot. For fun, do a Google search for "appcache is a douche" to find a wonderfully detailed rant about just how awful it can be to make use of the API.

The good news is, you don't have to worry about it! When you use Cordova to create an application, the files (HTML, CSS, JavaScript) are all bundled and put on the device itself. Whether or not the user is online (cell or WiFi) doesn't matter because the application has the content on the device itself. So, problem solved and you can move on. Not so fast!

6.3.1 *Problems with the application*

Consider the GitHub application you built in chapter 3. It was relatively simple—you enter a term and it hits GitHub's API to find projects that match your search term. What happens if you run this application on a device with no internet connection?

The first thing you'll notice is that when you enter a term and click Search, nothing happens. It's nearly impossible to know why, but luckily you'll learn how to debug Cordova applications soon. To make it easier, I'll tell you what failed:

```
<script type="text/javascript" src="http://ajax.googleapis.com/ajax/libs/
    jquery/2.1.0/jquery.min.js"></script>
```

Your application did what most people's did—used the Content Delivery Network (CDN) version of jQuery. This is typically a good idea, but in a Cordova application, using the CDN means that the moment the application is offline, it can no longer load jQuery!

That's easy enough to fix (download the jQuery file and copy it to your project). But what happens after you fix that and try to search while offline? Figure 6.6 demonstrates what the user will see.

You can see clearly that the app responded to the user input. It *says* it's searching, but nothing shows up. Because you're reading this book, you know what's going on, but the end user has no idea. Luckily, it isn't too difficult to correct this. You're going to modify your application to make two changes:

When the application starts, it will see if the user is offline, and if so, it will disable the form and tell the user why.

When the application starts, it will listen for network-related events. If the app goes online

Figure 6.6 Is the GitHub Search app working?

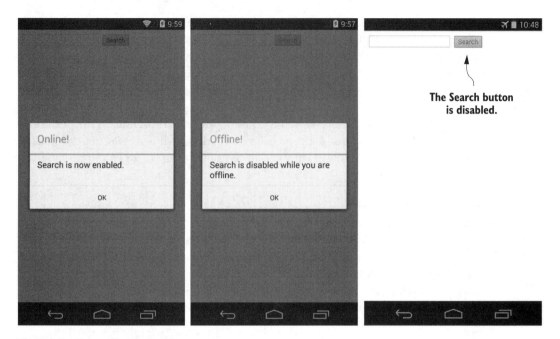

Figure 6.7   The application in different states

or offline, the application will respond accordingly. This is important because the application may start in one state and then flip back and forth as the user drives (or, hopefully, is driven).

Figure 6.7 demonstrates the changes made to the application.

6.3.2   *Adding offline support to the GitHub Search application*

To enable these changes, you'll add the Network Information plugin (`cordova-plugin-network-information`) as well as the Dialogs plugin (`cordova-plugin-dialogs`). The Dialogs plugin is only used for the prompts you see in figure 6.7. The Network Information plugin has two features. First, you can inspect a `navigator.connection.type` value to try to determine what type of connection the user has. This value can be unknown, offline, or one of a few different values representing different types of networks, for example, WiFi versus 4G. The second feature is support for responding to an `offline` and `online` event.

By listening to these events, you can modify the app to prevent searching when the user is offline. You can also tell the user what happened. Conversely, you can re-enable the form when the user goes back online and let the user know. Using Dialogs as you did earlier is an arbitrary design decision that makes sense to me. It may not make sense to you. But the important part here is to do *something* in response to the changing network conditions.

The code for this application is based on the GitHub sample from chapter 3, but with multiple modifications in order for this to work. Begin by creating a project and adding two plugins required (`org.apache.cordova.network-information` and `org.apache.cordova.dialogs`). You can find the source for the project in the c6/searchapp1 folder from the zip downloaded at the book's website. The following listing is the app's index.html page.

Listing 6.8 Search app's homepage (c6/searchapp1/index.html)

```html
<!DOCTYPE html>
<html>
  <head>
  <meta charset="utf-8">
  <title>GitHub Search Demo</title>
  <meta name="description" content="">
  <meta name="viewport" content="width=device-width">
  <script type="text/javascript" src="jquery.min.js"></script>    ← ① Loads in jQuery library
  <script type="text/javascript" src="app.js"></script>
  </head>

  <body>
    <input type="search" id="searchField">
    <button id="searchButton">Search</button>

    <div id="results"></div>

    <script src="cordova.js"></script>    ← 
  </body>                                    ② Loads in Cordova library
</html>
```

The first change is to refer to a local copy of jQuery ①. Obviously if the user is offline they still can't do much, but you want to ensure the library loads no matter what. The next change is to include the Cordova JavaScript library ②. You didn't need this in chapter 3 as you weren't really making use of Cordova features. Now your application does and will need this reference. Remember that the file will *not* exist in the www folder. It gets copied when you create builds. Now look at the JavaScript in the following listing.

Listing 6.9 Search app's JavaScript code (c6/searchapp1/app.js)

```javascript
document.addEventListener("deviceready", init, false);    ←  Switched to using
var lastStatus = "";                                       ① deviceready event
                                                           ⎱ Stores last status value ②
function init() {

    //listen for changes                                              ③ Listens for device
    document.addEventListener("offline", disableForm, false);    ←    to go offline
    document.addEventListener("online", enableForm, false);    ←  Listens for device
                                                                 ④ to go online
    $("#searchButton").on("click", function(e) {
```

```
    var search = $("#searchField").val();
    if(search === "") return;

    //disable button while we search
    $(this).prop("disabled",true);

    $("#results").html("<i>Doing a search for "+search+"</i>");

    //ok, hit the API
    $.get("https://api.github.com/search/repositories", {"q":search},
      function(res,code) {
        if(res.items && res.items.length) {
          var s = "<h2>Results</h2>";
          for(var i=0, len=res.items.length; i<len; i++) {
            var entry = res.items[i];
            s += "<p><strong>"+entry.name+"</strong><br/>";
            s += "By: " + entry.owner.login+"<br/>";
            s += "Updated: " + entry.updated_at+"<br/>";
            s += entry.description;
            s += "</p>";
          }
          $("#results").html(s);
        }
        $("#searchButton").prop("disabled", false);
      });

  });

}

function disableForm() {
  $("#searchButton").prop("disabled", true);
  if(lastStatus != 'disconnected') {
    lastStatus = 'disconnected';
    navigator.notification.alert(
      "Search is disabled while you're offline.",
      null,
      "Offline!");
  }
}

function enableForm() {
  $("#searchButton").prop("disabled", false);
  if(lastStatus != 'connected' && lastStatus != '') {
    lastStatus = 'connected';
    navigator.notification.alert(
      "Search is now enabled.",
      null,
      "Online!");
  }
}
```

❺ Handler for device going offline

❻ Handles noticing if handler has run more than once in a row

❼ Handler for device going online

❽ Handles noticing if app just started and device is online

The first big change is to switch from jQuery's document-ready block to Cordova's deviceready event **❶**. Now that you're using device features this is required. You then add two event listeners (**❸**, **❹**) to respond to changes in the device's online status.

For the most part, the handlers are mirror copies of each other. One will disable the form's Submit button and tell users they're offline ❺, while the other will enable the form and let users know they're back online ❼. But what's up with that last-Status variable ❻?

Cordova, like any open source project, will sometimes have bugs. During the writing of this book, I noticed that on Android the dialogs would sometimes show up more than one time in a row. I Googled and discovered this is a known bug. Cordova has a bug tracker that's viewable by anyone. Not only is it viewable by anyone, but anyone can report a bug as well. This bug can be found at https://issues.apache.org/jira/browse/CB-7787. The use of lastStatus handles the case where the plugin mistakenly fires off the event handler multiple times at once. The code isn't necessary on iOS, and in theory, you could add code to detect iOS and skip that, but because it's also *harmless* on iOS, there's no reason to do that.

What about that check against an empty string in the online handler ❽? One of the cool things about both event handlers is that they will fire automatically when you start the application. That means if the device starts offline, the user immediately gets a warning. That's nice—but you don't want the same if the application starts online. Because the variable begins empty ❷ you can check that and skip it using the dialog in that case.

6.4 Supporting the entire planet

Your application is a great success and has a large number of uses. You then get an irate phone call from someone who missed an important event. Why? Your app said the event was happening 2/4/2015. They showed up on the right date—April 2, 2015. But wait—that makes no sense. Wasn't the date February 4, 2015? And there's the rub—depending on where you live, dates may be written Month/Day/Year or Day/Month/Year. Similar issues happen with numbers.

It's important to remember that people outside your country may make use of your application, and how they read numbers and dates may be very different from how you read the same values.

This type of problem, and fixing it, fall under the category of Internationalization and Localization. *Internationalization* is the act of making your application work internationally. *Localization* is actually implementing support for a particular locale.

This process can be *very* involved, which is why a lot of people don't bother. If your application is sold on an app store then you may be walking away from money. A complete internationalization of an application would involve setting it up so that it can be read in any (or many) languages. For example, changing a Buy Product button to Le Buy Le Product for people in French-speaking countries. (No, I don't speak French. How did you know?)

6.4.1 Improving the GitHub Search application for the world

For the purposes here you're going to do something a bit more simple. The GitHub Search application displays date values for each matched result. You're going to make use of a Globalization plugin to display those dates in a locale-friendly format, as shown in figure 6.8.

In figure 6.8 you can see the same application running with the same search against GitHub. The screenshot on the left is a device using an American language setting. The one on the right is using U.K. English. Notice how the dates are displayed correctly for each locale. To make this work, you'll make use of the Globalization plugin (`cordova-plugin-globalization`). The plugin has methods for getting the current locale, as well as formatting dates, numbers, and currency values. In general, it's a simple plugin to use. But the biggest issue is that all of the methods are asynchronous. If you recall, the application calls the GitHub API and gets an array of results. You take that array and generate an HTML string to insert into the display.

Now you have a problem. You'll have a random number of results (based on the search). For each result you want to format the date correctly. So how then do you handle these multiple asynchronous results? The same way you did earlier when we discussed waiting for jQuery Mobile to start up as well as Cordova—Promises.

English (US)

English (UK)

| coldfusion | Search |

Results

ColdFusion
By: SublimeText
Updated: 1/8/2015 3:48 PM
ColdFusion Sublime Text Package

ColdFusion-Koans
By: bittersweetryan
Updated: 9/25/2014 12:17 AM

Fusebox-ColdFusion
By: fusebox-framework
Updated: 9/18/2014 5:34 AM
Fusebox is a free, easy to use framework for web development that organizes your code for fewer development bugs and faster maintenance. It has a low runtime overhead. It is mainly targeted to ColdFusion but also has versions for PHP and ASP.

chef-coldfusion10
By: wharton
Updated: 11/26/2014 10:00 AM
Chef cookbook to install ColdFusion 10

| coldfusion | Search |

Results

ColdFusion
By: SublimeText
Updated: 08/01/2015 15:48
ColdFusion Sublime Text Package

ColdFusion-Koans
By: bittersweetryan
Updated: 25/09/2014 00:17

Fusebox-ColdFusion
By: fusebox-framework
Updated: 18/09/2014 05:34
Fusebox is a free, easy to use framework for web development that organizes your code for fewer development bugs and faster maintenance. It has a low runtime overhead. It is mainly targeted to ColdFusion but also has versions for PHP and ASP.

chef-coldfusion10
By: wharton
Updated: 26/11/2014 10:00
Chef cookbook to install ColdFusion 10

Figure 6.8   Application displaying dates in a locale-friendly format

The new version of the application may be found in the searchapp2 folder. This is an updated version of the one you just improved with offline/online detection. To make this application work, you'll need three plugins: `cordova-plugin-network-information`, `cordova-plugin-dialogs`, and `cordova-plugin-globalization`. The only change code-wise is within the search handler, so the code snippet in the following listing focuses on that.

> **Listing 6.10 Handling globalization of search results (c6/searchapp2/app.js)**

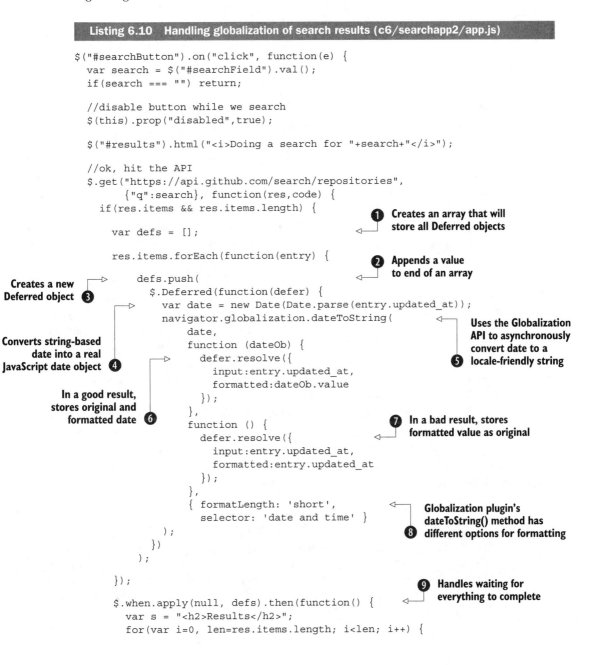

```
$("#searchButton").on("click", function(e) {
  var search = $("#searchField").val();
  if(search === "") return;

  //disable button while we search
  $(this).prop("disabled",true);

  $("#results").html("<i>Doing a search for "+search+"</i>");

  //ok, hit the API
  $.get("https://api.github.com/search/repositories",
      {"q":search}, function(res,code) {
    if(res.items && res.items.length) {

      var defs = [];

      res.items.forEach(function(entry) {

        defs.push(
          $.Deferred(function(defer) {
            var date = new Date(Date.parse(entry.updated_at));
            navigator.globalization.dateToString(
              date,
              function (dateOb) {
                defer.resolve({
                  input:entry.updated_at,
                  formatted:dateOb.value
                });
              },
              function () {
                defer.resolve({
                  input:entry.updated_at,
                  formatted:entry.updated_at
                });
              },
              { formatLength: 'short',
                selector: 'date and time' }
            );
          })
        );

      });

      $.when.apply(null, defs).then(function() {
        var s = "<h2>Results</h2>";
        for(var i=0, len=res.items.length; i<len; i++) {
```

1 Creates an array that will store all Deferred objects

2 Appends a value to end of an array

Creates a new Deferred object **3**

Converts string-based date into a real JavaScript date object **4**

5 Uses the Globalization API to asynchronously convert date to a locale-friendly string

In a good result, stores original and formatted date **6**

7 In a bad result, stores formatted value as original

8 Globalization plugin's dateToString() method has different options for formatting

9 Handles waiting for everything to complete

```
            var entry = res.items[i];
            s += "<p><strong>"+entry.name+"</strong><br/>";
            s += "By: " + entry.owner.login+"<br/>";
            s += "Updated: " + arguments[i].formatted+"<br/>";
            s += entry.description;
            s += "</p>";
        }
        $("#results").html(s);
    });

    }
    $("#searchButton").prop("disabled", false);
  });

});
```

When displaying, uses result passed in from deferreds ❿

Okay, let's take this a bit slow. As noted earlier, working with Promises (and a `Deferred` object is simply a version of that) can be a bit complex. This particular example is somewhat complex as it has to handle an unknown number of asynchronous calls. To do this, you use an array that will store the `Deferred` objects ❶. You can then loop over the array and add ❷ new `Deferred` objects ❸ to the array. Inside that loop, you convert the string-based date returned from GitHub's API into a proper JavaScript date object ❹. This can then be sent to the Globalization API ❺ with specific options ❽ specifying that you want a short version of the date and one that includes the time as well. The API either runs a success or error handler. For the success handler, the result is an object that contains the result ❻. You use `defer.resolve` as a way to "end" the asynchronous operation. You're returning an object for the result that contains both the original value and the prettier version. This isn't strictly necessary, but if you end up wanting the original date value later you'll have it ready. If an error occurs while parsing the value, you simply use the original value again ❼.

To wrap things up, you tell jQuery to wait ❾ for all of the asynchronous operations to finish. The handler run in the `then` block is sent one argument for every item in the original array. Because that matches the array of results, you can easily use the argument containing your date value ❿ when looping.

Perhaps "easily" is too strong a word. Obviously if you're working with one call to the Globalization API you could simply use a callback, even a callback inside a callback. But that won't work when the number of operations is unknown. At the end of the day this involves a bit of work, but it's worthwhile for the additional benefit given to your users.

Testing a new locale

Both real devices and emulators let you switch the locale to test what was just demonstrated. The actual setting to change will depend on your device platform and OS version, so if you have difficulty finding the right setting for your testing you may need to turn to Google, but do know that you can, and should, play with this setting while testing the globalization plugin.

6.5 Storing data on the device

For the final section of this chapter on building better Cordova applications, we'll look at storing persistent data on the user's device.

6.5.1 A real-world example

Imagine you're building a mobile application for your favorite restaurant. Let's call it Burrito Horn. No relation to that other fast-food Mexican restaurant—honest! You want the application to list all the locations where folks can pick up cheaply priced, semiauthentic Mexican cuisine. To handle this, you could use JavaScript to create a simple list of restaurants:

```
var restaurants = [
{address:"101 Elm Street, Lafayette, LA", openAllDay:true},
{address:"329 Green Street, Lafayette, LA", openAllDay:true},
{address:"9 Mayfair Street, Lafayette, LA", openAllDay:false},
{address:"7 Wayside Street, Lafayette, LA", openAllDay:true}
  ... and so on ...
];
```

The list of restaurants includes their addresses and a simple flag that determines if they're open 24 hours a day. This works well—until you realize that Burrito Horn is incredibly popular. A new restaurant opens about two or three times a month. This means you have to constantly update the application and resubmit it for approval in the various app stores.

So the solution is simple. Instead of using a hard-coded list of locations, use a server that speaks to a database and allows remote clients to connect. Then you can use simple AJAX to fetch the data:

```
$.get("http://something/service/getLocations", function(results) {
....
});
```

Cool! But we just discussed handling offline states in an application. Shoot! Now what do you do? Simple—you can store the restaurant data on the device. If the device is online, you can fetch the data and store it locally. If the device is offline, you can use the last set of downloaded data. Even if the device is online you could decide to use the local data just so that the app can respond quicker. Perhaps you remember when the data was fetched and use a rule like, "If I got restaurant data in the last seven days, just use that, otherwise try to fetch updated data."

6.5.2 Options for handling data storage

Cordova applications have multiple different ways they can store data locally. Which you use, and when, will depend on your application needs. Let's take a look at the available options.

LOCALSTORAGE

LocalStorage is not something Cordova provides functionality for—it works as a part of the web browser used to display your application. LocalStorage works by using a name/value system. Say you save a variable called `favoriteBeer` with a value, `Anchor Steam`. There's no search, although you can use code to enumerate all the values available. Data stored in LocalStorage is unique per application and not shared with anything else on the device. There are two flavors of LocalStorage: one that persists forever (technically a user can erase it) and one that lasts for a session, which on the desktop ends when the user closes the browser, and in Cordova ends when the application closes. (Technically, the name of the session-based version is SessionStorage.) Read more about this feature at https://developer.mozilla.org/en-US/docs/Web/API/Web_Storage_API. Storage limits range from 2 MB on the lower side to 10 MB on the higher side.

WEBSQL

WebSQL is a miniature database system. We're not talking a full-blown Oracle server here, but a basic single-user database system that supports the most common types of SQL statements developers use. Like LocalStorage, data stored here is unique per application. Also like LocalStorage this is provided by the embedded web view displaying the application and doesn't require a plugin. Read more about WebSQL at www.w3.org/TR/webdatabase/. If you do, you'll see a bright-yellow warning about how this specification is no longer being actively maintained. What this means is, going forward, WebSQL eventually will be removed from web browsers. Does this mean you shouldn't use it? No. If at some point in the future this feature is removed, it could be added right back in with a plugin. The "future" of storage for web browsers is another specification called IndexedDB, but unfortunately, IndexedDB support on mobile devices is very low. You could use it in a Cordova application if it were optional, but I'm not sure it makes sense to use this feature now. Storage limits vary more wildly here, but in general, an app can store up to 50 MB of data.

FILESYSTEM

You can also make use of the filesystem. Cordova applications have full access to at least part of the device's filesystem. Your app can't, for example, steal data from other apps or remove the OS. But it can work with certain common directories and work within an application-specific sandbox. Where possible, a Cordova application can read and write files and list, create, and delete directories. File access is provided by the File plugin (`cordova-plugin-file`). The limit of this is based on the storage size of the device itself.

6.5.3   *Selecting the type of data storage*

There are no hard-and-fast rules for when you should use one over the other, but in general, here are the guidelines I follow:

- *Data that's simple, or restricted to a known set of keys, is best stored within LocalStorage.* Examples include preferences, a stored username to make login quicker, and cached data from services (like the list of restaurants).
- *Data that's not restricted and can grow at will, like user-entered data, is best stored in WebSQL.* Examples may include a diary, a set of notes, and reviews of food (the

best of Burrito Horn!). If you need to search data, then this is the preferred storage mechanism.

- *Data that's binary, like pictures, is best stored on the filesystem.* Things like audio recordings, video, and images make sense here.

6.5.4 Improving the GitHub Search application

Let's once again enhance your GitHub application using LocalStorage. As mentioned, there are two flavors of LocalStorage, one that persists and one that expires when the application closes. You'll modify the application to make two changes.

First, you'll remember the last search term used by the user. If the last thing the user searches for is donuts, when the user opens the application again the input field will be automatically defaulted to donuts.

Second, you'll use the session-based version of LocalStorage to cache search results. If the user searches for donuts, you'll store the results in SessionStorage (the session flavor of LocalStorage). If the user searches for donuts again, you can skip hitting the remote service and just use the cached results.

The new version of the application can be found in the searchapp3 folder. As before, you can make a new application or simply copy the www assets in and update the existing app. If you make a new application, be sure to add the required plugins: `org.apache.cordova.file`, `org.apache.cordova.globalization`, and `org.apache.cordova.network-information`. The only change is within app.js and the init function, so let's take a look at that in the following listing.

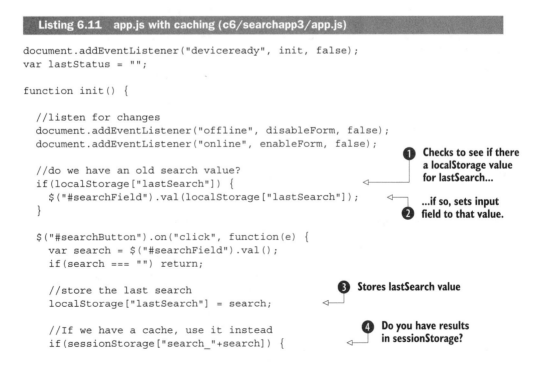

> **Listing 6.11   app.js with caching (c6/searchapp3/app.js)**

```
document.addEventListener("deviceready", init, false);
var lastStatus = "";

function init() {

  //listen for changes
  document.addEventListener("offline", disableForm, false);
  document.addEventListener("online", enableForm, false);

  //do we have an old search value?
  if(localStorage["lastSearch"]) {
    $("#searchField").val(localStorage["lastSearch"]);
  }

  $("#searchButton").on("click", function(e) {
    var search = $("#searchField").val();
    if(search === "") return;

    //store the last search
    localStorage["lastSearch"] = search;

    //If we have a cache, use it instead
    if(sessionStorage["search_"+search]) {
```

❶ Checks to see if there a localStorage value for lastSearch...

❷ ...if so, sets input field to that value.

❸ Stores lastSearch value

❹ Do you have results in sessionStorage?

```
    $("#results").html(sessionStorage["search_"+search]);
    return;
}
```
If so, then
⑤ use them.

```
//disable button while we search
$(this).prop("disabled",true);


$("#results").html("<i>Doing a search for "+search+"</i>");


//ok, hit the API
$.get("https://api.github.com/search/repositories",
      {"q":search}, function(res,code) {
  if(res.items && res.items.length) {

    var defs = [];

    res.items.forEach(function(entry) {

        defs.push(
          $.Deferred(function(defer) {
            var date = new Date(Date.parse(entry.updated_at));
            navigator.globalization.dateToString(
                date,
                function (dateOb) {
                  defer.resolve({
                    input:entry.updated_at,
                    formatted:dateOb.value
                  });
                },
                function () {
                  defer.resolve({
                    input:entry.updated_at,
                    formatted:entry.updated_at
                  });
                },
                { formatLength: 'short',
                  selector: 'date and time' }
            );
          })
        );

    });

    $.when.apply(null, defs).then(function() {
      var s = "<h2>Results</h2>";
      for(var i=0, len=res.items.length; i<len; i++) {
        var entry = res.items[i];
        s += "<p><strong>"+entry.name+"</strong><br/>";
        s += "By: " + entry.owner.login+"<br/>";
        s += "Updated: " + arguments[i].formatted+"<br/>";
        s += entry.description;
        s += "</p>";
      }
```

```
          //cache the rendered results:
          sessionStorage["search_"+search] = s;
          $("#results").html(s);
        });

      }
      $("#searchButton").prop("disabled", false);
    });

  });

}
```

Cache rendered results
in sessionStorage.

The first changes are simple. When the application starts up, you check `localStorage` ❶ for the value of the last thing the user searched for. If that value exists, you set it as the value of the input field ❷. Inside the search logic, you store the search term every time the user searches ❸.

When a search is performed, you cache the rendered results in `sessionStorage` ❻. Why not the actual data? You can only store simple string values in `localStorage` and `sessionStorage`. It would be trivial to convert the data into JSON, but if you store the rendered HTML, you don't need to build it again. You can check for that in the cache ❹ and take that string and display it as is ❺.

By using a bit of data persistence, you've made the application a bit nicer to use (especially if you commonly search for the same term) and quicker (no need to reuse the API for the same search).

6.6 *Summary*

Let's review the major topics covered in this chapter.

- A SPA has benefits for simple organizational purposes and for Cordova.
- A good Cordova application should respond intelligently when offline.
- Values like dates and numbers should be formatted in a way that's friendly to your end users—no matter what country they may be in.
- There are multiple ways to store data on a device and you should investigate which makes sense for your application.

In the next chapter we'll discuss multiple different ways to debug your Cordova applications.

Tools for debugging Cordova
and other hybrid apps

This chapter covers

- Why debugging is so important
- Debugging Cordova apps on Android
- Debugging Cordova apps on iOS
- Debugging with Weinre

I've been programming in some capacity or another since I was around 10 years old. In the 30 years or so of coding I've yet to write a computer program 100% correctly the first time. I hope to program for another 30 years, but I have no illusion about my ability to start writing perfect programs.

7.1 Finding the bug is nine-tenths the work of solving it

The absolute most important thing a developer can learn is how to properly debug an application. Things will go wrong. Period. Being able to determine the particular thing going wrong will take you a long way toward fixing it. You may not know how to fix an error, but being able to say "I get this error when I do this action" will give you something to Google where, most likely, you'll find an answer (probably multiple answers) to your question.

Unfortunately, debugging a Cordova application by itself is somewhat difficult. Normally when something goes wrong, no visible error will be printed to the device's screen. Instead, the usual response is for *nothing* to happen. Imagine your GitHub application suddenly becoming broken because of a typo. A user enters something in the text field, clicks Search, and nothing happens. Why? Because of some error that's invisible to the user.

In most cases, that's a good thing. A long, detailed error that makes sense to you and me would probably not make sense to a non-developer. But while developing the application you really need a way to see what's going on. This is where debugging comes in.

7.2 A broken app

As we progress through the different types of debugging techniques in this chapter, you'll use one main application that's full of bugs.

Figure 7.1 shows the application in all its glory. It has three buttons. Each button is meant to do *something*, but it doesn't matter what they do because every single one is broken. Let's first look

Figure 7.1   A broken app

at the HTML in the following listing. While simple, the HTML used is going to be part of a problem you'll need to fix later.

Listing 7.1   Broken application's HTML (c7/failingapp/index.html)

```html
<!DOCTYPE html>
<html>
    <head>
        <meta charset="utf-8">
        <meta http-equiv="X-UA-Compatible" content="IE=edge,chrome=1">
        <title></title>
        <meta name="description" content="">
        <meta name="viewport" content="width=device-width">
        <link rel="stylesheet" type="text/css" href="css/app.css" />
    </head>
    <body>

        <button id="runOne">Run One</button>
        <button id="runToorunTwo">Run Two</button>
        <button id="runThree">Run Three</button>

        <script src="cordova.js"></script>
        <script src="js/jquery-2.1.1.min.js"></script>
        <script src="js/app.js"></script>
    </body>
</html>
```

Pretty simple, right? Now let's look at the JavaScript in the next listing.

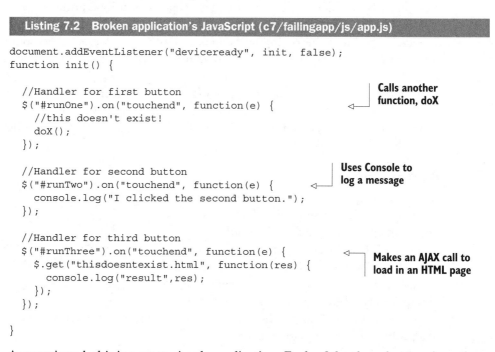

Listing 7.2   Broken application's JavaScript (c7/failingapp/js/app.js)

```
document.addEventListener("deviceready", init, false);
function init() {

  //Handler for first button
  $("#runOne").on("touchend", function(e) {
    //this doesn't exist!
    doX();
  });

  //Handler for second button
  $("#runTwo").on("touchend", function(e) {
    console.log("I clicked the second button.");
  });

  //Handler for third button
  $("#runThree").on("touchend", function(e) {
    $.get("thisdoesntexist.html", function(res) {
      console.log("result",res);
    });
  });

}
```

Calls another function, doX

Uses Console to log a message

Makes an AJAX call to load in an HTML page

As mentioned, this is a pretty simple application. Each of the three buttons has a handler that's meant to do something in particular. The exact functions aren't terribly important. What's important is that all three are broken.

If you create a new Cordova project with this source code and run it in your emulator, you'll notice that nothing happens when you click each button. There are any number of things that could be going wrong, but how do you determine what's happening?

7.3   *Working with Chrome remote debugging on Android*

For your first attempt at debugging the application, we'll look at Chrome remote debugging. Chrome remote debugging is specifically for applications running on Android devices. It works with the Chrome application on mobile devices as well as applications that make use of embedded web views, like Cordova. To use this feature, you must test against a device that's running Android 4.4 or higher. (According to the statistics as of the time this chapter was written, that's right at 40%.)

Bear in mind that even if you need to support older Android versions, you can still use this feature to quickly diagnose and fix issues that would crop up in *any* Android version. If you must debug against an older version of Android then see the Weinre section in the last part of this chapter.

Chrome remote debugging works on any OS you can run Chrome on. You'll also need to connect your device to your machine via a USB cable. When your device is connected, you must enable the debugging feature first. While this is something you have to do only once (per device), Android has added a somewhat stupid way of getting to the setting. (Note: You can perform the same steps using the Android emulator if you don't have a real device.)

7.3.1　*Preparing for Chrome remote debugging*

On your device, go to the Settings menu and choose the About phone option as shown in figure 7.2.

Click About phone to load the next page (figure 7.3), which contains information about the phone. At the very bottom will be a Build number setting. Click that seven times. Yes, seriously.

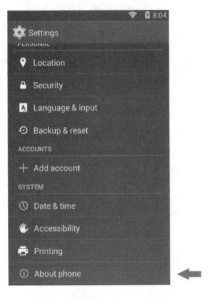

Figure 7.2　The About phone setting

Figure 7.3　Click the Build number setting seven times!

As you continue to click, you'll see a notice that you're close to becoming a developer. This "funny" message, shown in figure 7.4, is really trying to tell you that you're getting close to enabling developer options.

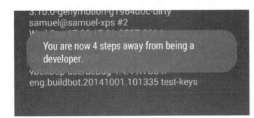

Figure 7.4　Google trying to make a funny

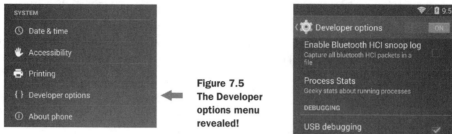

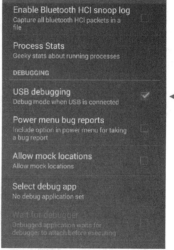

**Figure 7.5
The Developer
options menu
revealed!**

After you click seven times, click the Back button and you'll now see Developer options as an
available menu item, shown in figure 7.5.

Click this new option and scroll down until
you see USB debugging and choose it, as shown
in figure 7.6.

You'll get a scary warning when you enable
this, but it's okay. After all of this, you've finally
done what you need to do on the device. Again,
this is a one-time thing.

**Figure 7.6   Finally! Here is where you
enable USB debugging.**

Your device may differ

As an FYI, note that your device may require slightly different steps than what I described. On my HTC One M8, the build number was one menu deeper under the About
menu. Outside of that the process was the same.

Now that you've enabled debugging on the device side, it's time to test it on the
browser side. Chrome remote debugging requires Chrome, obviously. Any version
over 32 will work. You have two ways to get to the debugging screen for devices and
Chrome.

The first way is under the "hamburger" menu on the upper right corner of the
Chrome window, as shown in figure 7.7. Click this menu, navigate to the More Tools
submenu, and choose Inspect Devices.

Figure 7.7   Chrome's customize and control menu

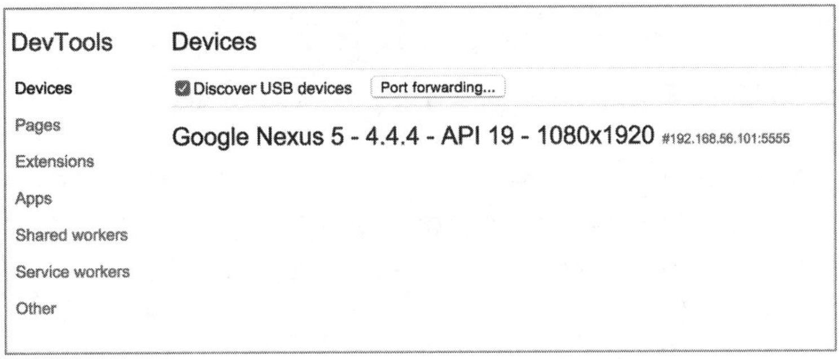

Figure 7.8 Chrome Devices menu

The second way of getting here is to simply enter chrome://inspect in Chrome's navigation bar. (And yes, you can also make a bookmark for this to make it easier to reach.) At this point you should see something like figure 7.8.

In figure 7.8, you can see one device listed, a Google Nexus 5. There isn't anything after it so you may think it isn't working, but what you see here is simply that there isn't anything running on the device that can be inspected. If you open the browser and press any web page, you'll immediately see the view update shown in figure 7.9.

In figure 7.9, what you're seeing is the result of my opening the browser on the device and doing a Google search for "cat." The Inspect link would open up the actual inspector. If I run a Cordova application, the view will change yet again as shown in figure 7.10.

In figure 7.10, you can see now two things are available to be inspected: the browser and a Cordova application. Recall when we first discussed the CLI, when you create a Cordova application you have the opportunity to give it an ID. This is a reverse-domain-style value that must be unique per app. When playing with Cordova

Figure 7.9 Inspect view showing the browser running

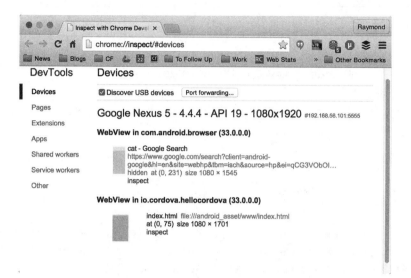

Figure 7.10   Inspect view showing both a browser application and Cordova

you can leave this blank and it will default to io.cordova.hellocordova. You can see this ID in figure 7.10. Clicking the Inspect link brings up the Inspector for the application, shown in figure 7.11.

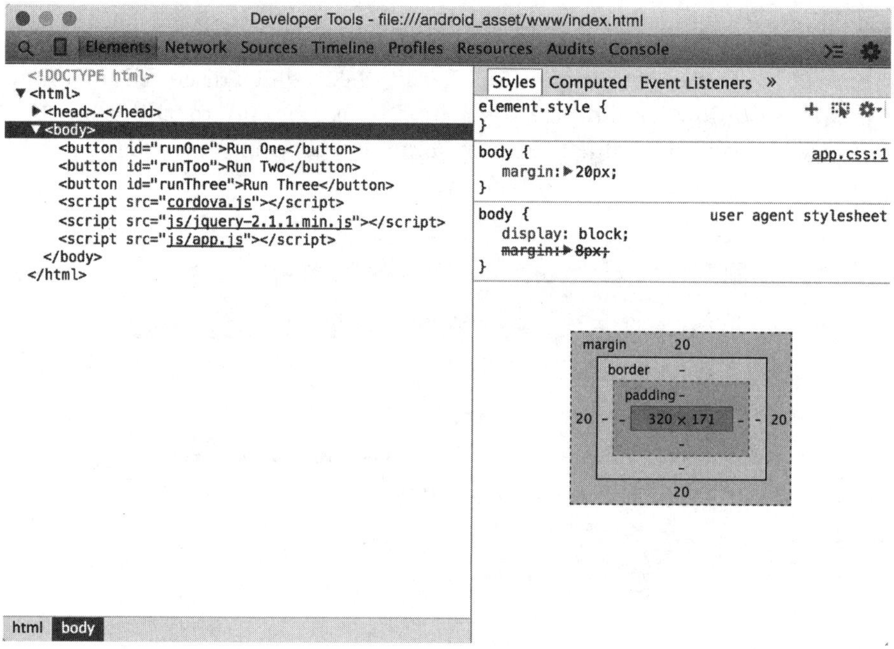

Figure 7.11   Inspector for the Cordova application running on the device

7.3.2　*Features of Chrome's developer tools*

As a web developer, you're probably familiar with Chrome's developer tools. They're one of the best features for debugging web applications. Chrome remote debugging gives you the same tools you (hopefully) use on the desktop for your mobile applications. While a full exploration of Chrome developer tools is outside the scope of the book, let's take a brief tour (table 7.1) through the major features as a refresher.

Table 7.1　Chrome debugger options

Tab	Purpose
Elements	Provides access to the DOM (DOM; tree structure) representing the layout of the current page. This is especially useful when JavaScript is used to generate new HTML on a page.
Network	Records all network requests made by the application. This includes images used in the HTML. This feature is especially useful for debugging applications using AJAX to load information. It can show you the complete request and response.
Sources	Lists all JavaScript files being used by an application and contains a complete JavaScript debugger. You can add breakpoints that tell the application to pause while running. This can be useful for debugging a complex issue.
Timeline	Represents a graphic view of activities occurring in your application. This includes rendering (the actual drawing of layout based on HTML and CSS) and memory use.
Profiles	Allows you to examine how much the CPU is working to handle your application.
Resources	Covers a variety of things: WebSQL, IndexedDB, LocalStorage, Cookies, and Application Cache. You can inspect the data stored in these mechanisms as well as edit them.
Audits	Analyzes a page (or in this case, an application) as it loads. It can provide feedback about improvements.
Console	Has a variety of uses. JavaScript can send messages to it and developers can execute JavaScript from it interactively.

Table 7.1 covers the major areas of the developer tools but doesn't cover every option. Also, Google is actively adding more and more tooling with each new version of the browser. For now, let's focus on how you can use these developer tools to debug the broken application.

7.3.3　*Putting Chrome remote debugging to use*

If you haven't already done so, be sure to create an instance of the bad application and run it on your Android device. You can find the full source code for the application in the zip you downloaded from the book's website. I hope you've already done this and have seen it fail to work properly.

If you've followed the steps to enable remote debugging on your device, open the device's inspection page in Chrome and find the application in the list. Refer to figure 7.10 for an example. Click Inspect and let's take a look.

The first thing you should do is click the Run One button (the first button). As a reminder, this is the code that handled that click:

```
//Handler for first button
$("#runOne").on("touchend", function(e) {
  //this doesn't exist!
  doX();
});
```

This is going to throw a Java-Script error because you never coded a function called doX. If you open the Console in the debugger you'll see something like figure 7.12.

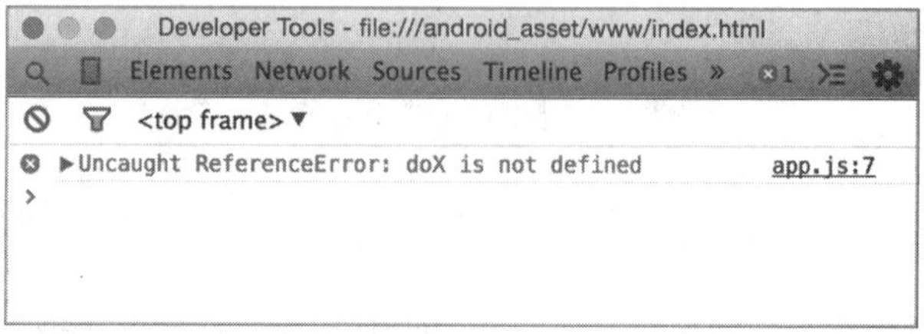

Boom! So while the application itself reported nothing, you can see the issue

Figure 7.12   Error reported in the Console panel

immediately with the remote debugger. Now consider the second button. If you don't remember the code for it, here's the handler:

```
//Handler for second button
$("#runTwo").on("touchend", function(e) {
  console.log("I clicked the second button.");
});
```

Nice and simple, right? As explained in table 7.1, the Console can report messages sent by JavaScript. You can see an example of this with the console.log call. This *should* send a message to the Console. But if you click it, nothing shows up. Also, nothing is reported as an error. So what could it be?

The jQuery selector is trying to find something in the DOM with the ID of runTwo. Also remember that the Elements panel lets you examine the HTML powering the application. Switch to the Elements panel (figure 7.13) to reveal the current DOM.

**Figure 7.13
The Elements panel reveals the DOM behind the application.**

If you mouseover the items in the Elements panel, you'll notice they highlight on the device itself. For example, mouseover the first button and you can see it highlighted on the device, as shown in figure 7.14.

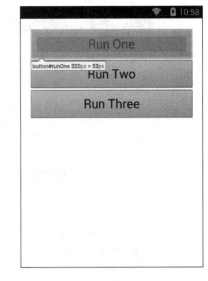

You can even edit the DOM directly from the Elements panel. This is useful for testing CSS or layout tweaks live on a device. In this case you simply want to see why that jQuery selector for runTwo didn't work. A careful look at the Elements panel will reveal that the second button actually has an ID of runToo. A typo. And while I could have probably fixed this with some simple double-checking of the HTML in my editor, it shows how useful the Elements panel can be in examining the HTML of your application. In real production applications where things are being generated dynamically and you can't look at the source code, this will be invaluable.

Figure 7.14 Live updating of HTML elements in the app

Yet another way to fix this same issue would be to use the Console. The Console is interactive, which means you can run commands within it. If you run the same selector your code uses, you can see it returns an empty array. In other words, the selector matched nothing. If you run the selector with the proper ID (figure 7.15), it matches.

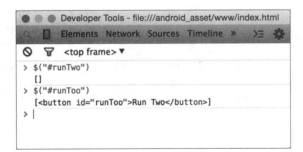

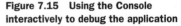

Figure 7.15 Using the Console interactively to debug the application

With the developer tools being so powerful, it's common for there to be multiple ways to find solutions to your problems. Now let's look at the final issue, button three. As a reminder, here's the code fired when it's used:

```
//Handler for third button
$("#runThree").on("touchend", function(e) {
  $.get("thisdoesntexist.html", function(res) {
    console.log("result",res);
  });
});
```

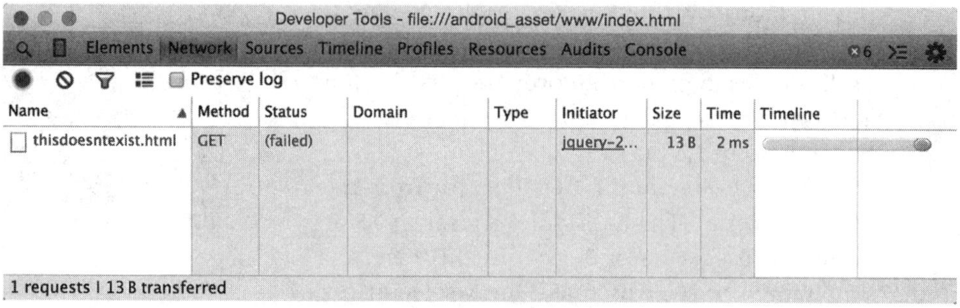

Figure 7.16   Network panel

Once again, it's fairly obvious why this is going to fail. The file, thisdoesntexist.html, doesn't exist. But let's see how it gets reported. Click the button and open the Network panel (figure 7.16) in the developer tools.

You can clearly see that the request failed. The bright-red color is a clue that something has gone wrong. You can also see this in the Console where it's reported as an error as well. In cases where the network request doesn't fail, like working with an API, it can be very useful to inspect the result. Clicking one line item in the panel returns details, and if the request was successful, it will include the response. Figure 7.17 demonstrates an example from the GitHub Search application.

Now that you've seen how Chrome remote debugging can help you with Android, let's take a look at iOS.

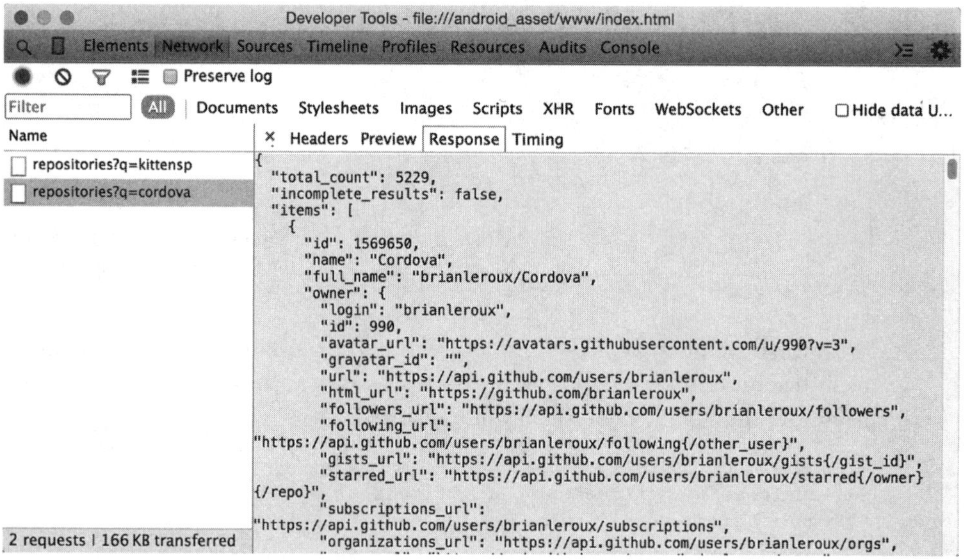

Figure 7.17   The Network panel can reveal details of remote APIs.

7.4 Remote debugging with iOS and Safari

With the introduction of iOS 6, Apple created a way for Safari to debug mobile applications. Like Chrome remote debugging, you can use Safari to debug both the mobile web browser and hybrid mobile applications. Unfortunately, you must use Safari on a Mac to debug your iOS applications. If you want to use a Windows or Linux machine you'll need to look at Weinre, discussed later in the chapter.

7.4.1 Preparing for Safari remote debugging

Luckily, preparing your device for Safari remote debugging is far simpler than what Google makes you do for Chrome. On your device, go to Settings, then Safari, and then Advanced. Then choose Web Inspector as shown in figure 7.18.

Next, open Safari. If you don't see a Develop menu, go to Safari's Preferences, the Advanced tab, and click Show Develop menu in menu bar, as shown in figure 7.19.

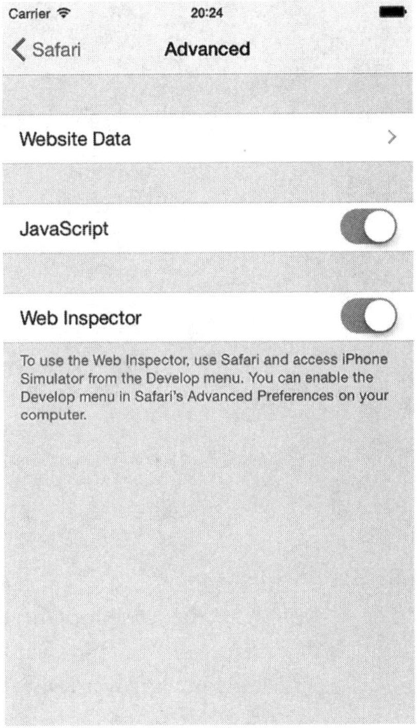

Figure 7.18 Enabling remote debugging on a device

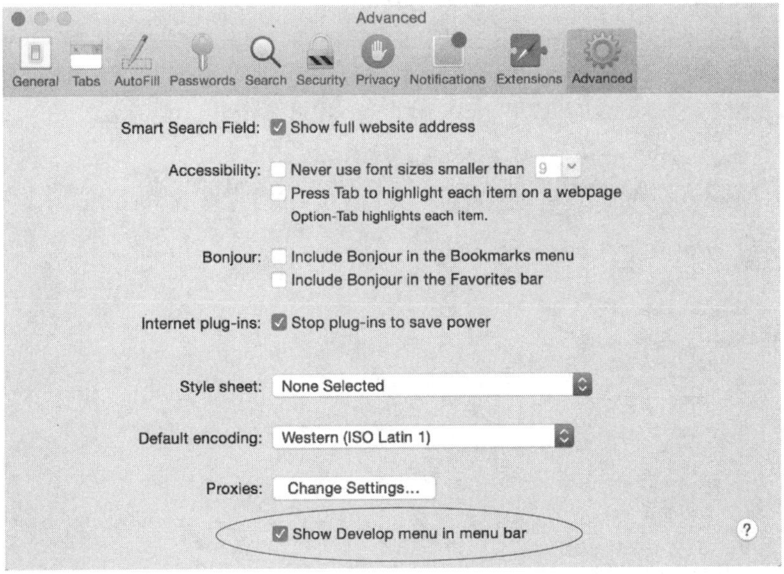

Figure 7.19 Enabling the Develop menu

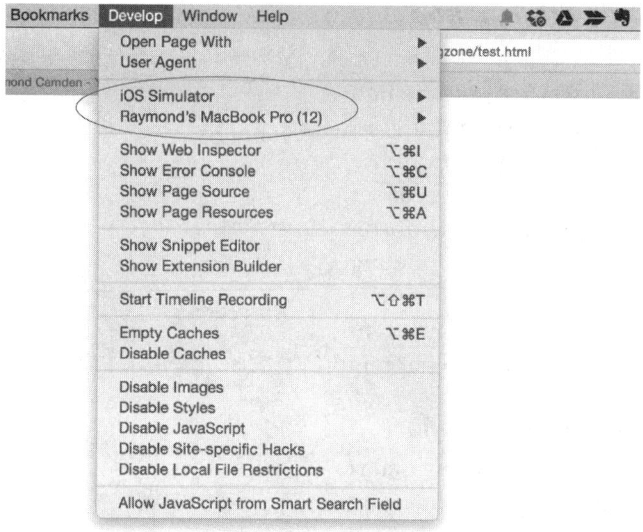

Figure 7.20   iOS device being recognized by Safari

Enabling the Develop menu is a one-time operation. If you've connected your iOS device to your machine via a USB cable, you can now go to the Develop menu in Safari and see your hardware listed like in figure 7.20.

As you can see in figure 7.20, not only does remote debugging work with iOS devices, but also with the iOS simulator. Once you select the hardware (or simulator), a submenu of inspectable applications will appear. This is any open web page in Mobile Safari or a hybrid application. If you have none of them open, then the menu will be empty. If you've been able to set up an iOS environment for Cordova and can run the broken application there, figure 7.21 shows how it would appear in the menu.

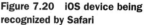

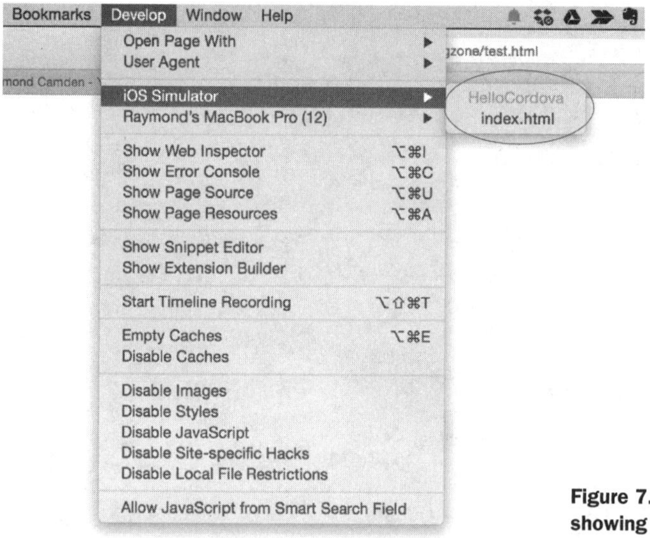

Figure 7.21   Cordova application showing up as an inspectable application

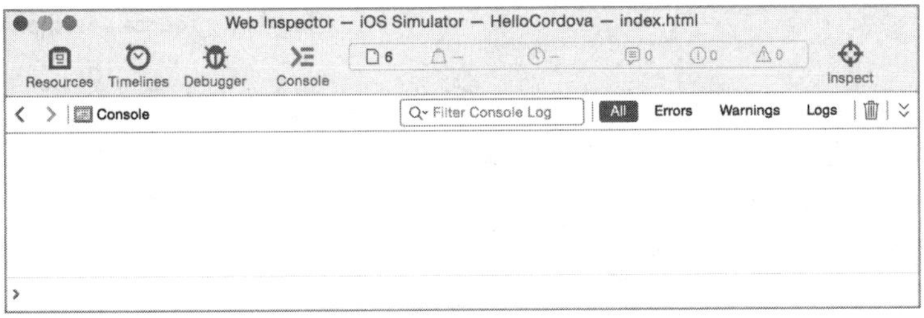

Figure 7.22 Safari's Web Inspector

If you then select the application, Safari will open a new window, shown in figure 7.22, containing its own developer tools for the application.

7.4.2 Features of Safari's developer tools

While I will bet many readers have some familiarity with Chrome's developer tools, Safari isn't usually the browser developers choose to use. Table 7.2 lists Safari's developer tools tabs and what each provides.

Table 7.2 Safari's developer tools

Tab	Purpose
Resources	Similar to both the Elements and Sources panels in Chrome. It provides access to the source code for every file being used in the application (HTML, CSS, and JavaScript), and can switch to a DOM tree toggle. When working with the DOM tree, it will also highlight the DOM elements on the device.
Timelines	Similar to both the Network and Timeline panels in Chrome, described earlier.
Debugger	Provides a full JavaScript debugger.
Console	Acts the same as the Console panel in Chrome's developer tools, described earlier.
Inspect	If you choose this and then click something on the application, the developer tool will display the matching HTML code that represents the item you clicked.

You know the three issues that plague the application in this chapter, but let's look at how they'd be displayed in Safari's developer tools. The first issue occurs when the first button is clicked and the unknown JavaScript function is called. Like in the Android test, this will be shown in the Console (figure 7.23).

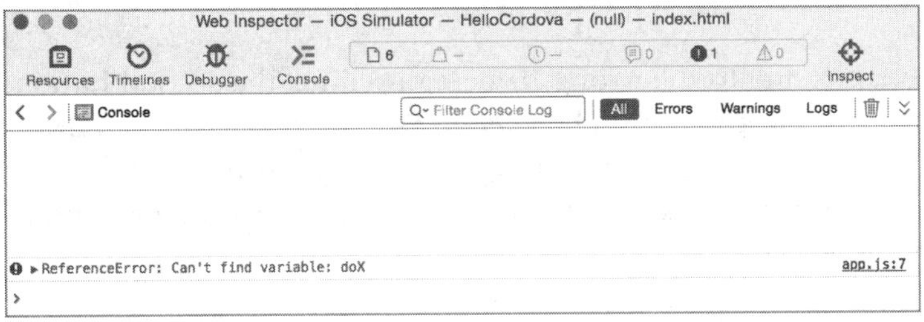

Figure 7.23 Error displayed in Safari's developer tools Console tab

Toggle for source and the DOM tree.

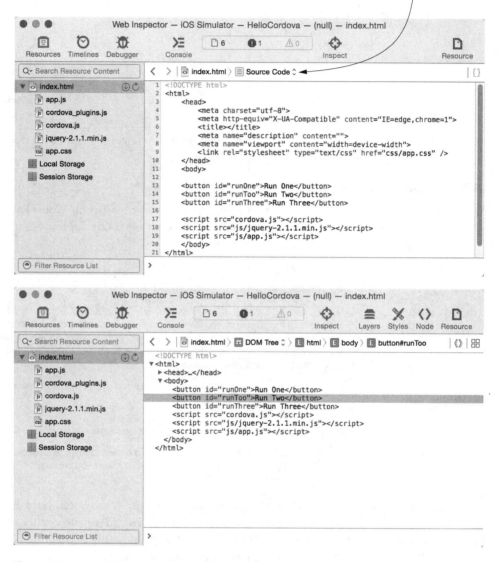

Figure 7.24   Switching between source code and DOM tree

The second error is due to the wrong ID being used for the second button. You can see the DOM tree of the application by selecting the Resources button. By default, the source code is shown, and that's probably enough to help you, but you may want to switch to the DOM tree view instead. As shown in figure 7.24, clicking Source Code lets you switch to the DOM tree.

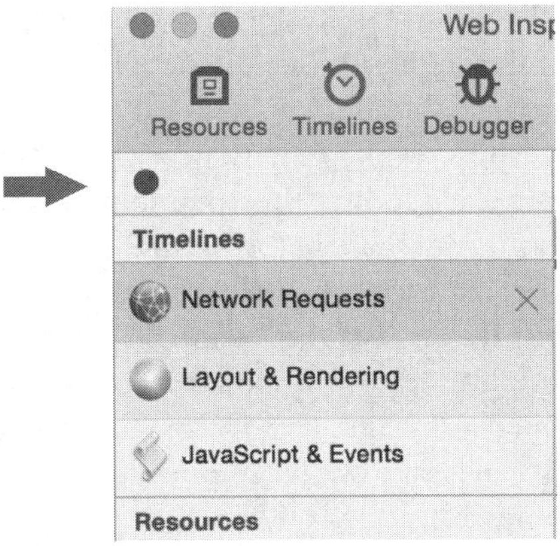

Figure 7.25 Timelines/Network Requests panel in the default state of *not* recording

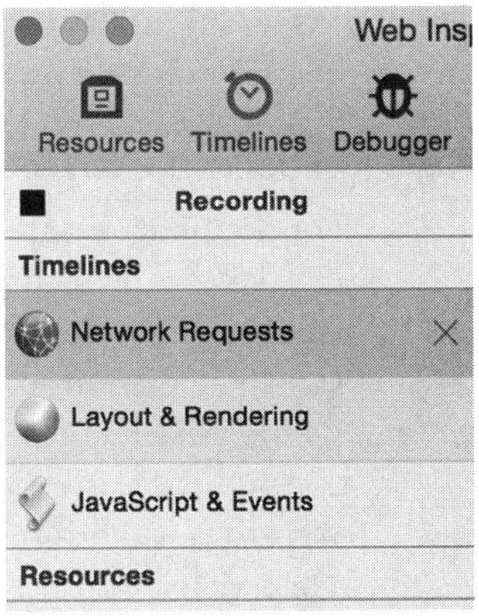

Figure 7.26 Times/Network Requests panel in Recording mode

The third issue involves making a network request to a resource that doesn't exist. Just like in Chrome, this error is reported in the Console, but you may want to use the Timelines panel to see it more clearly. By default, the Network Requests data is *not* recording, even though it has a bright-red circle that looks a lot like the light you see on a video camera (figure 7.25).

Clicking it one time will tell Safari's developer tools to actively start recording. As shown in figure 7.26, the red circle turns into a black square and it will say "Recording".

Now that you're actively recording, click the third button to see the failed network request, shown in figure 7.27.

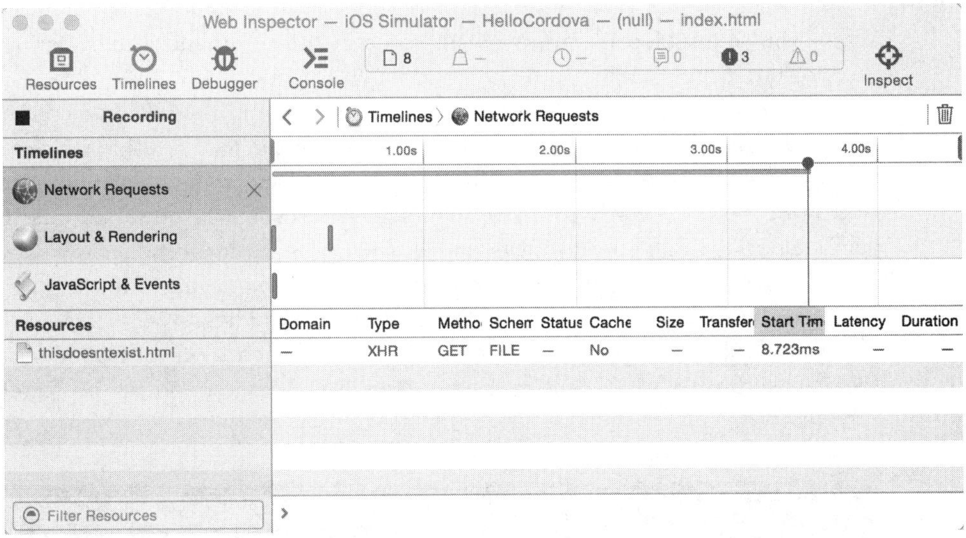

Figure 7.27 Failed network request

Just like with Chrome's developer tools, if you want to inspect a successful response to examine the result, you'd simply click on the request to see the details.

7.5   Working with Weinre

For the final example of remote debugging, we'll look at the open source Weinre project. Weinre is a somewhat old project and was built before remote debugging for Android and iOS existed. In general, I do *not* recommend using Weinre unless you can't get the earlier two options to work. If you visit the Weinre homepage http://people.apache.org/~pmuellr/weinre-docs/latest/, you'll see a very large, very direct message asking you if you're sure you need to use it. This isn't meant to imply that Weinre is bad; it simply isn't as useful as it once was. But it's important to know how to work with it in those few cases where you need it.

Weinre works by sending debugging information from your mobile device to a remote server. To make this work you need to include one script tag into your code. This script tag needs to be removed before you release your application. Let's walk through the process of installing, running, and using Weinre.

7.5.1   Installing Weinre

Weinre can be installed multiple ways, but the simplest is via `npm`. You used `npm` earlier in the book to install Cordova so now you get to reap the benefits of the tool again. At the command line, type this:

```
npm install -g weinre
```

On OS X you may need to prefix the above command with `sudo`. If you used `sudo` to install Cordova then do so again.

7.5.2   Running Weinre

Once you've installed Weinre, you can run it at the command line by typing `weinre`, as shown in figure 7.28.

This will fire up a default instance of the server on port 8080. The command line supports a variety of options. You can print help for the tool by using `weinre -h`. One option you'll most definitely need to use is `boundHost`. By default Weinre is active on localhost. But to use Weinre in your mobile devices, you need an address that your mobile device can connect to. The localhost address basically means myself, and on a mobile device localhost would refer to the device, not your machine running Weinre.

The best address to use for Weinre is the IP address your local network has assigned to you. How you get your local IP address depends on your OS. On a Mac, it is in the Network part of System Preferences. On Windows it can be found in the

```
→  ~  weinre
2015-01-24T21:24:57.272Z weinre: starting server at http://localhost:8080
```

Figure 7.28   Weinre running at the command line

```
 →  ~  weinre --boundHost 192.168.1.68
2015-01-24T21:42:33.125Z weinre: starting server at http://192.168.1.68:8080
```

Figure 7.29   Using Weinre on a specific host

Network application of the control panel. Once you have your IP address, pass it to Weinre using --boundHost as an argument, as shown in figure 7.29.

Once Weinre is running, open the address specified from the output in your browser (figure 7.30).

There are two important things to note in the homepage. The first is the Debug Client User Interface. This is the link you'll click to start monitoring the default information from your app. Before you can do that you have to copy the script tag in the Target Script section. This line can be placed within the head block of your index.html file, as noted in the following listing.

Listing 7.3   Head portion of the broken app with the Weinre script

```html
<head>
  <meta charset="utf-8">
  <meta http-equiv="X-UA-Compatible" content="IE=edge,chrome=1">
  <title></title>
  <meta name="description" content="">
  <meta name="viewport" content="width=device-width">
  <link rel="stylesheet" type="text/css" href="css/app.css" />
  <script src="http://192.168.1.68:8080/target/target-script-min.js#anony-
    mous"></script>
</head>
```

weinre - web inspector remote

Access Points

debug client user interface: http://192.168.1.68:8080/client/#anonymous
documentation: http://192.168.1.68:8080/doc/

Target Demos

The following links point to an already instrumented sample application, run in a couple of different environmental conditions.

First open a new browser window for the debug client user interface, as specified above. Then open another new browser window for one of the demos below. They should auto-connect and result in an active debug connection between the client and the target demo.

- the non-minified demo
- the minified demo
- the non-minified strict demo

Target Script

You can use this script to inject the weinre target code into your web page.

    http://192.168.1.68:8080/target/target-script-min.js#anonymous

Example:

    <script src="http://192.168.1.68:8080/target/target-script-min.js#anonymous"></script>

Target Bookmarklet

You can use this bookmarklet to inject the weinre target code into any web page you are viewing.

link you can drag to your bookmarks:

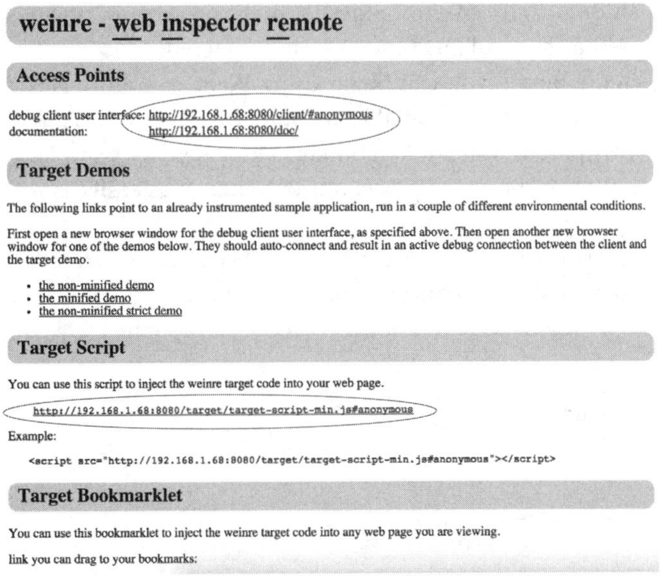

Figure 7.30   Weinre server homepage

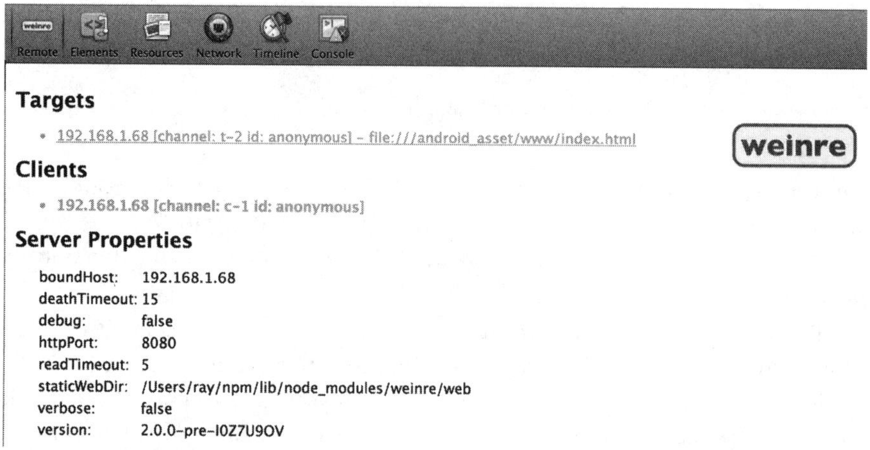

Figure 7.31 Weinre targets

After you've added the script, send the application to your device. Back in your web browser, click the link by the label Default Client User Interface. On the next page will be a "target" that represents your application. If you test with Android and iOS, or just multiple devices, then you'll have multiple targets (figure 7.31).

This next part is important. The tabs on top of the web page represent different parts of the debug interface you'll be able to use to debug your application. If you have multiple devices using Weinre at the same time, you must choose the target first. This tells the Weinre client which device you want to work with. Click the target you want to debug before using any of the other tabs. If you only have one target then it should be selected automatically. Weinre doesn't make it terribly obvious but the green link is the selected target and any blue link isn't selected.

Once you've selected a target, you can begin using Weinre. Weinre is based on an older version of the developer tools available in both Chrome and Safari. If you've used these tools in the past it will look familiar. The tabs have similar names as Chrome and follow similar purposes, so you can use them just as easily as you did with Chrome's remote debugger.

There is one serious issue with Weinre's console. JavaScript errors aren't reported in the console like they are with the two earlier examples in this chapter. If you have a general idea of where your problem code might lie, you could wrap it in a try-catch block:

```
//Handler for first button
$("#runOne").on("touchend", function(e) {
  //this doesn't exist!
  try {
  doX();
  } catch(e) { console.log("error", e); }
});
```

Because the preceding code is using `console.log` to report the error, it will correctly show up in the Weinre console. You could also use a global JavaScript error handler:

```
window.onerror = function(e) {
  console.log('global err', e);
}
```

Both of these suggestions require modifying your code a bit, but if you have to use Weinre, it will help.

7.6 *Other debugging options*

As they say, "But wait, there's more!" The previous three options are pretty powerful ways to debug your Cordova applications, but there are even more things you can try. Which one is best depends on what you're doing and what feels right to you as you work. If you're successful using a tool then use it! Let's look at two other ideas.

7.6.1 *Skip Cordova!*

While working with Cordova is pretty easy, you may run into situations where you're testing something that doesn't really *need* Cordova. Imagine you were having trouble with the GitHub API we've used a few times as an example. You could try running your code on a regular web server and use your desktop browser to execute it. This lets you skip the compile step and edit and reload in your browser. It's quicker than testing on a device or simulator, and you get to use your browser's developer tools directly. A lot of times I've found that the core Cordova features work just fine and it's things unrelated to Cordova itself that cause me grief. While I may need them for my Cordova application I can test them in a desktop environment to have quick turnaround. As a tip, if you have code like this:

```
document.addEventListener("deviceready", init, false);
function init() {
//stuff
}
```

then you may have trouble testing your code in a desktop browser because device-ready will never fire. Simple solution: use the browser's developer console to run `init` manually. Literally type in `init()`. To be clear, this doesn't magically make Cordova features like the camera and filesystem work, but it would run your application's `init` function as if Cordova had fired it itself.

7.6.2 *GapDebug*

GapDebug by Genuitec is a free desktop tool that wraps Chrome and Safari debugging tools within one Chrome tab. By itself that doesn't sound terribly exciting. It does let you skip opening Safari, which is nice. One thing it does really well is handle application reloads. When using both Chrome and Safari remote debugging, you'll notice that any time you recompile your application and send it to the device, the debugging window goes away. You have to reopen it to start debugging. GapDebug will notice when an application goes away and wait for it to return. When it does it will automatically reconnect.

If you need another reason to like it, consider this: it lets you debug iOS applications on a Windows machine! You can download GapDebug at www.genuitec.com/products/gapdebug/.

7.7 *Summary*

Let's review the major topics covered in this chapter.

- When a Cordova application throws an error, typically there's no way to tell what went wrong.
- Chrome remote debugging lets you debug Android 4.4 and higher-based Cordova applications from your desktop.
- Safari remote debugging lets you debug iOS-based Cordova applications from your desktop.
- Weinre can also be used in cases where Chrome or Safari remote debugging isn't available, but note that it will not correctly report JavaScript errors.

In the next chapter, you'll learn how to use native code to build your own plugins for Cordova projects.

Creating custom plugins

This chapter covers

- Why you'd write your own plugins
- The basic architecture of plugins
- How to build a sample Android plugin

In the past few chapters you've made use of a variety of plugins. Plugins to use the camera. Plugins to provide notifications. Plugins for globalization. You've also seen that an entire directory, (http://plugins.cordova.io) containing over 700 different plugins, exists.

8.1 Why write your own plugins?

But with all those choices, there's still a strong chance you may encounter a need that isn't covered by an existing plugin. Or perhaps a plugin exists, but it performs poorly and hasn't been kept up to date. Perhaps the iPhone 9 is released with an incredible new feature—a cowbell. This feature is available to folks building native applications, but there's no hook yet to use it with Cordova. A plugin would let you have access to this cool new feature. No matter the reason, one day you may need to create your own plugin.

8.2   *Plugin architecture*

Let's review the basic architecture of how plugins work, shown in figure 8.1.

In figure 8.1, you can see the basic layout of how a plugin built for Android devices would work. Your code makes a call to a JavaScript library specifically built for that plugin. The JavaScript plugin sends a request to Java code specifically written for the Android platform. That Java code then speaks to the device. Finally, everything gets passed up the chain of calls back to your own code. So that's a plugin for Android, but what about plugins that support multiple device types?

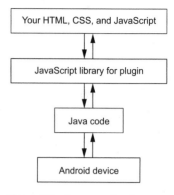

Figure 8.1   An example of an Android plugin

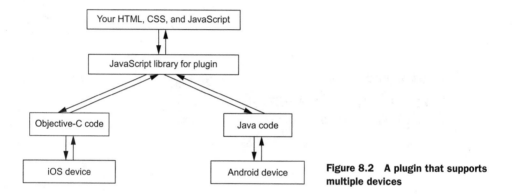

Figure 8.2   A plugin that supports multiple devices

In figure 8.2 the plugin has been updated to support both Android and iOS. In this case, the same JavaScript library for the plugin is used no matter what platform is supported, but on iOS the calls now go to a set of code written in Objective-C or Swift. What's powerful about this setup is that because the same JavaScript library is used, the code within your application remains the same. If the plugin provided an API that looked like `window.cowbell.ring()` and supported both iOS and Android, the developer wouldn't necessarily need to care how it was implemented in Android versus iOS.

Let's look at building a custom plugin and how your Cordova application can make use of it. As before, you're going to use Android versus iOS because anyone on any platform can build it. For folks who want to build an iOS plugin, the process will be similar, outside of the native code of course.

8.3   *Building an Android plugin*

Before we begin, a word of caution. Android plugins are built using Java. You do *not* need to know how to write Java to continue with this chapter. We're going to keep the code as simple as possible. But unlike HTML, if you make one small mistake in your

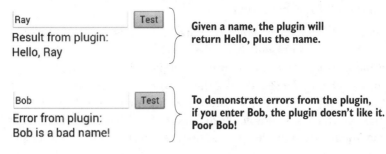

Given a name, the plugin will return Hello, plus the name.

To demonstrate errors from the plugin, if you enter Bob, the plugin doesn't like it. Poor Bob!

Figure 8.3   Two examples of the plugin in action

Java code, your application will fail to build. Later in the chapter you'll see an example of how the process fails when something is wrong in the Java code. The particular plugin you're building here will not make use of any particular device features, but will return a simple "Hello" message. While you wouldn't need a plugin like this in a production application, this chapter will illustrate the process of working with custom plugins. In figure 8.3, you can see an example of the plugin in action.

As noted before, this is a fairly trivial plugin. You'd normally do this in JavaScript alone. The plugin will take any input representing a name and return "Hello", plus the name sent to it. But if the name "Bob" is sent, the plugin will consider this an error and react accordingly. This functionality will demonstrate how plugins can take input, return output, and let the application know that something went wrong. Let's start building.

8.3.1   Setting up the plugin

In all other examples we've worked on in this book, you've created one folder per application. A plugin may not be tied to one application though. You could be building a plugin that you plan on releasing to the world, so, for this example you'll work with two different folders. The first folder will be for the plugin itself. The second folder will be for the application. If you copy the code from the zip file associated with this book, you'll find a plugin folder and a plugintest folder. The plugin folder (figure 8.4) is where you'll build your plugin and the plugintest folder is the actual Cordova application.

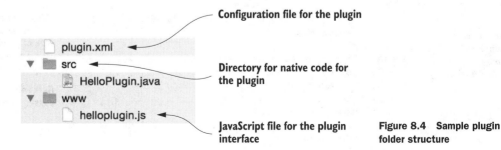

Configuration file for the plugin

Directory for native code for the plugin

JavaScript file for the plugin interface

Figure 8.4   Sample plugin folder structure

Plugins consist of three main parts:

- *The native code, HelloPlugin.java*—The native code is the Java, Objective-C, and so forth files that represent the native code for the device. This could be one file or many. For this example it will be one Java file.
- *The JavaScript code, helloplugin.js*—This is where you create the interface that Cordova developers will use to interact with your plugin. How simple or complex this interface is is completely dependent on what your plugin does. As you can imagine for this sample application, the interface will be rather simple.
- *A special file called plugin.xml*—This XML file helps Cordova understand how to package your plugin. It will tell Cordova where the native code exists, where the JavaScript code is, and provide identifying information about the plugin, like the name.

Figure 8.4 demonstrates how your sample plugin looks. If you didn't copy the code from the zip, you should create a folder for these files and call it plugin. (That folder name is a bit vague and you should feel free to name it something more precise if you want, like firstplugin. Just be sure to *remember* what you used.)

8.3.2   *Writing the plugin code*

Let's begin by looking at the Java code for the plugin shown in the following listing. Again, don't worry if you don't know how to use Java. The code here is rather simple and I'd be willing to bet you can get the gist of what's being done.

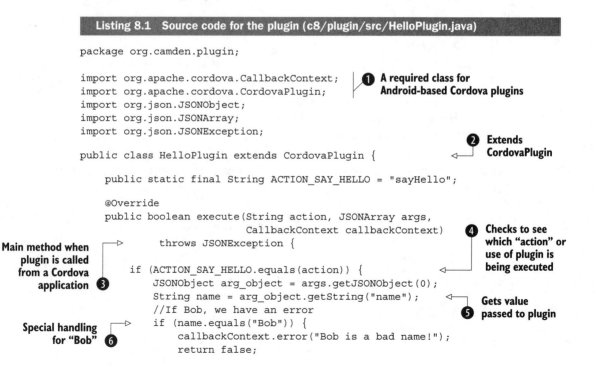

Listing 8.1   Source code for the plugin (c8/plugin/src/HelloPlugin.java)

```
package org.camden.plugin;

import org.apache.cordova.CallbackContext;          ❶ A required class for
import org.apache.cordova.CordovaPlugin;               Android-based Cordova plugins
import org.json.JSONObject;
import org.json.JSONArray;
import org.json.JSONException;
                                                       ❷ Extends
public class HelloPlugin extends CordovaPlugin {          CordovaPlugin

    public static final String ACTION_SAY_HELLO = "sayHello";

    @Override
    public boolean execute(String action, JSONArray args,
                           CallbackContext callbackContext)    ❹ Checks to see
                                                                  which "action" or
Main method when           throws JSONException {                 use of plugin is
plugin is called                                                  being executed
from a Cordova       if (ACTION_SAY_HELLO.equals(action)) {
application ❸            JSONObject arg_object = args.getJSONObject(0);
                        String name = arg_object.getString("name");    ❺ Gets value
                        //If Bob, we have an error                         passed to plugin
Special handling        if (name.equals("Bob")) {
for "Bob" ❻               callbackContext.error("Bob is a bad name!");
                            return false;
```

```
        }
        String result = "Hello, "+name;
        callbackContext.success(result);                    ◀─────
        return true;                                             ❼ Returns result
    }

    callbackContext.error("Invalid action");        ◀─────
    return false;                                       ❽ Handles invalid
                                                           uses of plugin

}

}
```

The Java code begins by importing the classes it needs to work properly, but most importantly it grabs Cordova-specific classes required for plugin development ❶. This allows the `HelloPlugin` class to extend `CordovaPlugin` ❷. The `execute()` method ❸ is run whenever a Cordova application speaks to the plugin and this is where all your logic will be run. An action string is passed to this method telling the plugin what exactly is being requested. Because a plugin may have a few different features (imagine you added a "goodbye" action to your plugin), the code within the `execute()` method has to see which particular action is being used this time. If the action is `sayHello` ❹ then the Java code grabs the input from a JSON data structure passed in ❺. The sample plugin is simple and only has one input value, but if your plugin needed additional inputs, you'd grab them from the JSON as well. There's a special bit of code ❻ to handle an input of "Bob," but if the name weren't Bob, you pass back the result ❼ using a `callbackContext` object. This comes from the imports done earlier ❶ and is part of the Cordova plugin API you get out of the box. If an invalid action was requested, an error ❽ is returned to the caller.

For the most part, any Android-based plugin you build will look very similar to this, with the main differences being within the `execute()` method. Even an incredibly complex plugin will still follow this same pattern. Now that you've seen the Java code, let's look at the JavaScript interface shown in the next listing.

Listing 8.2   Source code for the JavaScript interface (c8/plugin/www/helloplugin.js)

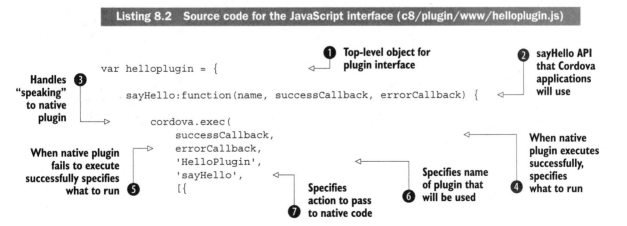

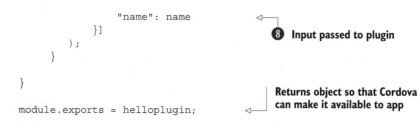

```
              "name": name
          }]
      );
    }

}

module.exports = helloplugin;
```

⑧ Input passed to plugin

Returns object so that Cordova
can make it available to app

Because the plugin is so simple, the corresponding JavaScript code is also rather simple. You begin by creating a top-level object ❶ that will store the various APIs. In this case, the plugin's API only supports a single action, `sayHello` ❷. The actual communication between JavaScript and the native code is done via `cordova.exec` ❸. If you're wondering where this is defined in the listing, it's not. When this code is run in context of a Cordova application, the `cordova` object, and the `exec()` method, will be available. The `exec()` method is passed two arguments that represent the code to run when things work well ❹ and what to do if something goes wrong ❺. In this example, you expect the user to pass functions in to handle those results. You then tell Cordova what plugin to call ❻ and what action ❼ to pass to the plugin. As a final step, you pass input ❽ to the plugin. What's passed to the plugin will depend on what the plugin is doing. Remember your plugin takes a name and returns a message.

Now that you've seen the native code and the JavaScript API, the final part is the XML configuration that puts it all together, as shown next.

Listing 8.3   Plugin definition file (c8/plugin/plugin.xml)

```
<?xml version="1.0" encoding="UTF-8"?>

<plugin xmlns="http://www.phonegap.com/ns/plugins/1.0"
        id="org.camden.plugin.HelloPlugin"
        version="1.0.0">
    <name>HelloPlugin</name>
    <description>Stupid Simple Cordova Plugin</description>
    <author>Raymond Camden</author>
    <keywords>hello,sample</keywords>
    <license>MIT</license>

    <js-module src="www/helloplugin.js" name="HelloPlugin">
        <clobbers target="window.helloplugin" />
    </js-module>

    <!-- android -->
    <platform name="android">
        <config-file target="res/xml/config.xml" parent="/*">
            <feature name="HelloPlugin">
                <param name="android-package"
                  value="org.camden.plugin.HelloPlugin"/>
            </feature>
        </config-file>
```

❶ Top-level XML declaration for the plugin

Human-readable data about the plugin ❷

❸ Controls how the JavaScript API is available to the plugin

❹ Specifies how the plugin works with a particular platform

Platform-specific directive for plugin ❺

Package and class of Java file ❻

```
            <source-file src="src/HelloPlugin.java"
               ➡ target-dir="src/org/camden/plugin" />
        </platform>
    </plugin>
```

◁─┐ **Specifies where source code**
❼ **for this platform exists**

Like any good XML file, the top-level element (`<plugin>`) ❶ wraps the entire content of the file and is required. Within this tag are two required elements, `id` and `version`. The `id` value should be a unique, reverse-domain-style identifier for your plugin. In some ways, this is much like the ID value you use for Cordova applications. The `version` value is also required, and while you can specify whatever version makes sense to you, it *must* follow a particular pattern; for example, `number.number.number`, where the first number represents a major version, the next a minor version, and the last a patch.

You've probably seen applications use versioning similar to this. The next version of Windows (at the time I write this chapter) is 10. That would be the major version. It could be written as 10.0.0. This represents the initial release of Windows 10. Let's say a week later a few very small bugs are patched. Microsoft could then release 10.0.1. Because this is an arbitrary decision, they could also name it 10.0.2. If, a few months later, there have been many small fixes and perhaps a new feature added, Microsoft could decide that it's time for a minor version update and use 10.1.0. To an end user, 10.1 should represent a version that's updated from 10.0.2. It should convey an important update. A user may decide not to update to 10.0.2, but 10.1.0 is probably important. (For folks curious to learn more about this type of versioning, see www.semver.org.)

Again, this is arbitrary but your version must follow the same format. Because this is the first release of the plugin, you'll use 1.0.0. If you used 10.0.0, no one would come arrest you, but you should try to be sensible and follow the norms here.

Next come four tags (`<name>`, `<description>`, `<keywords>`, and `<license>`) ❷ that provide human-readable metadata about the plugin. These help describe the plugins to developers who may be using them. The license you select is up to you. For more information about licenses and which may be best for you, see http://opensource.org/licenses. To be clear, a plugin does *not* have to be open source. You don't have to share your code.

The `<js-module>` ❸ block is where you tell Cordova how to make your JavaScript API available. The plugin.xml supports copying files to your project automatically via `<asset>` tags (not used in this plugin), but `<js-module>` is more powerful. This directive will copy your JavaScript code to the Cordova project, and when the application is actually running on a device, it can make the API available automatically to your Java-Script code. The code here uses the top-level `window` variable, but `navigator` could be used as well (as other plugins do).

The first attribute, `src`, points to the JavaScript you created. The inner tag, `<clobbers>`, is where the magic occurs. What happens here is that the module code you defined in your JavaScript will be made available to Cordova developers as `window.helloplugin`. As an example of this, consider the Camera plugin. When you add it to a project, you suddenly have access to `navigator.camera`. In a desktop environment, this doesn't exist, but Cordova makes it available via a plugin. In this example, you're telling Cordova you want it to be made available as part of the core browser window object. As you can guess, `<clobbers>` implies "blow away." If in the future a `window.helloplugin` object became part of the core browser API, then your code would blow it away, which would be bad, but at that point your Cordova application wouldn't need a plugin! There are other options available, including merging, instead of clobbering, but for your plugin you can use the clobbers to good effect. The name value is only important if you're using Cordova's `require` functionality, which isn't covered in this chapter.

Next there's a section ❹ that defines how the plugin should be integrated with the native platform. Your plugin supports only Android, but if it supported iOS, Windows Phone, and other platforms, you'd have repeated `<platform>` blocks for each. The particular items within a platform will depend on the platform itself.

For your plugin, you use the `<config-file>` ❺ tag to specify that you want text inserted into an Android configuration file. The text inside this block will be copied into the config file at the root level (due to the parent attribute). In this case, you're simply specifying to Android what your Java code's package and class value are ❻. The last part ❼ is a pointer to the source code itself for the plugin. The `target-dir` attribute is specifying where the code should be deployed on the native platform. In this case, you're specifying a subdirectory based on the package used in the Java code. This helps ensure your code doesn't mess with anyone else's code.

There are additional attributes you can specify for the plugin.xml but these are the minimum required to get your project working correctly. A full listing of the XML tags and their meanings can be found at http://cordova.apache.org/docs/en/4.0.0/plugin_ref_spec.md.html.

8.3.3   *Working with your plugin*

At this point, you've defined your native code (listing 8.1) and your JavaScript API (listing 8.2) and described to Cordova how to integrate the plugin with a project (listing 8.3). Now it's time to use the plugin!

Begin by creating a new project and adding the Android platform. (Remember that your plugin supports only Android.) The first file, index.html in the following listing, will handle the UI for the application.

Listing 8.4   Application HTML file (c8/plugintest/index.html)

```
<!DOCTYPE html>
<html>
  <head>
  <meta charset="utf-8">
  <title>Plugin Demo</title>
```

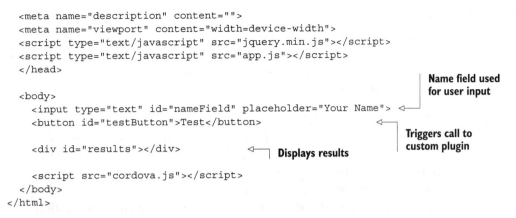

```
    <meta name="description" content="">
    <meta name="viewport" content="width=device-width">
    <script type="text/javascript" src="jquery.min.js"></script>
    <script type="text/javascript" src="app.js"></script>
    </head>

    <body>
      <input type="text" id="nameField" placeholder="Your Name">
      <button id="testButton">Test</button>

      <div id="results"></div>

      <script src="cordova.js"></script>
    </body>
</html>
```

Name field used for user input

Triggers call to custom plugin

Displays results

As the application is fairly trivial, there isn't much here. You've got a field for users to input their name, a button to click when they're ready, and a div to display the results from the plugin. Now look at the JavaScript in the following listing.

Listing 8.5 Application JavaScript file (c8/plugintest/app.js)

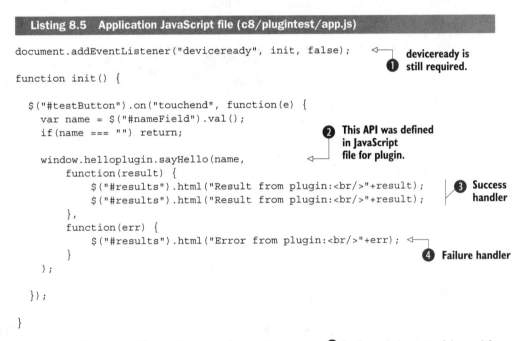

```
document.addEventListener("deviceready", init, false);

function init() {

  $("#testButton").on("touchend", function(e) {
    var name = $("#nameField").val();
    if(name === "") return;

    window.helloplugin.sayHello(name,
        function(result) {
            $("#results").html("Result from plugin:<br/>"+result);
            $("#results").html("Result from plugin:<br/>"+result);
        },
        function(err) {
            $("#results").html("Error from plugin:<br/>"+err);
        }
    );

  });

}
```

① deviceready is still required.

② This API was defined in JavaScript file for plugin.

③ Success handler

④ Failure handler

As a reminder, you still need to wait for deviceready ① before doing anything with the device. Just because your plugin is custom doesn't mean this requirement has changed. Because the plugin copied its JavaScript code to window.helloplugin, you can run window.helloplugin.sayHello to execute it from the application ②. You simply pass in the name to the API and then define a success ③ and failure ④ handler. In both cases you'll update a div with what the plugin returned.

8.3.4 *Adding the plugin*

So you're done, right? Nope! Don't forget you have to actually add a plugin to a project before you can use it. Previously you've seen examples of plugins that were hosted at the main plugin registry (http://plugins.cordova.io). This allowed you to add plugins via their ID, for example:

```
cordova plugins add org.apache.cordova.io
```

While you could add your plugin to this registry, most likely you don't want to do that while you're still testing it. Luckily the Cordova CLI also allows you to add plugins from local directories. In case you've forgotten, you can run `cordova help plugin` to see documentation about the plugin command.

If you followed the directory structure from the zip, you should have a folder called plugin for the plugin and one called plugintest for the application. (For the application, you should obviously install the Android platform first.) Both folders should be at the same level (that is, next to each other). Within the plugintest folder, you can then add your plugin with the following command:

```
cordova plugin add ../plugin
```

The result should be no different than adding any other plugin (figure 8.5).

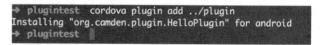

```
plugintest  cordova plugin add ../plugin
Installing "org.camden.plugin.HelloPlugin" for android
plugintest
```

Figure 8.5   Adding the custom plugin from the CLI

At this point you can either emulate or run the project and you should see the application as it was shown in figure 8.3. But what happens if you did something wrong? Perhaps you have a typo in your Java code? You can go back to HelloPlugin.java and on the first line add something that will break, for example:

```
<donut tag is not valid java>
package org.camden.plugin;

import org.apache.cordova.CallbackContext;
import org.apache.cordova.CordovaPlugin;
import org.json.JSONObject;
import org.json.JSONArray;
import org.json.JSONException;
```

This brings up an important issue. How do you update the plugin with your application? Changing the source code isn't enough. First you must remove the plugin from the application. While you added the plugin via a directory, you have to remove it by its ID value. If you don't remember it, run `cordova plugins` to list your currently installed plugins (figure 8.6).

```
plugintest  cordova plugins
org.camden.plugin.HelloPlugin 1.0.0 "HelloPlugin"
plugintest
```

Figure 8.6   Currently installed plugins

```
→ plugintest  cordova plugins
org.camden.plugin.HelloPlugin 1.0.0 "HelloPlugin"
→ plugintest  cordova plugins rm org.camden.plugin.HelloPlugin
Uninstalling org.camden.plugin.HelloPlugin from android
Removing "org.camden.plugin.HelloPlugin"
→ plugintest
```

Figure 8.7   Removing the custom plugin

Given the output in figure 8.6, you can remove your custom plugin by using an ID value of `org.camden.plugin.HelloPlugin` (figure 8.7).

Whether you're fixing bugs or adding features, you'll need to remove and then again add the plugin as you modify the source code. If you've modified the Java code to intentionally break it, go ahead and add it back. You won't get an error because the Cordova CLI simply copied in the plugin and got it ready. It hasn't actually *built* it yet. To make this happen you can either use the CLI `build` command or emulate or run to the device. Attempting to run your project with the bad plugin will return an error in your console, like that shown in figure 8.8.

```
    [javac] /Users/raymondcamden/Dropbox/Writing/Cordova book/code/c8/plugintest/platfor
ms/android/src/org/camden/plugin/HelloPlugin.java:17: error: not a statement
    [javac]          donut;
    [javac]               ^
    [javac] 1 error
    [javac] 3 warnings

BUILD FAILED
/Applications/android-sdk-macosx/tools/ant/build.xml:716: The following error occurred w
hile executing this line:
/Applications/android-sdk-macosx/tools/ant/build.xml:730: Compile failed; see the compil
er error output for details.
```

Figure 8.8   The failed build of your Cordova application

While it's a bit verbose, when you look at the output in figure 8.8, you can see both that it failed and how it failed. While you develop your plugin, your editor can provide helpful tips and help flag obvious errors before you get that far. To restore the plugin to working order, remove the invalid tag from the Java code, remove the plugin, add it again, and then try running it once more.

8.4   Summary

Let's review the major topics covered in this chapter.

- While numerous plugins exist, there may come a time when you need to build your own. Cordova provides a framework to make this possible.

- Custom plugins consist of the native code, a JavaScript API, and a plugin.xml file that describes how the plugin is integrated into an application.
- During development, a plugin can be added by using the CLI to point directly to the folder.
- Don't forget you have to remove and add the plugin as you develop it.

In the next chapter, you'll learn about ways to package your application, including adding support for splash-screens and icons.

Packing options for Cordova projects

9

This chapter covers

- Using config.xml to customize your Cordova project
- Using merges for platform-specific modifications
- Using hooks to enhance the build process

Whenever you create a Cordova project, you may have noticed that a file named config.xml is created in the root of the project, as shown in figure 9.1.

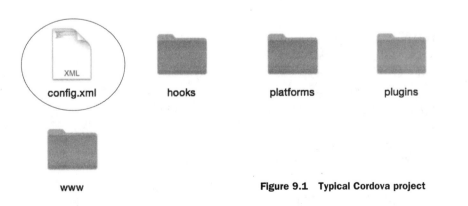

config.xml   hooks   platforms   plugins

www

Figure 9.1   Typical Cordova project

9.1 Using config.xml to customize your Cordova project

You've not had to worry about the config.xml file until now, but go ahead and open it. The following listing contains the default config.xml for a project created at the command line with no additional arguments. (For example, not specifying the ID or application name.)

Listing 9.1 Default config.xml

Application ID value ❶

Optional application description ❸

Optional application author element ❹

Application name ❷

File loaded ❺ by default

Special security tag used for accessing resources

```xml
<?xml version='1.0' encoding='utf-8'?>
<widget id="io.cordova.hellocordova" version="0.0.1" xmlns="http://
    www.w3.org/ns/widgets" xmlns:cdv="http://cordova.apache.org/ns/1.0">
    <name>HelloCordova</name>
    <description>
        A sample Apache Cordova application that responds to the deviceready
     event.
    </description>
    <author email="dev@cordova.apache.org" href="http://cordova.io">
        Apache Cordova Team
    </author>
    <content src="index.html" />
    <plugin name="cordova-plugin-whitelist" version="1" />
    <access origin="*" />
    <allow-intent href="http://*/*" />
    <allow-intent href="https://*/*" />
    <allow-intent href="tel:*" />
    <allow-intent href="sms:*" />
    <allow-intent href="mailto:*" />
    <allow-intent href="geo:*" />
    <platform name="android">
        <allow-intent href="market:*" />
    </platform>
    <platform name="ios">
        <allow-intent href="itms:*" />
        <allow-intent href="itms-apps:*" />
    </platform>
</widget>
```

This file is used by Cordova to define multiple different aspects of your application. You can see the ID value ❶, which is used to uniquely identify the application, as well as the name ❷. If you didn't specify these at the command line, then you get default values.

If you had specified them like so: `cordova create somefolder org.camden.myapp "My Cool App"`, you'd have seen them in the config.xml file:

```xml
<widget id="org.camden.myapp" version="0.0.1" xmlns="http://www.w3.org/ns/
    widgets" xmlns:cdv="http://cordova.apache.org/ns/1.0">
    <name>My Cool App</name>
```

If you forgot to specify these values when creating your application, then modifying them in the config.xml file is how you'd fix it later. Cordova will use this file when creating builds of your application.

The file also includes optional items like a description ❸ and author ❹, but they're useful to populate just for documentation purposes alone.

If you choose, you can tell Cordova to *not* use index.html as the default file ❹ loaded on your device when the application opens. While possible, I've yet to see a good reason for doing this, so you should probably avoid changing this.

The final option in the *default* config.xml is the `<access>` block ❺. This is a rather special tag as it dictates what *remote* resources (JavaScript files, CSS, images, remote APIs, etc.) your application can access. To be clear, we're talking about remote resources that aren't bundled within your www folder. The default value, *, means any and all resources are allowed. Typically that's probably okay. But imagine your application has dynamically generated user content. Maybe it lets people post comments about pictures, for example. You may wish to allow HTML within your comments, bold tags, italics, and perhaps links. It's possible that a person may include a link to someplace that you'd rather your users not go. This may come as a surprise to you, but there are certain places on the internet where people can find naughty things. While this is simply a fact of life on the internet, you may wish to lock down your application to specific domains.

The value you specify in the `<access>` tag's origin value can include the * character to make more flexible matches. You can specify as many `<access>` tags as you wish. For example, to allow access to anything on https://google.com, both secure and nonsecure, you could use the following:

```
<access origin="https://google.com" />
<access origin="http://google.com" />
```

To further allow for subdomains under Google, you can use a * to represent them:

```
<access origin="http://*.google.com" />
<access origin="https://*.google.com" />
```

Whether or not you lock down your access security is up to you and what your application is doing. The default behavior of allowing anything is certainly the *easiest* solution, but if your application isn't using user-generated content, you should consider restricting access to only what your application needs. For example, if your application uses only one remote API at https://raymondcamden.com, then you could use this:

```
<access origin="https://raymondcamden.com" />
```

Cordova refers to this feature as whitelisting. In the most recent version of Cordova, this feature was moved into a unique plugin that provides even additional features in iOS and Android. For further details, see https://github.com/apache/cordova-plugin-whitelist.

As a real example, Google has a few APIs it provides to developers. You'll see an example of this in chapter 12—the Google Feed API. To let your application use the Google APIs and nothing else, you could use this access block:

```
<access origin="https://www.google.com/jsapi">
```

The origin of config.xml

In case you're curious, config.xml's structure is based on a World Wide Web Consortium (W3C) specification for packaging web apps. It has always been a philosophy of Cordova to try to follow web standards as much as possible. In the ideal world, everything Cordova does would be supported by regular mobile browsers and Cordova could cease to exist. You can probably guess how soon that will come to pass.

Now that you've looked at the default config.xml file, let's discuss what else you can add here. At a high level, settings in config.xml fall into the following categories:

- General preferences that apply to all platforms.
- Preferences that only make sense on one platform.
- Icon and splash-screen settings.
- Settings for plugins.
- Settings that will only be applied to one platform. This is different from platform-specific settings. You can take any general setting that *would* have applied everywhere and make it work for only one particular platform.

Now that you've gotten a basic idea of the types of settings you can use, let's tour them and show examples.

9.1.1 General (or global) preferences

There are five global preferences, although some aren't truly global and apply only to a few of the major platforms. They're listed in table 9.1.

Table 9.1   Preference options

Name	Purpose	Where applicable
Fullscreen	Determines if an app covers the entire screen	All but iOS
Orientation	Lets you lock an app to one orientation	Everything but iOS
DisallowOverscroll	Prevents an app from "shifting" off screen	Only Android and iOS
BackgroundColor	Specifies an application background color	Android and Blackberry
HideKeyboardFrom-AccessoryBar	Hides an additional toolbar that appears over the keyboard	iOS and Blackberry

Using these preferences is a simple matter of adding a new tag to your config.xml file:

```
<preference name="THE PREFERENCE" value="THE VALUE" />
```

To specify that an application should use the `Fullscreen` preference you'd type the following:

```
<preference name="Fullscreen" value="true" />
```

Preference names are *not* case sensitive. Let's look at the first three of these preferences as they can have the most dramatic impact on your application. They're also the ones that most developers end up tweaking in their applications.

CREATE YOUR APPLICATIONS

Before we begin, create two new Cordova applications. If you created one to see the default config.xml file earlier, then make one more. You'll use these two applications to compare how these preferences can change your application. Remember the application IDs should be unique. When you use the default ID for your testing and run the apps on your device or emulators, Cordova overwrites the previous installation. You can use the following two commands to create two applications for testing the preferences:

```
cordova create test_with_nopreferences org.camden.nopreferences
    "NoPreferenceTest"
cordova create test_with_preferences org.camden.withpreferences
    "PreferenceTest"
```

These will also match the directories created in the zip file you downloaded with this book.

Open the config.xml file in your second application, or if you downloaded the code, the test_with_preferences folder. The following listing demonstrates the modified config.xml file.

Listing 9.2 test_with_preferences/config.xml

```
<?xml version='1.0' encoding='utf-8'?>
<widget id="org.camden.withpreferences" version="0.0.1" xmlns="http://
    www.w3.org/ns/widgets" xmlns:cdv="http://cordova.apache.org/ns/1.0">
    <name>PreferenceTest</name>
    <description>
        A sample Apache Cordova application that responds to the deviceready
        event.
    </description>
    <author email="dev@cordova.apache.org" href="http://cordova.io">
        Apache Cordova Team
    </author>
    <content src="index.html" />
    <access origin="*" />

    <preference name="Fullscreen" value="true" />          ← Fullscreen preference
    <preference name="Orientation" value="portrait" />     ← Orientation preference
    <preference name="DisallowOverscroll" value="true" />  ← DisallowOverscroll preference

</widget>
```

The three lines you'll want to add (if you aren't using the file from the zip) are the three preference lines at the end of the listing.

Add your platform of choice, and then run it in the emulator. To really see how these preferences modify your application, you'll need to run one app first, and then the next app. In theory, you could try running one on a device and one on an emulator. iOS

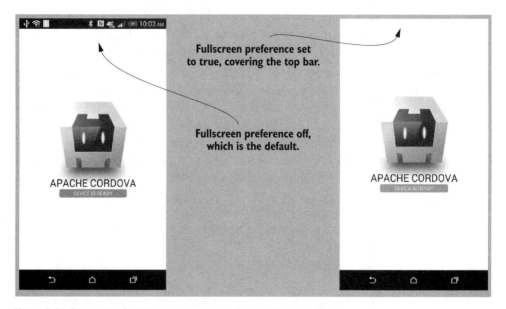

Figure 9.2   Demonstrating the Fullscreen preference in an emulator

will only let you use one emulator at a time. Android will let you use multiple different emulators, but not the same one twice (although you could build two emulators using the same version, size specifics, etc.).

FULLSCREEN PREFERENCE

Let's first look at how the Fullscreen preference changes the application. Remember that this doesn't work in iOS. If you're interested in a similar feature for iOS, see the Statusbar at plugin at http://plugins.cordova.io/#/package/org.apache.cordova .statusbar.

In figure 9.2, the default behavior (Fullscreen set to false) is shown on the left. On the right, you can see how the application now takes over that top bar. Whether or not you use this is purely an aesthetic decision.

ORIENTATION PREFERENCE

Let's look now at how the Orientation preference works. Remember that by default your Cordova application will work in either orientation. By specifying landscape or portrait, you can lock your app into one orientation. Figure 9.3 shows the Orientation preference set to portrait.

As you can see, when the device is rotated, the application with a specific Orientation preference setting doesn't rotate. As with the Fullscreen preference setting, whether or not you use this is up to you and is dependent on what your application requires. (If you're testing with the Android emulator, you can use Ctrl+F12 to rotate the view.)

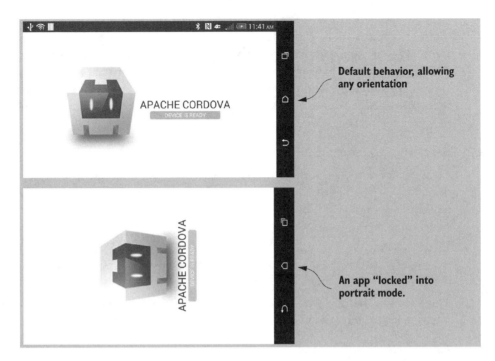

Default behavior, allowing any orientation

An app "locked" into portrait mode.

Figure 9.3 Orientation **preference is locked and therefore cannot change.**

This is the area being exposed by dragging down.

DISALLOWOVERSCROLL PREFERENCE

The DisallowOverscroll preference is a bit difficult to demonstrate in book format. In figure 9.4, you have to imagine my finger has touched the screen and dragged down.

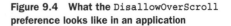

Figure 9.4 What the DisallowOverScroll preference looks like in an application

As my finger shifts down, the black space above the app grows. When my finger is lifted, it bounces back. While this doesn't necessarily break anything, it may confuse users. As native applications don't have this behavior, DisallowOverscroll also flags the application as a hybrid application versus a "pure" native application. Because it takes mere seconds to add the DisallowOverscroll preference, it's almost always recommended. Note: You can see this effect in the simulator by clicking the mouse and dragging the cursor up or down.

9.1.2 Specifying preferences for a platform

Earlier when I specified the types of preferences you can add to a project, I mentioned it was possible to specify a preference for only one platform. If you wish to use a preference and only apply it to one platform, you wrap it within a </platform> tag, as demonstrated here:

```
<platform name="ios">
    <preference name="DisallowOverscroll" value="true" />
</platform>
```

This specifies that the DisallowOverscroll preference is only true for iOS. You can put as many preferences in here as you'd like.

9.1.3 Finding other preferences

How do you find the other globally useful preferences? If you go to the Cordova documentation site at http://docs.cordova.io, you'll see a link in the left navigation bar for Platform Guides. This takes you to a list of links for all the major platforms supported by Cordova. In most of these platforms there's a specific link for configuration, as shown in figure 9.5.

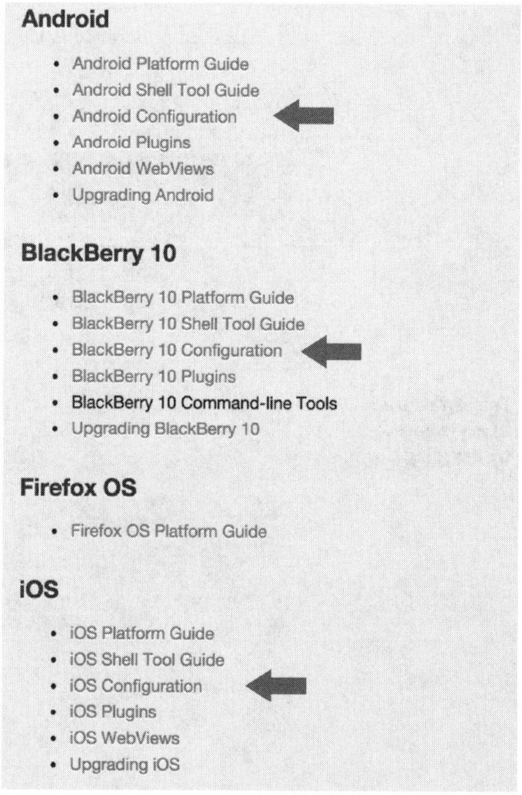

Android

- Android Platform Guide
- Android Shell Tool Guide
- Android Configuration
- Android Plugins
- Android WebViews
- Upgrading Android

BlackBerry 10

- BlackBerry 10 Platform Guide
- BlackBerry 10 Shell Tool Guide
- BlackBerry 10 Configuration
- BlackBerry 10 Plugins
- **BlackBerry 10 Command-line Tools**
- Upgrading BlackBerry 10

Firefox OS

- Firefox OS Platform Guide

iOS

- iOS Platform Guide
- iOS Shell Tool Guide
- iOS Configuration
- iOS Plugins
- iOS WebViews
- Upgrading iOS

Figure 9.5 Platform guides and configuration links

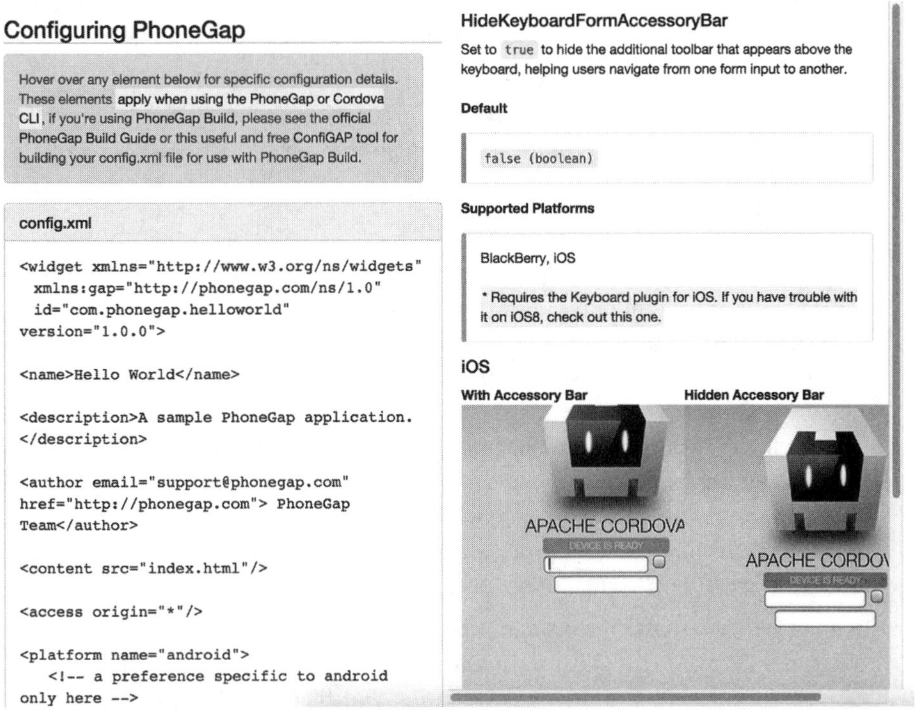

Figure 9.6   Holly Schinsky's interactive config.xml guide

Each link will take you to a list of preferences specific to that platform. Another way to learn about these preferences is via an excellent tool created by PhoneGap team member Holly Schinsky: http://devgirl.org/files/config-app/. This tool is an interactive guide to the config.xml. In figure 9.6, you can see that as you hover over each section, you get detailed docs as well as screenshots where appropriate.

I highly recommend bookmarking this tool and referring to it as you configure your application.

9.1.4   *Working with icons and splash-screens*

All applications that are going to be released to the wild need a custom icon and splash-screen. Hybrid apps are no exception. The config.xml makes it easy to specify icons and splash-screens, assuming that you've spent the time to design them. For testing here, you'll be using source images from the Dynamic Dummy Image Generator website at http://dummyimage.com. This is a web service that generates images based on query parameters. It's useful when creating mockups where you need quick images of certain sizes. So for example, the URL http://dummyimage.com/600x400/000/fff.png creates a 600 × 400 image with the color hex code 000 (black) for a background, fff (white) for text, and .png as the file extension to generate a PNG format image. We're doing this because you absolutely don't want me generating icons for the book. My three-year-old draws better than I. That's not a joke.

SPECIFY AN ICON OR SPLASH-SCREEN

Specifying an icon or a splash-screen by itself isn't too difficult. For example, this would be all you need to do for one icon and one portrait splash-screen:

```
<icon src="res/icon.png" />
<splash src="res/splash.png" />
```

The paths in the preceding code are relative to your project root, *not* the www folder. The subdirectory and filename themselves are completely arbitrary, but it certainly makes sense to name them something logical.

Splash-screens require one additional small step: you must include the Splash-screen plugin. This plugin provides additional ways to work with splash-screens that you probably won't ever need, but you must install it before the lines in your config.xml file. Run `cordova plugin` and add `cordova-plugin-splashscreen` to add the plugin to your project.

To test this feature, either create a new project yourself and the respective images or use the test_with_icon_splash folder from the zip file for this book.

ICON DESIGN AND DISPLAY CONSIDERATIONS FOR ANDROID AND IOS

Figure 9.7 shows the custom icon (again, created by http://dummyimage.com). Notice that it's *not* a well-designed icon. The black background makes it disappear

Figure 9.7   Custom application icon

into the list of apps. Obviously it isn't very creative either. Covering the design of a good icon or splash-screen is beyond the scope of this book, but you can check with the documentation for your platform for guides. Android and Apple provide guides (http://developer.android.com/design/style/iconography.html) for creating icons. (https://developer.apple.com/library/ios/documentation/UserExperience/Conceptual/MobileHIG/IconMatrix.html).

And this opens up another can of worms! As you're aware, the variety of devices available to users in the mobile world has exploded. At a broad level, you have phones and tablets. Phones started out around 3 inches or so wide and have steadily increased in size. Tablets typically come in two main sizes, 10 inches and 7 inches, but 8-inch models exist and apparently Apple is working on a 12-inch model. To make matters even more interesting, you have different screen resolutions. Apple introduced the world to "retina" displays, which pack twice the pixels on a screen of the same size.

As stated previously, the guides provided by each platform will help you figure out how to support each device type, but how does Cordova help with the process?

First, recall that I demonstrated earlier how you can specify a preference for one particular platform by wrapping it in the </platform> tag. So if you had built an iOS and Android icon, you could use the following snippet to specify one per platform:

```
<platform name="android">
    <icon src="res/android/icon.png" />
</platform>
<platform name="ios">
    <icon src="res/ios/icon.png" />
</platform>
```

In this snippet, you've told Cordova to use res/android/icon.png for the Android icon and res/ios/icon.png for the iOS one. The subdirectories are arbitrary, but organizing your assets by platform will help you in the long run. Now this is where things get interesting.

To support different types of Android icons, you specify a particular density value. Android and Cordova support density values of ldpi, mdpi, hdpi, and xhdpi. These equate to an *approximate* density value:

- ldpi: 120 dpi
- mdpi: 160 dpi
- hdpi: 240 dpi
- xhdpi: 320 dpi

Assuming you've created icons at these resolution values, specifying them in config.xml is rather simple:

```
<platform name="android">
    <icon src="res/android/icon_low.png" density="ldpi" />
    <icon src="res/android/icon_medium.png" density="mdpi" />
    <icon src="res/android/icon_high.png" density="hdpi" />
    <icon src="res/android/icon_xhigh.png" density="xhdpi" />
</platform>
```

Android supports xxhdpi and xxxhdpi settings, but these aren't yet supported by the config.xml file.

iOS is, not surprisingly, a bit more complex. For iOS, you'll specify the dimensions of your icon as a means of targeting a particular platform, size, and OS. This particular example targets the iPhone 6 Plus:

```
<platform name="ios">
    <icon src="res/ios/icon-60@3x.png" width="180" height="180" />
</platform>
```

The name of the icon is up to you, but following standard naming for icons may make it easier to work with others who have experience with native mobile apps. The Cordova platform guide lists the currently supported iOS icon sizes and dimensions: http://cordova.apache.org/docs/en/4.0.0/config_ref_images.md.html#Icons and Splash Screens.

SPLASH-SCREEN DESIGN AND DISPLAY CONSIDERATIONS FOR ANDROID AND IOS
For splash-screens, you've got a similar situation, but you must deal with portrait and landscape modes. For Android, once again you use a density value, but now it can include the prefix land or port, representing landscape and portrait. Here's an example:

```
<platform name="android">
    <splash src="res/android/ss_low_p.png" density="port-ldpi" />
    <splash src="res/android/ss_med_p.png" density="port-mdpi" />
    <splash src="res/android/ss_low_l.png" density="land-mdpi" />
    <splash src="res/android/ss_med_l.png" density="land-mdpi" />
</platform>
```

And as before, iOS will use height and width:

```
<platform name="ios">
  <splash src="res/ios/Default~iphone.png" width="320" height="480" />
  <splash src="res/ios/Default-Portrait~ipad.png" width="768" height="1024" />
  <splash src="res/ios/Default-Landscape~ipad.png" width="1024" height="768" />
  <splash src="res/ios/Default@2x~iphone.png" width="640" height="960" />
</platform>
```

As before, you can use the Cordova reference for a full list of supported iOS devices and resolutions, and don't forget you can add comments to your config.xml file to help you remember what's what:

```
<platform name="ios">
  <!—regular iphone -->
  <splash src="res/ios/Default~iphone.png" width="320" height="480" />
  <!-- ipad in portrait, non-retina -->
  <splash src="res/ios/Default-Portrait~ipad.png" width="768" height="1024" />
  <!-- ipad in landscape, non-retina -->
  <splash src="res/ios/Default-Landscape~ipad.png" width="1024" height="768" />
  <!-- awesome retina enabled iphone -->
  <splash src="res/ios/Default@2x~iphone.png" width="640" height="960" />
</platform>
```

> ## Ionic is awesome—and here is why ...
>
> I've mentioned the Ionic framework earlier, and recommended *Ionic in Action* for a full look at that platform, but for a quick example of why Ionic is awesome, consider this: One of the features of the Ionic CLI is a resource generator. You create one icon and one splash-screen, and Ionic can automatically generate *all* of the relative-sized assets for you. Not only does it generate the assets, it even updates your config.xml file for you!

9.2 *Using merges for multiple platforms*

While you can use one code base to create applications for all the platforms Cordova supports, you typically will want to create an experience that's tailored to a particular platform. For example, it's a common Android UI design to have tabs on top of the app, while on iOS, tabs will be on the bottom. Given that you have one www folder within a Cordova project, how do you handle that?

One way would be to generate a build for one platform, edit the www files, and then generate a build for the other platform. That's simple, but error-prone. Another way would be to use the Device plugin. It gives you access to information about the device that your application is running on. That works too but it could be complex to use JavaScript to assign CSS based on different factors.

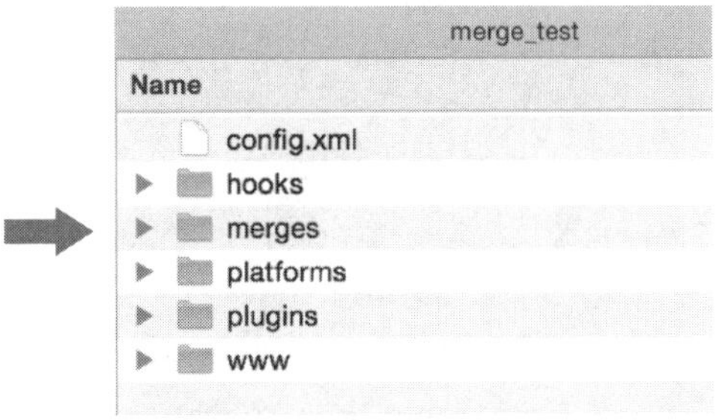

A much easier solution is to use the merges folder. This folder does *not* exist by default. To test it, create a new folder called merges at the root of your project, as shown in figure 9.8.

Figure 9.8 A project with the merges folder

Inside this folder you can create a new directory for each platform you want to customize. For testing purposes, create one named android and one named ios, as shown in figure 9.9.

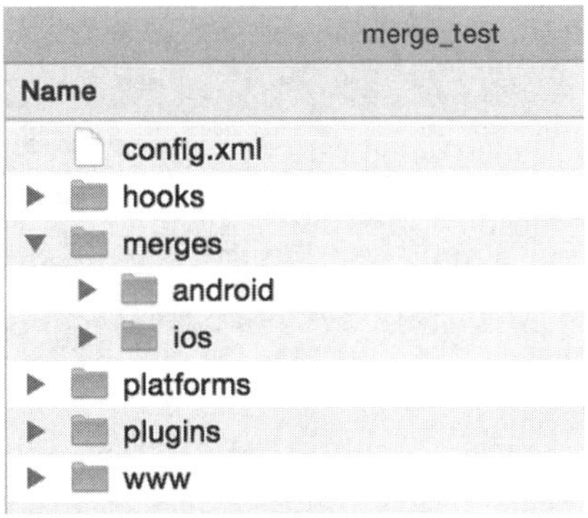

When you use the Cordova CLI to create projects, the merges folder will be checked for each platform you support. If a file exists in the platform-specific merges folder that matches one in www, it will be replaced. If there's a file in the platform-specific merges folder that doesn't exist in www, it will be added. The subdirectory in the merges folder should be named the same as the

Figure 9.9 Two new directories for Android and iOS

platform you want to modify. Case doesn't matter. Let's look at a simple example of this in action.

You'll begin by creating a new application and making a simple "Hello World" HTML page. You can find this in the merges_test folder from the zip you downloaded for the book.

Listing 9.3 Application homepage (merges_test/www/index.html)

```
<!DOCTYPE html>
<html>
    <head>
        <meta charset="utf-8" />
        <meta name="format-detection" content="telephone=no" />
        <meta name="msapplication-tap-highlight" content="no" />
        <meta name="viewport" content="user-scalable=no, initial-scale=1,
    maximum-scale=1, minimum-scale=1, width=device-width, height=device-
    height, target-densitydpi=device-dpi" />
        <link rel="stylesheet" type="text/css" href="css/index.css" />
        <link rel="stylesheet" type="text/css" href="css/platform.css" />
        <title>Hello World</title>
    </head>
    <body>

            <h1>Hello World</h1>
            <p>
            Hello folks!
            </p>

        <script type="text/javascript" src="cordova.js"></script>
    </body>
</html>
```

Default CSS for all platforms ❶

Specific CSS file for a platform ❷

Notice that the application loads two different CSS files. The first one ❶ is meant to contain CSS for all platforms. The second one ❷ will be platform-specific. The main index.css is pretty minimal, as shown in the following listing.

Listing 9.4 CSS file for all platforms (merges_test/www/css/index.css)

```
/* Apply to all */
h1 {
    font-family: sans-serif;
}

p {
    font-family: sans-serif;
    color: black;
}
```

Here's the platform.css file:

```
/* Blank by default */
```

Yes, that's it. Why is there a (essentially) blank file? You're going to use the merges feature to provide custom CSS for one or more platforms. For platforms that don't need this feature, you want to provide a blank file so that when the application requests the CSS file, it doesn't create an error. That error wouldn't really hurt anything, but if you're debugging then you don't want a bogus error message to get in the way.

You're going to customize the Android platform only. To do that, you'll create an android folder under a merges folder in the project root, and then a css folder, and finally a platform.css file, as shown in figure 9.10.

The end result will now be different for just Android when creating builds. Cordova will notice that a file exists in the android merges folder and use that instead of the version in www. The result is a different look for Android versus iOS. The following listing shows the Android-specific platform.css.

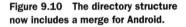

Figure 9.10   The directory structure now includes a merge for Android.

Listing 9.5   Android-modified CSS (merges_test/merges/android/css/platform.css)

```css
body {
    background-color: aquamarine;
}

p {
    font-family: sans-serif;
    color: black;
    font-size: 40px;
    font-style: italic;
}
```

When running the application on both iOS and Android you can immediately see the differences, as shown in figure 9.11.

Figure 9.11   An example of how a merge can modify an application by platform

9.3   *Using hooks to enhance the Cordova CLI*

Another powerful feature of the Cordova CLI is the hook. Hooks allow you to modify the behavior of the Cordova CLI within a project. They're scripts that interact with the CLI based on what action you may be taking. In general, they fall into two broad categories: scripts that run before actions and scripts that run after actions. For example, when you add a platform via the CLI, that's an opportunity for a hook to run, both before the platform is added and after. When you add a plugin, that's another opportunity for a hook to run, before and after.

9.3.1   *Why do you use hooks?*

The most obvious question you probably have now is ... so what? Hooks aren't a feature you'll use terribly often. You'll certainly not (most likely) ever use *all* of the hooks. It's important to know that the feature exists. If you ever find yourself performing some particular action with your Cordova projects, you should look at hooks as a way of possibly automating those actions so you don't have to repeat them. As a real-world example, imagine you're working on a project that makes use of a few plugins. Every time you add a new platform, you need to remember to add those required plugins. It would be nice to automate that, wouldn't it? If you look at the list of hooks that follow, you'll see one exists for `after_platform_add`. This means you can create a hook that will run after a platform is added.

9.3.2   *Defining hooks*

Hooks can be defined two ways. By default, the Cordova CLI will look for hook scripts with a subdirectory of the hooks folder. All Cordova projects have an empty hooks folder by default. If you then create a subdirectory with the same name as a hook, Cordova will look for executable scripts in that folder to run. In that subdirectory, hooks will be executed in alphabetical order as defined by their filename.

Hooks can also be configured in config.xml. This allows for the use of `</platform>` tags to specify hooks for particular platforms.

Scripts can be written in any language that works on your computer, but JavaScript scripts run via Node are preferred as they're the most portable. (By that I mean that the script can run on Windows, Mac, and Linux machines.)

9.3.3   *Hooks: before and after CLI commands*

So what hooks exist?

- `before_build` and `after_build`
- `before_compile` and `after_compile`
- `before_emulate` and `after_emulate`
- `before_platform_add`, `before_platform_ls`, `before_platform_rm`, and `after_platform_add`, `after_platform_ls`, `after_platform_rm`
- `before_plugin_add`, `before_plugin_ls`, `before_plugin_rm`, `before_plugin_install`, `before_plugin_search`, `before_plugin_uninstall`, and after

      `_plugin_add, after_plugin_ls, after_plugin_rm, after_plugin_install, after_plugin_search`

- `before_prepare` and `after_prepare`
- `before_run` and `after_run`
- `before_serve` and `after_serve`
- `pre_package` (Windows 8 and Windows Phone only)

As you can see, hooks are named based on when they occur (before or after) and what CLI command they're bound to. A hook for `before_build` would run before `cordova build`. A hook for `after_emulate` would run after `cordova emulate`.

9.3.4 Example: use a hook to add plugins for a platform

This example uses a hook created by PhoneGap team member Holly Schinksy. You can find this hook, and a few more, at her blog post: http://devgirl.org/2013/11/12/three-hooks-your-cordovaphonegap-project-needs/.

The following listing demonstrates how a hook could be created.

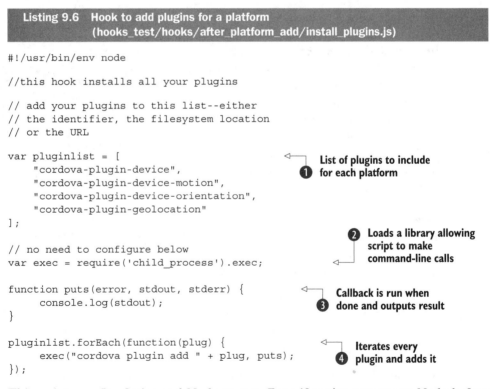

Listing 9.6   Hook to add plugins for a platform (hooks_test/hooks/after_platform_add/install_plugins.js)

```
#!/usr/bin/env node

//this hook installs all your plugins

// add your plugins to this list--either
// the identifier, the filesystem location
// or the URL

var pluginlist = [                                    ← ❶ List of plugins to include
    "cordova-plugin-device",                               for each platform
    "cordova-plugin-device-motion",
    "cordova-plugin-device-orientation",
    "cordova-plugin-geolocation"
];

// no need to configure below                          ❷ Loads a library allowing
var exec = require('child_process').exec;                 script to make
                                                        ← command-line calls

function puts(error, stdout, stderr) {                ← ❸ Callback is run when
    console.log(stdout);                                  done and outputs result
}

pluginlist.forEach(function(plug) {                   ← ❹ Iterates every
    exec("cordova plugin add " + plug, puts);             plugin and adds it
});
```

This script uses JavaScript and Node to run. Even if you've never seen Node before now, you should be able to understand the JavaScript used in the script. If you installed the Cordova CLI via `npm`, then you have Node and this script can run once you've set it as executable. The plugin list ❶ is arbitrary for this example—in a real

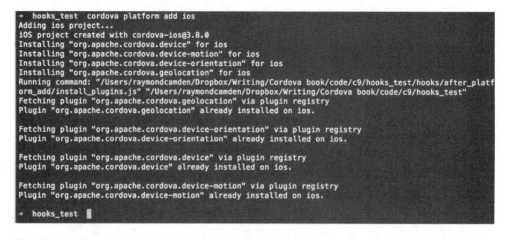

Figure 9.12   An example of the hook automatically adding hooks

project it would match your needs. Node can load ❷ in various libraries, and this script loads in one that allows it to call other programs via exec ❹. The result is spit back out to the screen ❸.

Now when a new platform is added, plugins for the platform will be installed automatically, as shown in figure 9.12.

For this to work, the file must be in the correctly named folder. Because you want this to run after a platform is added, that folder is hooks/after_platform_add (figure 9.13).

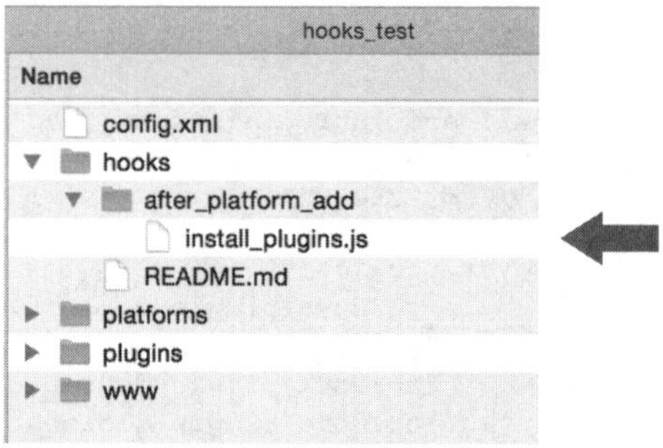

9.3.5   *Using hooks with config.xml*

While the filesystem is the preferred way of using hooks, you can also specify hooks within your config.xml file. You really only need this feature if:

Figure 9.13   Putting the hook in the proper place

- You don't want to use default behavior of "folder X and so is used for hook X" and want to specify a custom folder.
- You want to specify a hook but only for a particular platform.

At the simplest level, you can specify a hook in config.xml with a <hook> tag:

```
<hook type="after_platform_add" src="myhooks/install_plugins.js" />
```

Given a subdirectory myhooks, if you had put the earlier script there instead and then added this line to config.xml, you'd get the same behavior as before. Most likely, though, you'd use this feature when you want to specify a hook for one particular platform only:

```
<platform name="android">
<hook type="after_platform_add" src="myhooks/install_plugins.js" />
</platform>
```

Note that Cordova will execute your hooks in the order you define them in config.xml and not alphabetically.

9.3.6 *Working with hook arguments*

Your hook scripts will also be passed information that includes the type of hook being executed, the path to the script itself, and the arguments passed in to the current command. If your hook needs access to these values for whatever reason, your code can access them and respond accordingly. How this data is passed to your hook is a bit complex.

If you're using the "directory hook" setup, and by that I mean you use the default hooks folder and not the config.xml definitions, then this data is passed as a series of environment variables: `CORDOVA_VERSION`, `CORDOVA_PLATFORMS`, `CORDOVA_PLUGINS`, `CORDOVA_HOOK`, and `CORDOVA_CMDLINE`. Accessing environment variables depends on what the language you used to write your script. If you had used JavaScript as demonstrated in listing 9.6, then it could look like so:

```
console.log(process.env.CORDOVA_HOOK);
```

If you're using config.xml to define what hooks to run, you have to write your hook slightly different to use this information. If you look at listing 9.6, you'll see it's a simple script that's run as is—pretty much top to bottom. To work the numerous arguments the hook script has access to, you'll need to define a main function that's exported from the script. That sounds confusing, but it really comes down to wrapping your code with the following block:

```
module.exports = function(context) {
//your stuff here;
}
```

This block essentially means: "This function is what I'm exporting, or sharing, with the command line." When the Cordova CLI executes your hook, it will look for that exported function and call it. The context argument will contain all the information about how the hook was executed, command-line arguments, and so on. The following listing is an updated version of the earlier hook that makes use of this format.

> **Listing 9.7   Updated hook (hooks_test2/myhooks /install_plugins.js)**

```
var pluginlist = [
    "cordova-plugin-device",
    "cordova-plugin-device-motion",
    "cordova-plugin-device-orientation",
```

```
    "cordova-plugin-geolocation"
];

var exec = require('child_process').exec;

function puts(error, stdout, stderr) {
    console.log(stdout);
}
```
① Module wrapper
```
module.exports = function(context) {
    console.log("This hook is "+context.hook);
    pluginlist.forEach(function(plug) {
            exec("cordova plugin add " + plug, puts);
    });
}
```
② Context variable

The main logic of this hook (looping over a plugin list) is now wrapped in an export ❶. When the Cordova CLI executes this hook, it will run this function and pass in information. You can use that information by using an appropriate value from the context variable. In this case, you simply log the hook name ❷. The last thing needed to make this work is to edit config.xml to point to this script:

```
<hook type="before_platform_add" src="myhooks/install_plugins.js" />
```

If you've downloaded the code for this book you can find this example in the hooks_test2 folder.

9.4   *Summary*

Let's review the major topics covered in this chapter.

- When the CLI is used to create mobile applications, there are multiple ways you can configure how that application is created.
- The config.xml file has different options allowing for customization of the application.
- Merges let you easily swap out or add files on a per-platform basis.
- Hooks allow for script-based programs to run in any particular part of the development process.

In the next chapter, you'll discover a whole new way to create Cordova applications using Adobe PhoneGap Build.

Using PhoneGap tools

This chapter covers

- Using PhoneGap Build to create mobile apps
- Configuring PhoneGap Build apps
- Updating PhoneGap Build apps with Hydration
- Using the PhoneGap Developer App to develop mobile apps

In chapter 1 we discussed how PhoneGap relates to Cordova. PhoneGap is the name most developers use when talking about building hybrid mobile applications, but Cordova is the actual open source project. As part of Adobe, PhoneGap offers a few alternatives to working with mobile apps that may be enticing for users. In this chapter we'll look at some of these tools. To be clear, these aren't things you *must* use, and in some cases they may not be helpful if you've already got your entire environment set up correctly. But knowing about these options may make it easier to bring other coworkers into your team. Also, both of the options discussed in this chapter will enable you to build for iOS devices from a Windows or Linux machine.

10.1 Working with PhoneGap

In this chapter we'll look at the PhoneGap Build service. This lets you create hybrid mobile applications with absolutely *no* setup on your machine. You can skip installing SDKs and command-line programs and instead use your favorite editor. The only requirement is an Adobe ID.

We'll then look at the PhoneGap Developer App. It lets you test your application from an Android or iOS device. All you need for that is the actual app (a free application you download on your device) and the PhoneGap command-line program (easily installed via npm).

In both cases, you'll be using *real* devices, not emulators, to test these features.

10.2   PhoneGap Build service

PhoneGap Build is a web-based service (http://build .phonegap.com) that provides compilation services for hybrid mobile applications. That's a fancy way of saying that it handles converting your HTML, CSS, and JavaScript into a mobile application. If you remember all the steps you had to do in chapter 2 to set up your machine to build applications for Android, you can skip *all* of this. Remember how you used the Cordova CLI? You can skip that too! All you need to do is write your HTML and then let the PhoneGap Build service take it from there. Figure 10.1 demonstrates this process.

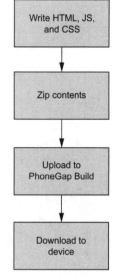

Figure 10.1   Phone Gap Build process

10.2.1   Create a PhoneGap Build account

To begin, create an account on the website. To be clear, PhoneGap Build is a *commercial* service. You have to pay to get this convenience, but you can use PhoneGap Build for free in a limited fashion. At the time this chapter was written, there were three levels of accounts available for PhoneGap Build:

- *The free plan*—Allows you to create one private application and unlimited open source apps. The exact meaning of how those types of apps differ will be explained next. For the purpose of this book, the free plan is sufficient and will let you get a feeling for how the service works.
- *The paid plan*—(At the time of writing, $9.99 a month, because obviously $10 would be far too much.) Allows for larger applications and more private applications.
- *Adobe's Creative Cloud*—If you join, you get to work with even larger applications. (Adobe's Creative Cloud provides access to a large stable of design tools as well.)

To begin the signup process, click Sign Up from the top of the website and select your plan. Again, you do *not* have to pay anything to get started. You will, however, be asked to sign up for an Adobe ID. As you can guess, this is a login you can use for other Adobe services, and if you already have an Adobe ID, you should use the Sign In link instead.

Also note that if you happened to already be logged in at www.Adobe.com, you may be redirected immediately to the website. In other words, PhoneGap Build will recognize that you've already logged in at Adobe (figure 10.2).

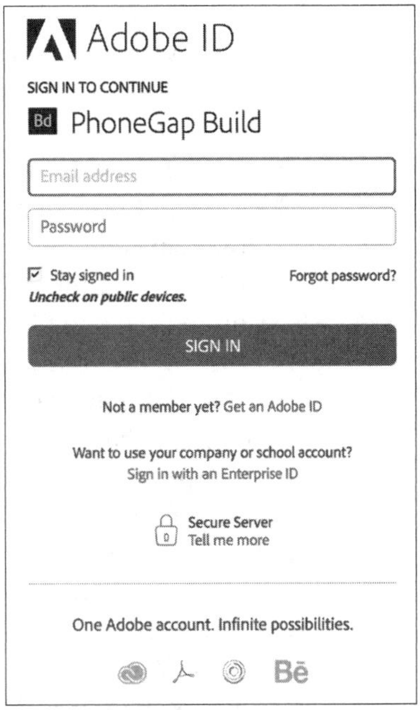

10.2.2 Creating your first PhoneGap Build application

Immediately after logging in, you're prompted to create your first application, as shown in figure 10.3. Here's where you first get to see the difference between private and open source applications.

PhoneGap Build lets you source your applications from two different places. A private application is one that's created from a folder on your machine. You write HTML (and CSS, JavaScript, etc.), zip the folder, and then upload it to PhoneGap Build. An open source application is one that's sourced from a GitHub repository. You can also create a private application from a GitHub repository.

Figure 10.2 Signup form for PhoneGap Build

This option lets you create an application from a GitHub repository.

This option lets you create an application from code on your machine.

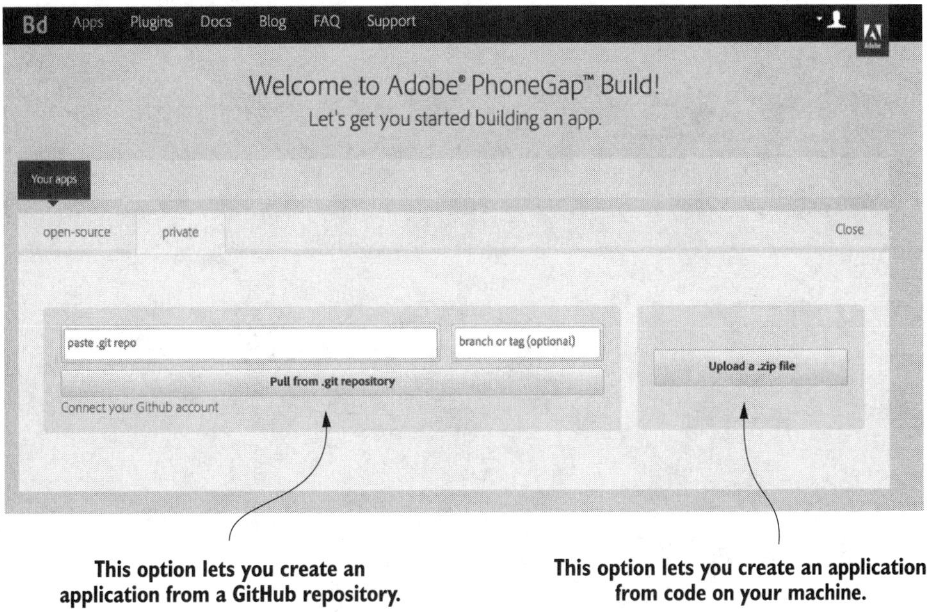

Figure 10.3   Creating your first application

For the purposes of this first demo, use the zip option. To keep things simple, you'll create a hybrid application that consists of one file. That one file *must* be called index.html, which is hopefully a standard you follow when building websites. What you put in that index.html is completely arbitrary for now, but you can get by literally with this: `<h1>Hello World!</h1>`. You then want to ensure that this file exists in a folder by itself. The name of the folder doesn't matter.

Now comes the important part. PhoneGap Build is asking for a zip. But you *must zip the folder* containing your assets, not just the file. Obviously a real application will have more than one file so you wouldn't be sending only one zipped file, but you want to ensure you're always zipping the folder, not the contents inside it. As an example, on a Mac you right-click on the folder and choose Compress, as shown in figure 10.4.

Once you have a zipped file you can then choose the Upload a .zip File back in PhoneGap Build. After the file uploads, you're presented with a new screen allowing you to name your project and enable a few options (figure 10.5).

The screen you get may be a bit different from figure 10.5, but it should be relatively similar. There's both a warning and a tip that you can safely ignore for now—we'll be covering what they imply later. All you should worry about here is the application name. You can leave it as is, or give it a name that's more descriptive. For the purpose of this chapter, we'll assume you named it FirstPGB App. Click Ready to build and stand back.

PhoneGap Build is now creating your mobile application for you. Much like how the Cordova CLI took your web resources and built out a native application, the PhoneGap Build service performs the same action, but on its server instead. On the

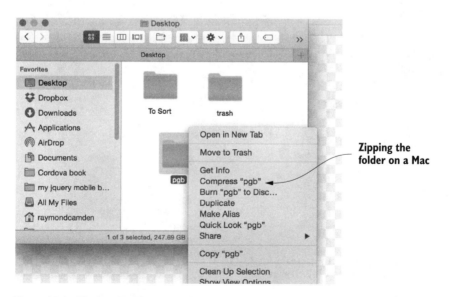

Figure 10.4   Zipping the folder on a Mac

This is a default name for
your new application.

This warning, and this tip, can be
ignored for now.

Figure 10.5 New application screen

new screen, you'll see three icons at the bottom left, representing the three PhoneGap Build supports and what state the build is in. From left to right they are iOS, Android, and Windows Phone. As you already know, when the Cordova CLI creates an application, it takes a few seconds. The same happens when PhoneGap Build creates an application. Depending on how busy the server is, it may take a bit longer. At first, each of the icons will be a gray, disabled color, like those shown in figure 10.6.

As each platform is complete, the icons will update to reflect their status, as shown in figure 10.7.

If everything worked typically, you'll see a bad (red) status for iOS and a good status for Android and Windows Phone. iOS will *always* fail at first. That's because iOS building requires you to have a developer account with Apple and you must create a certificate to sign the application with. Both Android and Windows Phone allow you to create development versions of your application and test them right away. You can create certificates for *all* platforms and upload them to PhoneGap Build to sign your apps if you

Figure 10.6 PhoneGap Build is currently updating the applications

Figure 10.7 PhoneGap Build is done creating the applications. Successful builds are shown in a blue (the two rightmost here) while errors are rendered in red (far left here).

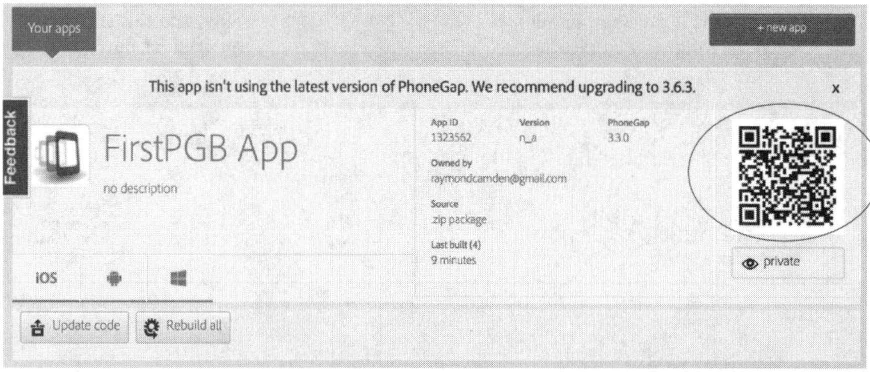

Figure 10.8   Look—a real use for QR codes!

wish. That would be required if you wish to distribute your apps commercially. Signing and distributing applications will be covered in the next chapter. So how do you test?

Clicking the icon for the platform will download the binary file for your application and that particular platform. While you can install files like this to your device via command-line tools, the easiest way to get the download is to take your device, open the browser, and go to PhoneGap Build. That will take a bit of typing though. You have to go to the website (http://build.phonegap.com/apps), log in, select your application, and then click the icon. It's even easier if you simply use the Quick Response (QR) code (figure 10.8).

In case you don't know, QR codes are those funky black-and-white symbols that marketers have been trying to get consumers to use the last few years. They should give up—it's never going to work. PhoneGap Build's use of the technology is one of the few places where they make sense. Get your device, open a QR reader app, and point it at the QR code. When the URL is discovered in the QR code and your browser opens it, PhoneGap Build is smart enough to recognize what type of device you're using. If you use an iPhone, it will send the iPhone version (again, assuming it was built); if you're using an Android device, it will send that one instead.

Go ahead and use the QR code to download the Android version. When opened, you're prompted to install the application, as shown in figure 10.9.

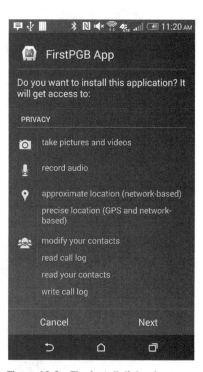

Figure 10.9   The install dialog for your new application

One thing you may notice right away is that the application you create, the simple "Hello World!", is asking for a *lot* of access. Pretty much it wants to be able to do *everything* with your phone. That's scary, and is something you'll want to correct. We'll discuss it later in this chapter when we get to configuration. Once you finish the installation and open it, you'll see your application in all its awesome glory (figure 10.10).

Okay, it isn't stellar, and it doesn't do anything, but just remember what happened here. You made a file, zipped up a folder, and uploaded it. That's it. No software development kits (SDKs) were installed. You didn't configure any system paths. You literally wrote HTML and uploaded it to a web page. Now obviously this

Figure 10.10 Your application

process is a bit slower than running from the command line. In your testing you may see the Android build created very quickly, or a bit more slowly, depending on how well the PhoneGap Build service is running at any particular time. And like any service, PhoneGap Build *can* go down. But for people who may find SDK installation a bit complex and only want to sample PhoneGap Build, this is a great alternative. Another thing to consider is client testing. Your PhoneGap Build application can be shared with a client, who can then download the application themselves using their QR readers.

10.2.3 Digging deeper into PhoneGap Build

A lot of detail may be found on your application's main detail page. With only one application it may be confusing to recognize that you're probably on the Apps listing page—that is, the listing page for all your applications. If you see https://build.phonegap.com/apps in the browser's location bar, then you're still on the listing page. Click the *name* of your application to go to the detail page, as shown in figure 10.11.

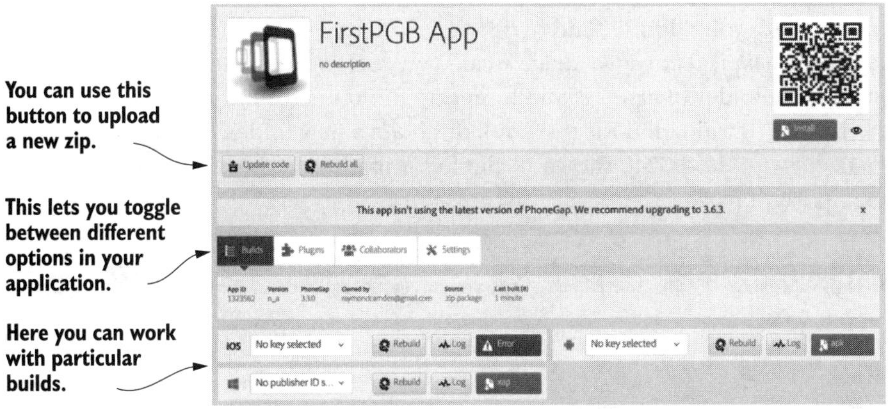

You can use this button to upload a new zip.

This lets you toggle between different options in your application.

Here you can work with particular builds.

Figure 10.11 Application's detail page

There's a heck of a lot of information on this page so let's focus on the more important bits called out in figure 10.11 First, if you want to update the code, you can use the Update Code button to send a new zip file. If you had used the GitHub option, this button would retrieve the files from your repository instead. At the bottom of the page you can see your builds. For each one you can ask for a rebuild, look at a log, and either see the status for the platform or download the bits. In the middle of the page are four tabs. This lets you switch between builds, plugins, collaborators, and other settings. Now is a great time to talk about plugins.

10.2.4 Using plugins with PhoneGap Build

If you click the Plugins tab for your application you'll see a notice saying that the application isn't using any plugins. Unlike the command line where you manage plugins by adding or removing them, with PhoneGap Build you have to *tell* it what plugins your application uses. This is done via a special file, config.xml.

The config.xml file is responsible for multiple things. It provides metadata about your application (version number, name, etc.), as well as details about the plugins the application uses. It lets you configure application options including icons and splashscreens. While you were able to create your first application without one, it's generally recommended to *always* use this file when working with PhoneGap Build.

To test this feature, you'll build a simple application that makes use of the Device plugin (http://plugins.cordova.io/#/package/org.apache.cordova.device) which cre-ates a simple JavaScript object representing the device your application is currently running on. It really isn't even an API per se—it's an object. That makes it a good candidate for your first test. The demo application will simply start up and display the `device.model` property (figure 10.12).

To begin work on this application, note that you don't, and

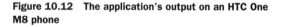

Figure 10.12   The application's output on an HTC One M8 phone

shouldn't, do the typical `cordova create` calls you've done in earlier chapters. Remember that a simple folder of assets is all PhoneGap Build needs. Either use the code as is from the zip you downloaded for the book or create a new folder for this section.

Let's begin with the HTML shown in the following listing. It's relatively simple, but has one important part.

Listing 10.1   App homepage (c10/pgbapp2/index.html)

```
<!DOCTYPE html>
<html>
  <head>
    <meta charset="utf-8">
```

```
      <title></title>
      <meta name="description" content="">
      <meta name="viewport" content="width=device-width">
   </head>
   <body>

      <h2>An App</h2>

      <div id="deviceArea"></div>

      <script src="phonegap.js"></script>
      <script src="js/app.js"></script>
   </body>
</html>
```

**Loads main ❷
phonegap.js
library**

**❶ Blank div the JavaScript
will update**

**Application's
❸ JavaScript code**

Like previous applications, the HTML has a blank div ❶ that will be updated by JavaScript ❸. In this case, the blank div is what gets populated with the device model name. The truly important part of this application is the line including phonegap.js ❷.

Earlier in the book you learned that your code should include cordova.js. This file did *not* exist in your www folder, but was injected by the CLI. PhoneGap Build, and the PhoneGap platform behind it, employs a similar mechanism. In this case, you won't create a file called phonegap.js—you'll only reference it. When PhoneGap Build works on your project, it will place the correct file in each platform. What if you mess up and use cordova.js instead? The good news is that it will work just the same.

Now let's look at the JavaScript in the following listing.

Listing 10.2 App JavaScript (c10/pgbapp2/js/app.js)

```
document.addEventListener("deviceready", init, false);
function init() {

   var s = "Your device is a " + device.model + ".";
   document.querySelector("#deviceArea").innerHTML = s;

}
```

No big surprise that this file is so small. As stated before, the device API is only an object. Because it's that simple, you can create a simple string including the model and then write it out in the HTML.

For this application to work correctly via PhoneGap Build, you need to include a config.xml file in the root of the folder. There are *numerous* things you can include in your config.xml file, but start simple using the code from the following listing.

Listing 10.3 Configuration file (c10/pgbapp2/config.xml)

```
<?xml version="1.0" encoding="UTF-8"?>

<widget xmlns     = "http://www.w3.org/ns/widgets"
        xmlns:gap = "http://phonegap.com/ns/1.0"
        id        = "com.camden.pgbapp2"
        version   = "1.0.0">
```

**Arbitrary ❷
version
for app**

❶ Gives app unique ID

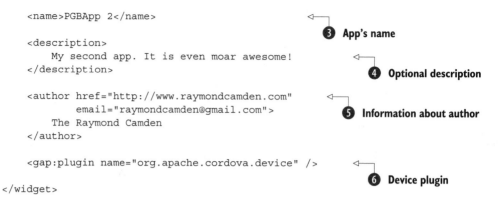

```
<name>PGBApp 2</name>
                                                        ❸ App's name
<description>
    My second app. It is even moar awesome!
</description>
                                                        ❹ Optional description

<author href="http://www.raymondcamden.com"
        email="raymondcamden@gmail.com">
    The Raymond Camden                                  ❺ Information about author
</author>


<gap:plugin name="org.apache.cordova.device" />
                                                        ❻ Device plugin
</widget>
```

As you learned in chapter 9, the config.xml file is based on a W3C specification for describing web apps. You don't need to know that to use the feature, but it's an interesting aside. The first thing of note is the application ID ❶. If you recall, you could use this with the Cordova CLI when creating new applications. It provides a unique identifier for your application and follows what's known as the reverse-domain style. You can use whatever you want here, but like the earlier recommendation, using com.yourlastname.appname is a good idea. Next up is the version number ❷. This is arbitrary and can be whatever you'd like. The application name ❸ is what you'll see on the PhoneGap Build website and when the application is installed on your device. The description ❹ is optional and only used on PhoneGap Build. A good use for this is differentiating between multiple apps that may share the same name. The author area ❺ is also optional. The truly critical piece here is the <gap:plugin> tag ❻ that specifies the application is using the device plugin.

The <gap:plugin> tag takes the same ID values you used earlier in the chapter. By default, these plugins are hosted at PhoneGap Build itself, and may be behind the version hosted at http://plugins.cordova.io. How can you tell? In the top navigation bar of the PhoneGap Build website is a link for Plugins. Clicking that and then choosing PhoneGap Plugins takes you to a page that lists all the core plugins. If you find the Device plugin, you can click it for details. At the time this book was written, the Device plugin at PhoneGap Build (https://build.phonegap.com/plugins/1163) was version 0.2.10. But the Device plugin at plugins.cordova.io (http://plugins.cordova.io/#/package/org.apache.cordova.device) is version 0.30.

If that sounds confusing, or you simply need to compare one version to another, you have options. The first is that you can tell PhoneGap Build to use the version from plugins.cordova.io. That's done by adding a source attribute to your XML:

```
<gap:plugin name="org.apache.cordova.device" source="plugins.cordova.io" />
```

The default value is pgb, which uses the version at PhoneGap Build. You have another option to specify the plugin version itself. This is done by adding a version attribute:

```
<gap:plugin name="org.apache.cordova.device" source="plugins.cordova.io"
    version="0.2.7" />
```

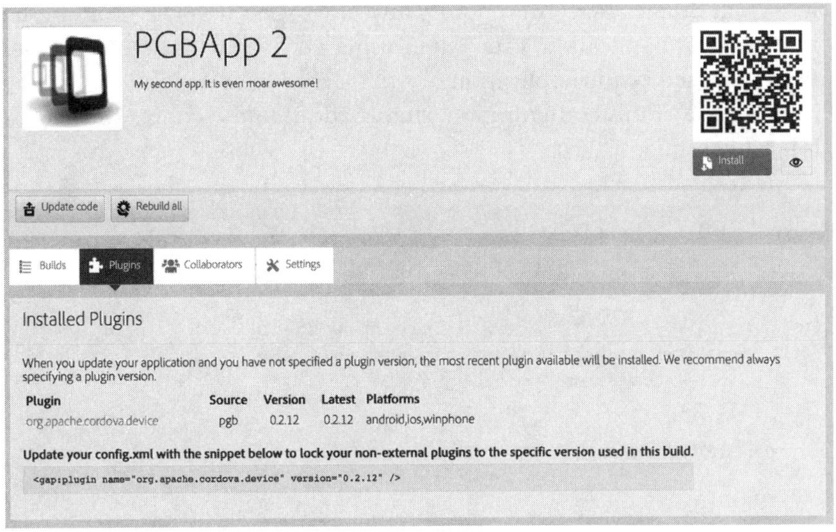

Figure 10.13   PhoneGap Build recognizes the plugins your application uses.

You can even get fancy with the versioning and specify a fuzzy version like ~2, which means any 2.X version.

You can now zip this folder and upload to PhoneGap Build. Remember that the free tier only lets you upload one zip. Because you're just testing you can replace the one you uploaded earlier, or if you shelled out for a paid version, you can make a new application. Another option is to delete your first application. You can delete a PhoneGap Build app by going into the Settings tab. Once uploaded, go into your app's detail page and click the Plugins tab you saw in figure 10.10. Now you should see the device plugin listed, as shown in figure 10.13.

10.2.5 *More configuration options*

There are numerous configuration options available within config.xml. Some apply globally (that is, to all platforms), some are platform-specific. The PhoneGap Build docs (http://docs.build.phonegap.com/en_US/index.html) go into deep detail about all these options, but let's look at a few simple ones you can use right away.

First, let's see if you can fix that scary installation screen you saw in figure 10.8. You'll want to remove the application from your device before continuing as you're testing an installation change. There's an Android-specific configuration option that lets you specify what permissions your application needs:

```
<preference name="permissions" value="none"/>
```

This tag only applies to Android. You can find a full list of possible permissions at the Android SDK documentation page: http://developer.android.com/reference/android/Manifest.permission.html. For your use here, you can use the none value because your application isn't doing anything special. Note that in terms of a PhoneGap Build application, even when using none, the INTERNET permission is still required and used by the application.

To make use of this configuration, simply add it to the config.xml file as shown in the following listing.

Listing 10.4   Updated configuration file (c10/pgbapp2/config.xml)

```xml
<?xml version="1.0" encoding="UTF-8"?>

<widget xmlns     = "http://www.w3.org/ns/widgets"
        xmlns:gap = "http://phonegap.com/ns/1.0"
        id        = "com.camden.pgbapp2"
        version   = "1.0.0">

    <name>PGBApp 2</name>

    <description>
        My second app. It is even moar awesome!
    </description>

    <author href="http://www.raymondcamden.com"
            email="raymondcamden@gmail.com">
        The Raymond Camden
    </author>

    <preference name="permissions" value="none"/>          New preference

    <gap:plugin name="org.apache.cordova.device" />

</widget>
```

Now it's only a matter of zipping the folder, uploading it to PhoneGap Build, and testing it within your device. Now when the application is installed, the warnings screen is much simpler and shorter. If you didn't uninstall the app first as mentioned earlier, you won't see a change. Android won't tell you that an updated app has *fewer* permissions, it will simply say it isn't adding *new* permissions. So to see this change better, uninstall the app on your device and then reinstall. Figure 10.14 demonstrates the new, friendlier installation screen.

Figure 10.14   The application with much nicer (that is, less scary) permissions

Now let's consider icons. You learned how to use them via the Cordova command line in chapter 9. While you can support icons specific to particular devices and resolutions, and you *should* build optimized versions, at the simplest level you can specify a default icon with one line in your preferences file:

```
<icon src="theicon.png" />
```

Multiple arguments exist for each version of this tag to let you target devices and different sizes; see the reference at http://docs.build.phonegap.com/en_US/ configuring_icons_and_splash.md.html#Icons%20and%20Splash%20Screens for more information. For now, though, let's give this a test with some simple graphics. In the zip file containing all the code for this book, you'll find a pgapp3 folder. There you'll find a Resources folder with one file: icon.png. The names are arbitrary, but in this case they obviously give you a clue as to what they represent. The following listing shows an updated config.xml file that makes use of these elements.

> **Listing 10.5 Updated configuration file (10/pgbapp3/config.xml)**

```
<?xml version="1.0" encoding="UTF-8"?>

<widget xmlns     = "http://www.w3.org/ns/widgets"
        xmlns:gap = "http://phonegap.com/ns/1.0"
        id        = "com.camden.pgbapp3"
        version   = "1.0.0">

    <name>PGBApp 3</name>

    <description>
        My third app. It is even moar awesome!
    </description>

    <author href="http://www.raymondcamden.com"
            email="raymondcamden@gmail.com">
        The Raymond Camden
    </author>
                                                    ❶ Icon configuration line
    <icon src="resources/icon.png" />           <──┘

    <preference name="permissions" value="none"/>

    <gap:plugin name="org.apache.cordova.device" />

</widget>
```

In the icon configuration line ❶, the path to the resource is determined from the root of the application. Because the assets are in a resources folder, you need to include that path in the value.

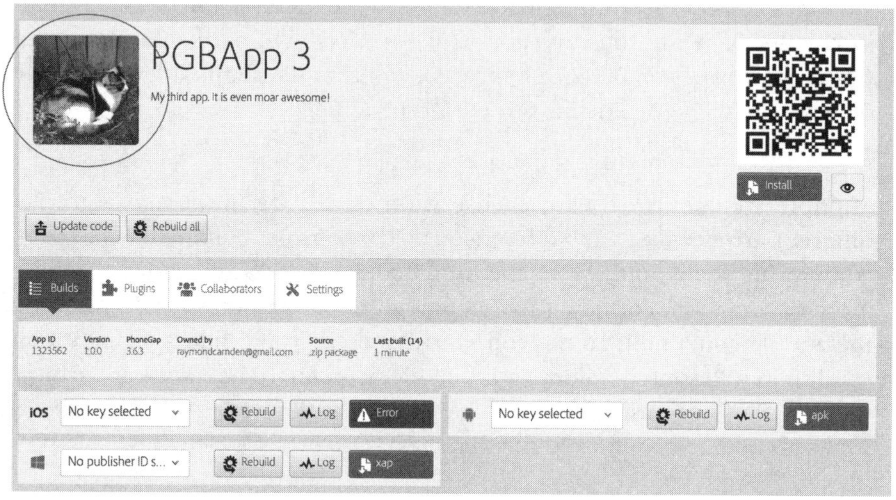

Figure 10.15   The application with a custom icon

Zip up the folder and upload it to PhoneGap Build, as you did previously. You'll notice that PhoneGap Build recognized that you're using an icon and will update the application page, as shown in figure 10.15.

And now if you install the application on your device, you should see the custom icon shown in figure 10.16.

10.2.6 *More PhoneGap Build features*

PhoneGap Build has even more features, including the ability to add other users to your project and set the visibility of your app on the website, but let's end our look at the service with one very cool feature: Hydration.

Imagine you've shared your PhoneGap Build app with a client. They can simply point their QR reader to the website to grab your application and test it on the device. This is a great way to distribute your application during development. But unlike a website that can be refreshed in a browser, for a client to get a new version of the application they have to go back to the website and

Figure 10.16   Here's the application with the amazing new cat icon!

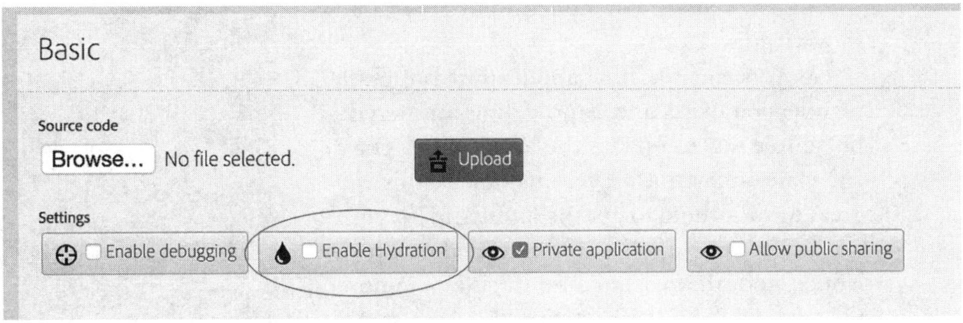

Basic

Source code

[**Browse...**] No file selected.   [⬆ Upload]

Settings

[⊕ ☐ Enable debugging][💧 ☐ Enable Hydration][👁 ☑ Private application][👁 ☐ Allow public sharing]

Figure 10.17   Settings for a PhoneGap Build application

redownload the app. That isn't difficult. But, you know clients. You may have fixed a few bugs and the client insists they still exist. The client says they updated the application, but you're worried they may not have. This is where Hydration comes in. If you click the Settings tab (figure 10.17) on the PhoneGap Build website, you'll see a few different options.

Click Enable Hydration to turn on the feature. Hydration creates a new version of your application with a powerful new feature: update detection. To be clear, this is for *development purposes* only. It isn't valid once your application goes live on the various app stores. During development, Hydration creates an automatic system to check for

and install new versions. Let's see this in action. Enable Hydration and click Save. Then reinstall the application.

Now when running the application, you'll briefly see a new message, as shown in figure 10.18.

This screen shouldn't last long and will automatically go away. Where things get interesting is when you update your application. Create a new zip (you don't have to change anything in the source code) and upload it to PhoneGap Build. Relaunch your application (both Android and iOS provide a way to "close" an application and you want to ensure

Figure 10.18   An application loading with Hydration enabled

you do that first), and notice what Hydration shows (figure 10.19).

As you can see, the application notices a new version exists and is providing an incredibly simple way to update the application. For a client who may not be very technical, this is a great way for them to get the latest and greatest version of your application as you develop it. Notice, too, that users could decide to ignore the update if they wish. Again, this isn't something you can use with a released application, but during development it can be a great way to ensure everyone is testing with the most recent version.

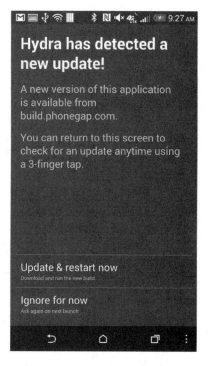

Figure 10.19   Hydration has detected an update

10.3   *PhoneGap Developer App*

As you've seen, the PhoneGap Build website offers a number of interesting features, but one of the most powerful things it does is let you create a hybrid application without installing *anything* on your computer (outside of an editor). There's another way to start building hybrid applications with minimal setup work—the PhoneGap Developer App (http://app.phonegap.com/). With this tool, you can write your HTML, CSS, and JavaScript and view the results on a real device. Your local machine essentially hosts the files and makes them available to the app running on the device. Figure 10.20 explains this process.

10.3.1   *Installing*

Preparing to use the PhoneGap Developer App requires only two main steps: installing the PhoneGap CLI and installing the application.

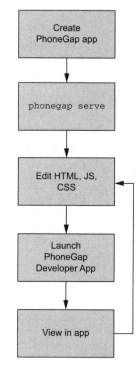

Figure 10.20   PhoneGap Developer App process—edit in your machine and view in the application

Technically, installing the PhoneGap CLI is two steps because the PhoneGap CLI is installed via npm, just like the Cordova CLI. Assuming you have npm already installed, you get the Phone-Gap CLI by running this at your command prompt:

```
npm install -g phonegap
```

Remember that you may want to prefix that command with sudo on OS X. The PhoneGap CLI works much like Cordova. It lets you create applications, add platforms and plugins, and run builds to emulators or devices. Because we've focused on using the Cordova CLI we won't spend any time looking at those options.

The second thing you need to install is the PhoneGap Developer App which you can download from the app store. It's available for iOS, Android, and Windows Phone and is free to install. Open the app store on your device of choice and search for "PhoneGap Developer App." Figure 10.21 shows the Android Play Store version of the application.

Figure 10.21   PhoneGap Developer App in the Android Play Store

10.3.2   Using the PhoneGap Developer App

To use the PhoneGap Developer App, you begin by creating a new application on your computer. The syntax is *exactly* like Cordova:

```
phonegap create helloWorld
```

Enter that directory and then run

```
phonegap serve
```

You should see a message stating that an app server has fired up and is now listening (figure 10.22).

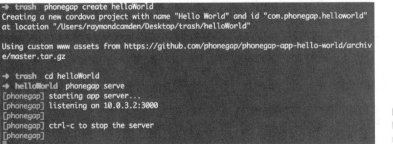

Figure 10.22 PhoneGap is now running a server

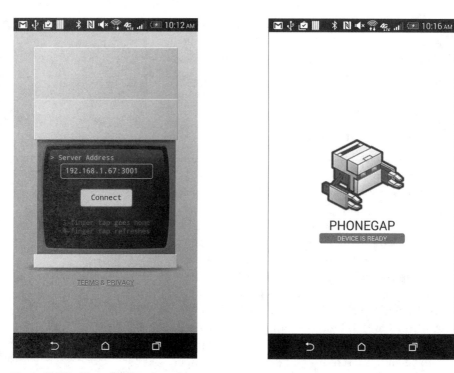

Figure 10.23   PhoneGap Developer App prompting for server address

Figure 10.24   PhoneGap Developer App running your application

What's happening here is that PhoneGap is actually running a server on your machine. It's taking the HTML assets for your application and making them available on your network.

Next, open the PhoneGap Developer App on your device. When it launches, it will prompt you for the server address, as shown in figure 10.23.

Begin by changing the IP and port values to what you saw in your command prompt. Once you've done that and press Connect, you should see your application start up. If you didn't touch the HTML assets created by the PhoneGap CLI, it will look like figure 10.24.

What you're seeing here is the app on your device "talking" to your computer and running your code directly from your machine. If you open those files in your editor and modify them, the application on your device will update automatically! It takes a few seconds, so if you don't want to wait, refer to figure 10.23. It shows that tapping the app with your finger four times will force a refresh.

As you can guess, this is an incredibly cool way to test out hybrid mobile development. The only thing you can't do with this setup is run custom plugins. By default, the PhoneGap Developer App includes all of the core plugins. As a reminder, those plugins include filesystem access, the camera, the device accelerometer and geolocation, native dialogs, and media (audio/video support).

Problems connecting?

For the PhoneGap Developer App to work correctly, your device must be able to access your desktop machine. Some network environments, especially many corporate and conference environments, will prevent this from happening. As a quick test, you can open your browser on the device and try to press the IP address of your PhoneGap server manually. If your device can't connect, it means the PhoneGap Developer App can't connect. Another possible issue can arise from using virtual private network (VPN) software on your machine. Typically you'll not have any way around this. But if you find the PhoneGap Developer App very appealing, it may be worthwhile to purchase a cheap WiFi router just for testing this feature. Simply put your computer and your device on the same network and they should be able to speak to each other. I've found a small travel router to be great for this.

10.4 *Summary*

Let's review the major topics covered in this chapter.

- While a Cordova developer probably should go through the process of installing native SDKs, PhoneGap Build is an alternative that lets you skip that process.
- With PhoneGap Build you can create new applications by uploading a zip file or pointing to GitHub repositories.
- You can configure PhoneGap Build apps using a config.xml file.
- PhoneGap Build also has other features, including an automatic way of pushing new builds to users.
- The PhoneGap Developer App lets you test out hybrid apps by running a small web server on your machine and connecting your code and the native app.

In the next chapter you'll learn the steps you need to take to publish your application to both the Android and iOS app store.

Part 3

Application release

In these two final chapters, you'll put it all together. Chapter 11 describes in deep detail the process of submitting your application to both the Android and Apple stores. You'll build a real application in chapter 12 that puts together many of the core concepts you learned in the rest of the book.

Submitting your app

This chapter covers

- Packaging your application for distribution on Android
- Packaging your application for distribution on iOS
- Becoming fabulously rich from app sales (or not)

Like every proud parent, there comes a day when your little app is all grown up (and properly debugged!) and ready to be shared with the world. Releasing an application for sale, or for free, to the mobile markets follows a generally similar path for all platforms:

- *You must create a release version of your application.* This is an application that is signed using a password. You can think of this as a way of saying that this application belongs to you and you only.
- *You submit your application to the store.* This typically requires you to write up descriptions for the application and create screenshots of it running. You can, and possibly should, think of this a bit like an ad campaign for your

175

application. You'll want to describe your app in the best way possible. You'll want to take screenshots that show off your app in the best light.

At this point, the paths diverge.

11.1 Releasing your app

Android's market allows anyone to publish anything (within reason; some types of applications are illegal). Once you've signed your application and released it to the market, anyone can download it.

Apple, of course, is a bit different. Apple can reject any application for any reason. People using hybrid technologies like Cordova may run into this problem if they don't actually use the device features Cordova gives them access to. What does that mean? You could use Cordova to build a native application that does nothing more than what a regular web page does. Apple will recognize this and rightly tell you that your app doesn't need to be an application. You want to ensure your application does something that a web page can't do. Unfortunately, there is no hard-and-fast rule for what you must do to pass Apple's muster, but that's the world iOS developers live in.

Also note that the screenshots in this chapter represent the UI of the various websites at the time of publication. Obviously they may differ slightly in the future or in your browser of choice.

11.2 Submitting your Android app

Because Apple can be a bit of a crapshoot, let's begin with a platform we know we can get our app published on: Android. As mentioned earlier, releasing an application begins with creating a release version of the application. At a high level, the process looks like this:

- Sign the application with a key made at the command line
- Create a release build of the application by slightly modifying how you use the Cordova command line
- Upload your application to the website Google uses for Android apps
- Supply various pieces of information about your app (title, icons, etc.)
- Mark your application as published

11.2.1 Signing your app

Signing your application requires a key store and a key. The key is really the important part. Think of the key store as, well, a store of keys. A box. The process we'll use will make it fairly easy for you to create both. It is crucial, though, that you keep your key store safe. If someone were to get the physical file, and somehow guess your password, they'd be able to release applications as you. They'd also be able to change the application in the Android market to whatever they want. Obviously, you also want to ensure you don't forget the password. If you do, you'll not be able to sign the application with the same key, which means you can't release an update to the application. With those warnings out of the way, let's get started.

Signing your application is done via a command-line call. The command is a bit complex, so we'll look at an example and then explain the bits:

```
keytool -genkey -v -keystore my-release-key.keystore
    -alias alias_name -keyalg RSA -keysize 2048 -validity 10000
```

This command will begin the key store creation process. It will also create one key at the same time. There are two values in that command that need your attention.

The first is the argument after `-keystore`. This will be the filename for your key store. You're welcome to keep it as described, but you may wish to use a more descriptive name. If you were building an application for a client, using the client's name in the key store file may be a good idea.

The second argument to (possibly) change is the alias (the argument after `-alias`). This gives the key store a nice plaintext name. While you can also leave this as is, it makes sense to make it resemble the filename.

For your purposes here, let's assume `mykeystore.keystore` and `mykeystore` will be used. When you press Enter, the command-line tool will ask you questions, as shown in figure 11.1.

These questions concern your name and your organization. For an individual, you can simply use your name.

At this point, you've created both your key store and a key, but how do you use them? Cordova's command-line tool makes this fairly easy. By appending `--release` to the build command, you can tell Cordova to create a release version of the application:

```
cordova build --release
```

```
→ mar6 keytool -genkey -v -keystore mykeystore.keystore -alias mykeystore -keyalg RSA -keysize 2048 -validity 10000
Enter keystore password:
Re-enter new password:
What is your first and last name?
  [Unknown]:  Raymond Camden
What is the name of your organizational unit?
  [Unknown]:  Raymond Camden
What is the name of your organization?
  [Unknown]:  Raymond Camden
What is the name of your City or Locality?
  [Unknown]:  Lafayette
What is the name of your State or Province?
  [Unknown]:  Louisiana
What is the two-letter country code for this unit?
  [Unknown]:  LA
Is CN=Raymond Camden, OU=Raymond Camden, O=Raymond Camden, L=Lafayette, ST=Louisiana, C=LA correct?
  [no]:  yes

Generating 2,048 bit RSA key pair and self-signed certificate (SHA256withRSA) with a validity of 10,000 days
        for: CN=Raymond Camden, OU=Raymond Camden, O=Raymond Camden, L=Lafayette, ST=Louisiana, C=LA
Enter key password for <mykeystore>
        (RETURN if same as keystore password):
[Storing mykeystore.keystore]
```

Figure 11.1 Answering questions about you and your organization

```
-release-prompt-for-password:

-release-nosign:
     [echo] No key.store and key.alias properties found in build.properties.
     [echo] Please sign /Users/raymondcamden/Desktop/trash/mar6/platforms/android/ant-build/MainActivity-release-unsigned.apk manually
     [echo] and run zipalign from the Android SDK tools.
[propertyfile] Updating property file: /Users/raymondcamden/Desktop/trash/mar6/platforms/android/ant-build/build.prop
[propertyfile] Updating property file: /Users/raymondcamden/Desktop/trash/mar6/platforms/android/ant-build/build.prop
[propertyfile] Updating property file: /Users/raymondcamden/Desktop/trash/mar6/platforms/android/ant-build/build.prop
[propertyfile] Updating property file: /Users/raymondcamden/Desktop/trash/mar6/platforms/android/ant-build/build.prop
```

Figure 11.2   Cordova's output complaining about key store and alias values

Doing so though will create a problem. Cordova doesn't know how to actually sign the application. You'll see this in the output returned to the screen after trying to build your application.

As seen in figure 11.2, Cordova doesn't know where your key store exists nor what the alias value is for that key store. A clue to how to fix that is provided in the output itself.

Open the Android platform folder under your project and create a file called ant.properties. Not build.properties as seen in figure 11.2, but ant.properties (figure 11.3).

Name	^
.DS_Store	
config.xml	
▶ hooks	
mykeystore.keystore	
▼ platforms	
.DS_Store	
▼ android	
.DS_Store	
.gitignore	
.project	
AndroidManifest.xml	
▶ ant-build	
▶ ant-gen	
ant.properties	
▶ assets	
build.gradle	
build.xml	
▶ cordova	
▶ CordovaLib	
custom_rules.xml	
▶ libs	
local.properties	
▶ platform_www	
project.properties	
▶ res	
▶ src	
▶ plugins	
▶ www	

Figure 11.3   Cordova project with the new ant.properties file

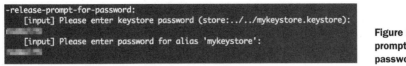

Figure 11.4 Cordova prompting you for your password

Open this file in your editor and add what you see in the following listing.

Listing 11.1 ant.properties file for signing an Android project

Before saving this file, you should change both values. In the first line ❶, notice how I've used ../../ to reference two folders above the location of ant.properties. I generated my key store in the root of my Cordova application. If you had built your key store file elsewhere, you should either enter the complete path, or a relative path from the Android platform folder. If I had put my key store file in the same folder as ant.properties, I could have left off the ../../. Obviously, you also want to change the filename itself. If you called your key store `superhappyfuntime.keystore`, then you should enter that value. The second line ❷ should also be changed to whatever you used for the alias.

Now run your release build again: `cordova build -release`. This time Cordova will find your key store file and prompt you for your password, as shown in figure 11.4.

You'll be asked not once, but twice, for the password. This is the password you entered while creating the key store. If everything worked okay, you'll see a `BUILD SUCCESSFUL` in the output.

You can also verify that you have a release version by opening the ant-build folder in the Android platform directory and looking for MainActivity-release.apk. If you're curious, APK is the standard file type for Android application files and stands for Android Application Package. Yes, I know that doesn't match APK, but go with it.

11.2.2 Publishing to the Android market

Now that you've got a signed release application, how do you get it to the masses? You can, if you choose, email the APK file to people who want to test it. You could also distribute the APK file via your website. But most likely you want it in the main market that Android users use—Google Play. Using Google Play gives you a large number of benefits, with the biggest benefit being discoverability. If your app meets some particular need, like being yet another Flappy Bird clone (remember that?), then people can discover your application simply by searching. Google Play will also provide analytics about how many people are installing your application and what issues they may be having. To begin, open your browser to Google Play's Developer portal: http://developer.android.com/distribute/googleplay/index.html. Then click the Developer

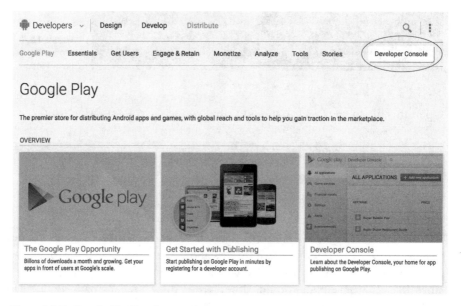

Figure 11.5   Google Play Developer portal

Console button in the upper right corner, shown in figure 11.5. (You may be looking for a Sign Up or Register button but those don't exist.)

At this point you'll need to log in, unless you've already logged into another service like Gmail. Next you'll need to accept an agreement (be honest, you won't read it), pay the registration fee ($25 for North America), and finish your account details (figure 11.6).

Sign-in with your Google account	Accept Developer Agreement	Pay Registration Fee	Complete your Account details

YOU ARE SIGNED IN AS...

This is the Google account that will be associated with your Developer Console.

If you would like to use a different account, you can choose from the following options below. If you are an organization, consider registering a new Google account rather than using a personal account.

Sign in with a different account   Create a new Google account

BEFORE YOU CONTINUE...

Read and agree to the Google Play Developer distribution agreement.

☐ I agree and I am willing to associate my account registration with the Google Play Developer distribution agreement.

Review the distribution countries where you can distribute and sell applications.

If you are planning to sell apps or in-app products, check if you can have a merchant account in your country.

$25

Make sure you have your credit card handy to pay the $25 registration fee in the next step.

Continue to payment

Figure 11.6   Account creation process

Figure 11.7 Adding the new application

Note that the registration fee is a *one-time* fee. Apple charges a yearly fee (approximately four times higher), but Google will charge you only one time. After you've completed registration, you can add your first application, as shown in figure 11.7.

Enter an appropriate title, and then choose Upload APK. This takes you to the next page where you'll select the APK you generated earlier (figure 11.8).

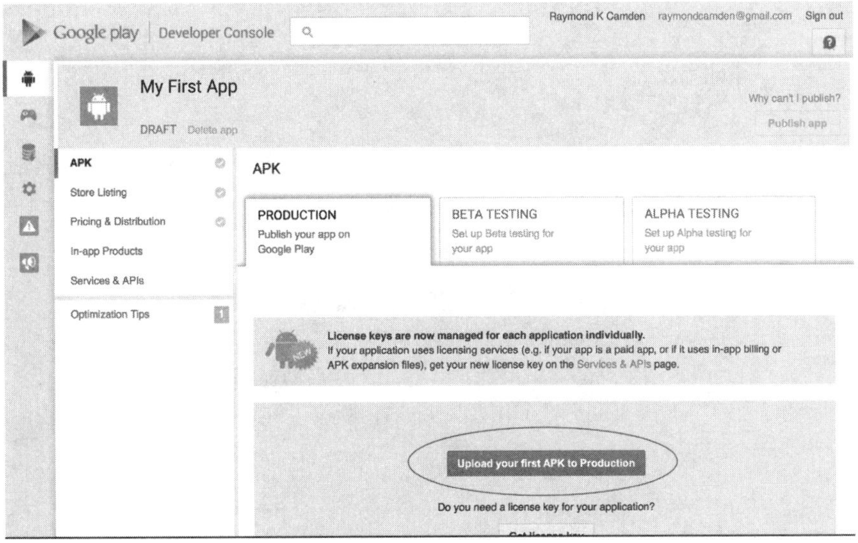

Figure 11.8 Preparing to select the release APK

UPLOAD NEW APK TO PRODUCTION

Upload failed

You need to use a different package name because "io.cordova.hellocordova" already exists in Google Play.

Upload another APK

Cancel

Figure 11.9   Uh oh, that looks familiar, doesn't it?

Remember that your APK will be located in the platforms/android/ant-build folder under your Cordova project. The name will be something-release.apk, where "something" will differ based on your application name. After you've selected the APK, you may encounter the error shown in figure 11.9.

As you remember from chapter 4, the CLI provides multiple options when you initially create the project. One is the ID value used for the application. If you don't specify this, then a default value of `io.cordova.hellocordova` will be used. This value must be unique across the entire Google Play store. If you forgot to change this value, then edit your config.xml file and change the ID. (Remember that the ID value is the first argument to the `<widget>` tag in config.xml.) Once you've done that, create your release build again. If everything worked okay, you should see something similar to figure 11.10.

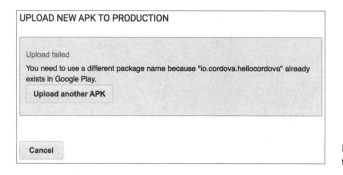

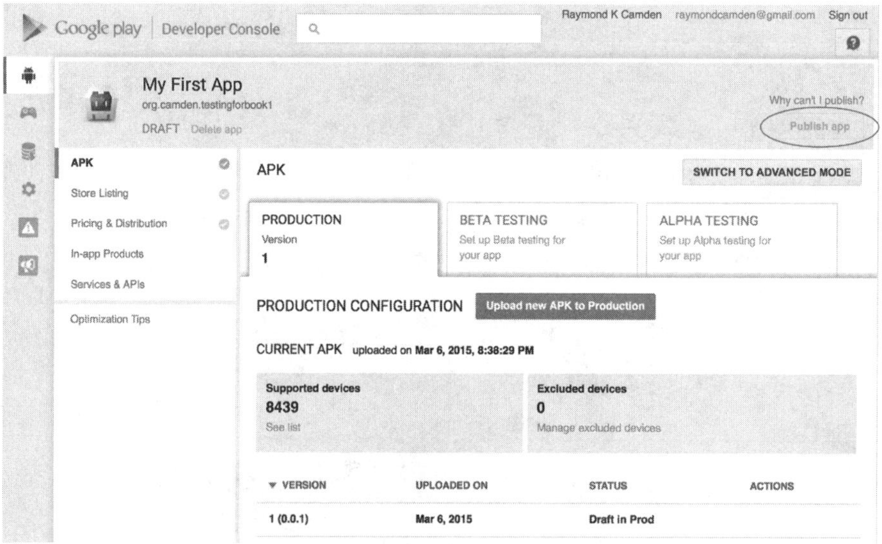

Figure 11.10   Your app preparing for publication

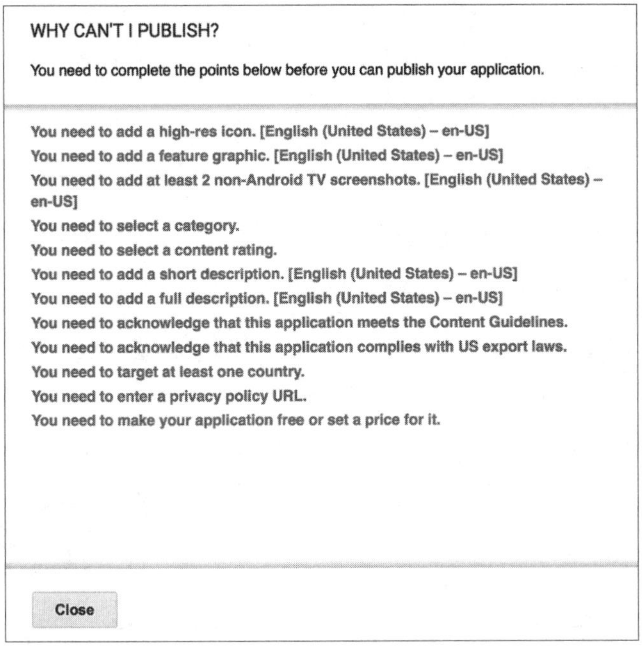

WHY CAN'T I PUBLISH?

You need to complete the points below before you can publish your application.

You need to add a high-res icon. [English (United States) – en-US]

You need to add a feature graphic. [English (United States) – en-US]

You need to add at least 2 non-Android TV screenshots. [English (United States) – en-US]

You need to select a category.

You need to select a content rating.

You need to add a short description. [English (United States) – en-US]

You need to add a full description. [English (United States) – en-US]

You need to acknowledge that this application meets the Content Guidelines.

You need to acknowledge that this application complies with US export laws.

You need to target at least one country.

You need to enter a privacy policy URL.

You need to make your application free or set a price for it.

Close

Figure 11.11 A list of things you must fix.

Google Play does a great job of calling out that you can't publish your application yet. Not only is the Publish App button disabled, but there's a clear link right above it telling you *why* you can't publish yet. Clicking it will provide you a nice long list of requirements, as shown in figure 11.11, you'll need to meet before publishing.

That may seem like quite a bit, but you don't have to take care of everything immediately. Google won't delete your app if you handle some items today and some tomorrow. Begin by clicking Store Listing in the left navigation bar. This will load a form with various fields related to how your app will show in the Google Play marketplace. Most fields on this form should be self-explanatory. As you work, you can click the Save Draft button to save your settings. You can also check your progress by clicking the Why Can't I Publish link as you work.

Selecting the graphical assets may be a more difficult task. You need to select screenshots that show off the worth of your application. No book can tell you what's best for your application, but obviously try for the most professional, most interesting aspects of your application. You'll need, at minimum, two screenshots, one icon, and a feature graphic, which is used when displaying your application in the store.

After selecting and uploading your graphical assets, click Pricing & Distribution. This is where you'll decide your price, if any, and what countries will be allowed to download your application.

Once you've completed everything, you'll notice that the Publish App button is now active. Click it to publish, and make note of the warning that it may take several

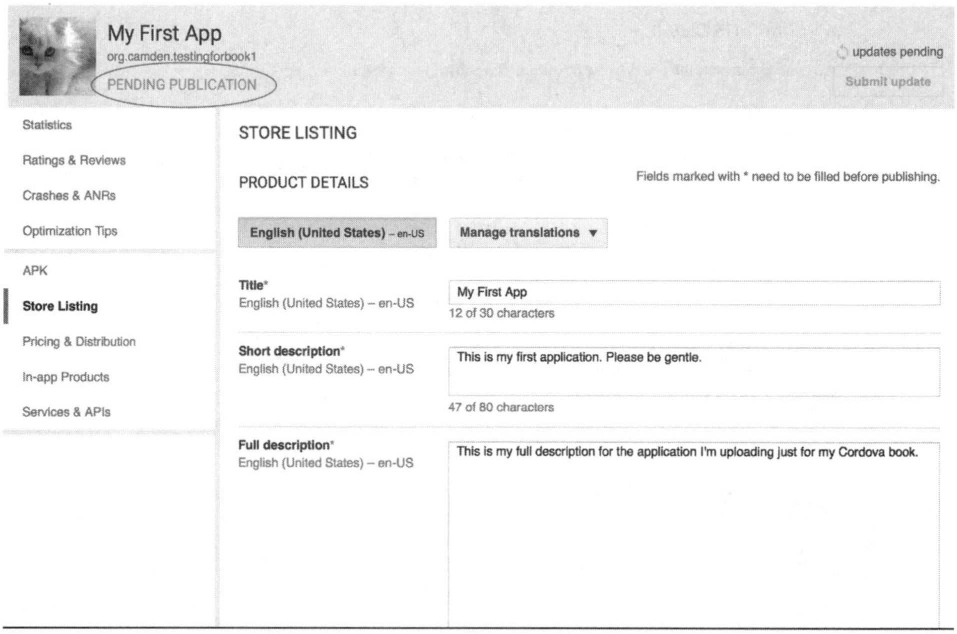

My First App
org.camden.testingforbook1
PENDING PUBLICATION

updates pending

Submit update

Statistics

Ratings & Reviews

Crashes & ANRs

Optimization Tips

APK

Store Listing

Pricing & Distribution

In-app Products

Services & APIs

STORE LISTING

PRODUCT DETAILS   Fields marked with * need to be filled before publishing.

English (United States) – en-US   Manage translations ▼

Title*
English (United States) – en-US

My First App
12 of 30 characters

Short description*
English (United States) – en-US

This is my first application. Please be gentle.

47 of 80 characters

Full description*
English (United States) – en-US

This is my full description for the application I'm uploading just for my Cordova book.

Figure 11.12   Your application awaiting its release to the world

hours for your application to go live. During this process, your application will be labeled as a pending publication as shown in figure 11.12.

Within a few hours, the status will change to Published, and you can see your application in the Google Play app store on your mobile device (figure 11.13).

11.3   *Submitting your iOS app*

Now let's look at releasing and submitting your application to Apple's market. This section will assume you're working on an Apple machine. You cannot sign applications using a Windows machine. At a high level, the process looks like like this:

- Sign the application with certificates created at the Apple developer site

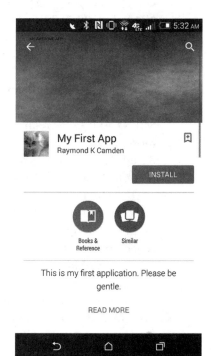

Figure 11.13   Your application released to the masses!

- Create a release build of the application by slightly modifying how you use the Cordova command line
- Upload your application to the website Apple uses for iOS apps
- Supply various pieces of information about your app (title, icons, etc.)
- Tell Apple your app is ready to be reviewed and cross your fingers

11.3.1 Signing your app

To begin, you must create a developer account with Apple. Begin at the iOS Developer page (https://developer.apple.com/devcenter/ios/index.action) and either sign in with an existing Apple ID (which you'll have if you own an iOS device) or register a new one.

After you've completed this process, you'll be returned to the iOS Developer page and should see an option to download Xcode. This is a free software package and is the primary tool for iOS developers to create applications. Earlier in the book we walked through setting up the Android SDK for development. If you instead followed the directions for doing iOS development, then you may have Xcode already installed.

Now that you've signed in, you need to register to become an iOS developer. This is separate from logging in to the developer website itself. If you don't see a link suggesting you join, you can point your browser to https://developer.apple.com/programs/ios/. Now be prepared for a bit of sticker shock (figure 11.14).

Currently the price tag to distribute apps in Apple's App Store is $99 per year. And you must continue to pay this even if you aren't adding new apps. Your app needs to be signed annually for it to be available to the public.

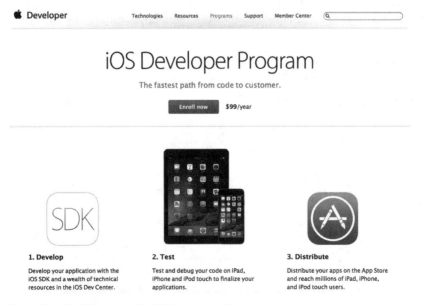

Figure 11.14   Welcome to the iOS Developer Program.

Figure 11.15   iOS Developer Member Center page

Once you've registered, you can go to the iOS Developer Member Center page (https://
developer.apple.com/membercenter/index.action). There are a number of resources
on this page, but there are two in particular you'll need to use (figure 11.15).

The first link to make note of is Certificates, Identifiers & Profiles. This is where
you'll create the assets you'll need to sign your application. The next is iTunes
Connect. This is the tool you'll use to submit your app and track its progress. To get
started, click Certificates, Identifiers & Profiles.

On the next page, shown in figure 11.16, you want to focus on iOS Apps, but which
link should you click first? Apple's process to sign applications is a bit more complex

Figure 11.16   Main portal for certificates, identifiers, and profiles

than what you did for the Android version. To properly sign an application requires three parts:

- *An app identifier*—This is pretty much what you expect. It is a way of identifying your application.
- *The certificate*—Think of it as placing your physical signature on the app.
- *The provisioning profile*—This is kind of like a final "package" around the app to prepare it for distribution.

To get started, click Identifiers. On the next page, click the plus (+) sign to create a new identifier. The next form will ask you to name your application. The name should be, obviously, the name of your application. The App ID Prefix value is preset for you and can be left alone (figure 11.17).

App ID Description

Name: Cordova Test

You cannot use special characters such as @, &, *, ', "

App ID Prefix

Value: 7V26N59B3E

Figure 11.17 Creating the app ID

In the next section, Explicit App ID (figure 11.18) should be selected. Leave that as is and enter the bundle ID. This should match the ID value you used in your Cordova project's config.xml file. It is the same reverse-style domain name system (DNS) type name you've seen before and it will have to be unique for the entire app store.

The next section, App Services, is where you'd tell Apple if your application is using any special services. For now, leave this as is and click Continue. The next page will ask you to confirm your details so be sure to finalize the app ID creation by clicking Submit one more time.

Explicit App ID

If you plan to incorporate app services such as Game Center, In-App Purchase, Data Protection, and iCloud, or want a provisioning profile unique to a single app, you must register an explicit App ID for your app.

To create an explicit App ID, enter a unique string in the Bundle ID field. This string should match the Bundle ID of your app.

Bundle ID: com.camden.cordovatest

We recommend using a reverse-domain name style string (i.e., com.domainname.appname). It cannot contain an asterisk (*).

Wildcard App ID

This allows you to use a single App ID to match multiple apps. To create a wildcard App ID, enter an asterisk (*) as the last digit in the Bundle ID field.

Bundle ID:

Example: com.domainname.*

Figure 11.18 Entering the bundle ID

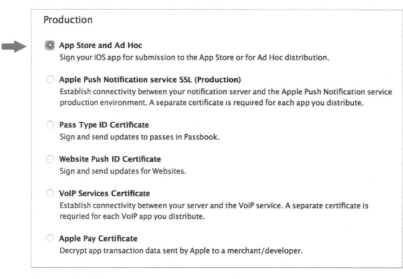

Figure 11.19   Selecting the certificate type

Now click Certificates and, once again, click the plus (+) sign to add a new certificate. The next screen asks you what type of certificate you want. Because you're going to release the application, you'll want to select App Store and Ad Hoc under Production, as shown in figure 11.19.

Next, you'll be instructed to create a certificate signing request (CSR) file. The Apple page describes how to do this so we won't repeat it here, but the end result is a file called CertificateSigningRequest.certSigningRequest. The next step will ask you to upload that file. Select it and click Generate. If everything went okay, your certificate is generated and you should download it (figure 11.20). Much like the warnings for Android, you want to keep this certificate in a safe place. Do not lose it.

Figure 11.20   The completed certificate

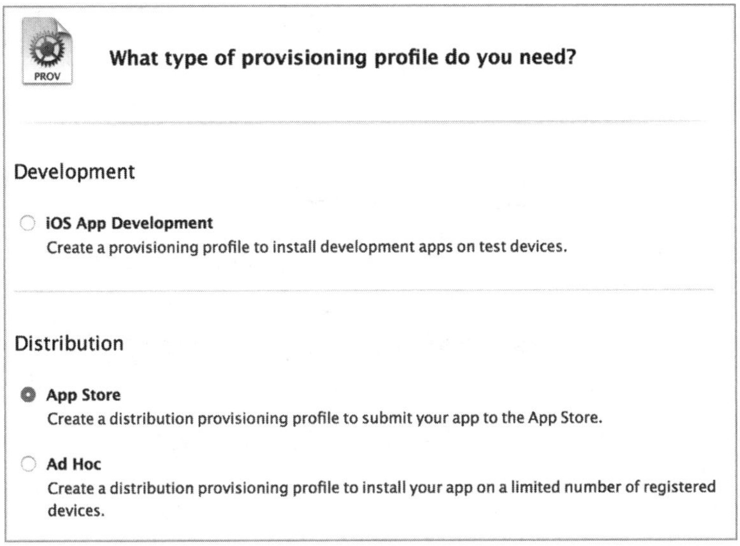

What type of provisioning profile do you need?

Development

○ **iOS App Development**
  Create a provisioning profile to install development apps on test devices.

Distribution

◉ **App Store**
  Create a distribution provisioning profile to submit your app to the App Store.

○ **Ad Hoc**
  Create a distribution provisioning profile to install your app on a limited number of registered devices.

**Figure 11.21
Deciding the type of
provisioning profile**

Now for the next step—creating the provisioning profile. As before, click the appropriate link in the left navigation bar and then the plus (+) sign to create a new provisioning profile. The type will be App Store, as shown in figure 11.21.

On the next page, select the App ID you created (figure 11.22).

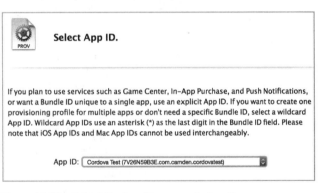

Select App ID.

If you plan to use services such as Game Center, In–App Purchase, and Push Notifications, or want a Bundle ID unique to a single app, use an explicit App ID. If you want to create one provisioning profile for multiple apps or don't need a specific Bundle ID, select a wildcard App ID. Wildcard App IDs use an asterisk (*) as the last digit in the Bundle ID field. Please note that iOS App IDs and Mac App IDs cannot be used interchangeably.

App ID: | Cordova Test (7V26N59B3E.com.camden.cordovatest) |

Figure 11.22   Select the App ID you created earlier.

Next, select the certificate you created (figure 11.23).

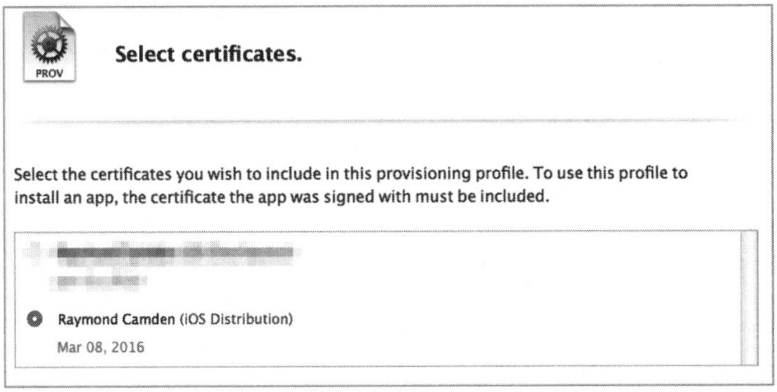

Select certificates.

Select the certificates you wish to include in this provisioning profile. To use this profile to install an app, the certificate the app was signed with must be included.

◉ **Raymond Camden** (iOS Distribution)
  Mar 08, 2016

**Figure 11.23   Select
the certificate you
created earlier.**

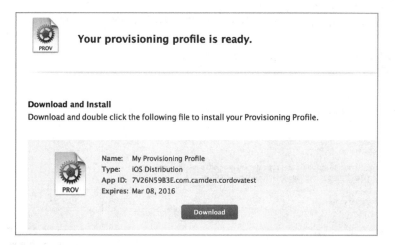

Figure 11.24   Naming the provisioning profile

For the final part of this process, give a name to the provisioning profile and click Generate (figure 11.24).

And finally, you can download the provisioning profile (figure 11.25). As before, keep this in a safe place, preferably next to the certificate.

Figure 11.25   The provisioning profile is done!

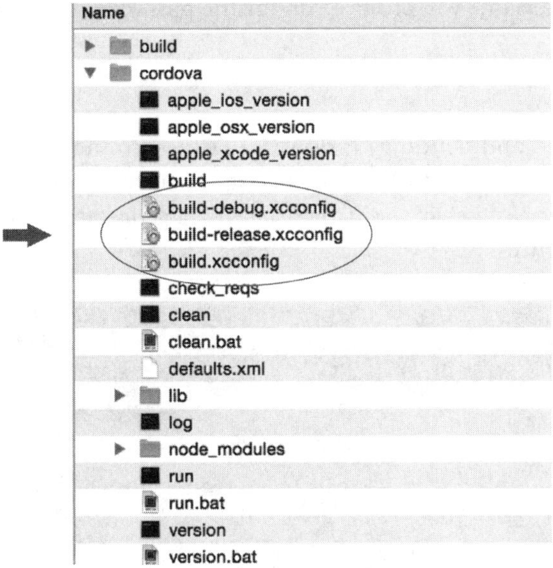

Figure 11.26 The xcconfig files

Before you sign the application you have one final step—installing the certificate and provisioning profile. In both cases it is a simple matter of double-clicking. Double-clicking the certificate file will open the Keychain Access application. You can then close it. Double-clicking the provisioning profile file will open Xcode, and again, you can then close the app.

As with Android, you can sign your application as part of the build process. Given that you've got a Cordova project already with the iOS platform, navigate to the platforms/ios/cordova folder. Inside you'll see two files, build-debug.xcconfig and build-release.xcconfig, as shown in figure 11.26. These files will be used when you create a release (or debug) version of your application.

Open build-release.xcconfig in your editor and make note of these two lines:

```
CODE_SIGN_IDENTITY = iPhone Distribution
CODE_SIGN_IDENTITY[sdk=iphoneos*] = iPhone Distribution
```

You'll need to replace iPhone Distribution with the name and type of your certificate. If you forgot what you selected, go back to the Certificates section in the iOS Developer website and look at your recently created certificate. In figure 11.20 you can see that type is iPhone Distribution and the name was Raymond Camden. So the correct text for the build-release.xcconfig file would be:

```
CODE_SIGN_IDENTITY = iPhone Distribution: Raymond Camden
CODE_SIGN_IDENTITY[sdk=iphoneos*] = iPhone Distribution: Raymond Camden
```

At this point you can now run almost the same command you did for Android: cordova build --device --release. The change here is to add the --device flag.

Unlike the Android platform, the iOS one will prompt you for the password only once, not with every build.

11.3.2 Publishing to the iOS market

Managing your apps (both released and pending) is done via iTunes Connect. If you return to the iOS Developer page, the iTunes Connect link is right beneath the one for Certificates, Identifiers & Profiles. Note that you'll be asked to log on again when entering this part of the portal (figure 11.27).

Figure 11.27   The iTunes Connect website

Click My Apps and then the plus (+) symbol (this time on the left side of the screen) to begin the process of adding a new application (figure 11.28).

New iOS App

Name ?	Version ?
My Cool App	0.0.1
Primary Language ?	SKU ?
English	10
Bundle ID ?	
Cordova Test - com.camden.cordovatest	

Register a new bundle ID on the Developer Portal.

Cancel   Create

Figure 11.28   New app dialog

Every field in this dialog is required but should be simple to fill out. Ensure the bundle ID matches the one you made earlier. The version should match the version string used in your app's config.xml file. SKU is an identifier for your product that's only used within your own company. It must have at least two characters, so using something like 10 for your first app is fine, just be sure to use 11 for the next one, and so on and so on.

The next page lets you enter information about your app and upload screenshots. It's pretty large and intimidating. The page also doesn't do a good job of telling you what the bare minimum requirements are. Therefore, I recommend a simple hack. Just click the Submit for Review button with nothing done. Immediately the form will highlight everything you need to enter before your app can be submitted.

In general, the required fields should be simple enough to understand. The icon can be uploaded by dragging a file onto the field, but note that it must be 1024 × 1024 with no alpha channels and transparencies. You must also click the Pricing tab to set a tier and availability date.

As a final step, submit the file containing your application. If you scroll down to the Build section you should see two methods described for doing this, as shown in figure 11.29.

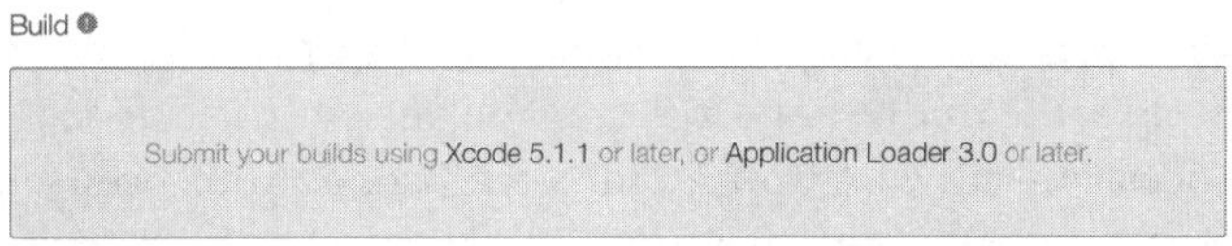

Build ❶

Submit your builds using Xcode 5.1.1 or later, or Application Loader 3.0 or later.

Figure 11.29   The Build submission UI

Clicking Application Loader 3.0 will prompt your browser to download an application. Once downloaded, install Application Loader. When it's done installing, run it. You'll be prompted to log in, and once there, you'll want to select Deliver Your App (figure 11.30).

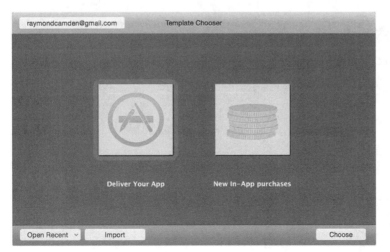

Figure 11.30   Using the Application Loader

This will prompt you to select the application binary, but here you'll run into a problem. The application expects an IPA file. Your earlier use of the Cordova command line only created an APP file. You can still use the command line to generate an IPA file, but you must use another tool. Credit for this particular tip goes to Dave Burt (you can see his StackOverflow answer at http://stackoverflow.com/questions/24061063/how-can-i-deploy-create-ipa-iphone-app-using-cordova-build-ios-release/25006630#25006630).

At the command line, change directories into platforms/ios/build/device. In this directory you should have an app file based on the project's name. In my test, this file was Mar62.app. (This is based on my using a folder called Mar62. It isn't a really friendly name for an app!) To convert the APP file into an IPA, run the following snippet:

```
/usr/bin/xcrun -sdk iphoneos PackageApplication "$(pwd)/Mar62.app" -o
    "$(pwd)/Mar62.ipa"
```

Note that I modified Dave's command a bit to specify an exact filename for both the APP and IPA file. When done, the xcrun command won't output anything, but you'll now have an IPA file in the same directory.

Select that IPA with Application Loader, and you'll see a confirmation screen, as shown in figure 11.31)

Click Next and the application will begin sending the bits to Apple. This may take a while, but when done, you'll get a success message like the one in figure 11.32.

Okay, take a deep breath. You're almost there. You've sent the bits to Apple, but now you need to associate it with your app submission. Back in your browser, go back to the Build section of your app, and click the plus (+) symbol next to it. This will open a popup that will let you select the IPA you just uploaded (figure 11.33).

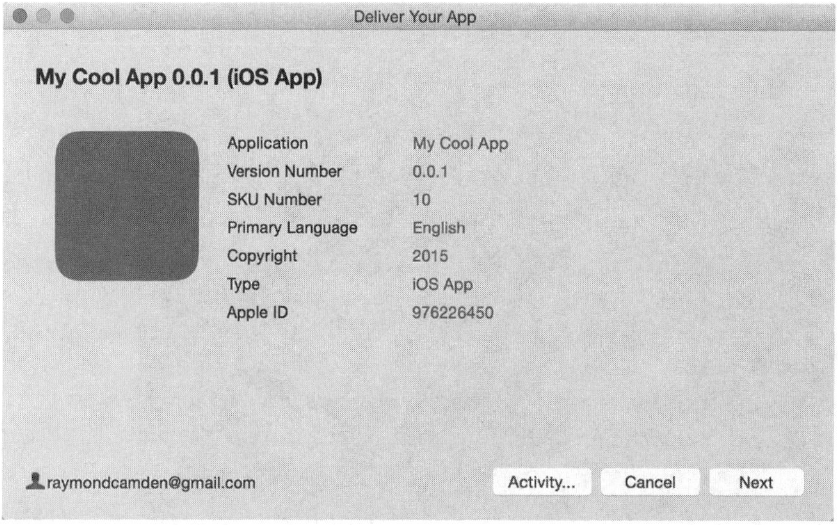

Figure 11.31 Confirmation screen for your app

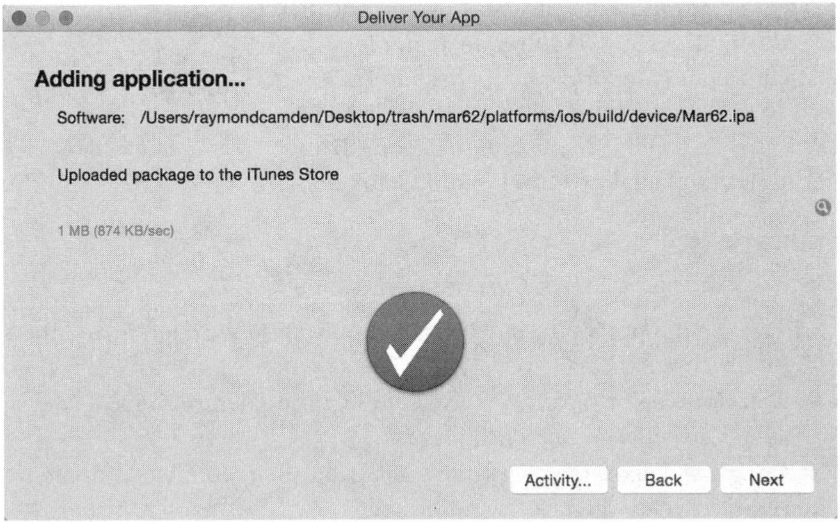
Deliver Your App
Adding application...
Software: /Users/raymondcamden/Desktop/trash/mar62/platforms/ios/build/device/Mar62.ipa
Uploaded package to the iTunes Store
1 MB (874 KB/sec)
Activity...
Back
Next

Figure 11.32 The app has been delivered!

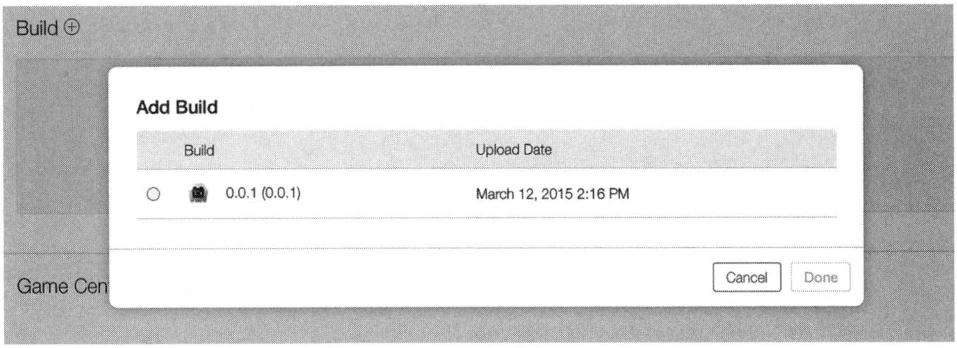
Build ⊕
Add Build
Build
Upload Date
0.0.1 (0.0.1)
March 12, 2015 2:16 PM
Game Cen
Cancel
Done

Figure 11.33 Selecting the IPA

My Cool App
iOS
0.0.1 Waiting For Review
Versions
Prerelease
Pricing

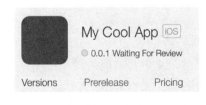

Figure 11.34 Miracle of miracles—the process is complete!

Select that file, click Save back on top of the form, and then click Submit for Review one more time. You may have additional errors—for example, more required screenshots. There will be yet another screen of prompts related to things like export compliance and content rights, at which point you can really, really, submit the app for review (figure 11.34).

Of course, now after all that hard work you're completely at the mercy of Apple. If your app is rejected, you'll at least be given a reason why and hopefully it will be something you can address.

My test application will most likely not be accepted, but figure 11.35 shows an example of an app that has been approved. It's Instant Halloween, a soundboard app built with Cordova. This was created by a good friend of mine, Andy Trice. You can download it now (or wait until October).

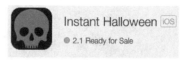

Figure 11.35   An example of an approved app in the store.

11.4   *Summary*

Let's review the major topics covered in this chapter.

- The general process for releasing an application is to sign in and then upload it to the store.
- App stores will typically require you to provide descriptions of your app as well as various different screenshots.
- Google will allow any app (that's legal) on their store while Apple reserves the right to decide what can be published.

In the final chapter, you're going to take everything you've learned so far and build a new application!

Building an RSS reader
app with Ionic

This chapter covers

- Designing a simple RSS reader application
- Using Ionic for Cordova development
- Enhancing the application with native plugins

For the final chapter, you're going to build a real, if simple, application—an RSS reader.

12.1 Designing a simple RSS reader application

RSS is an XML format commonly used by blogs as a way to syndicate their content. While not as popular as it once was, a website using RSS can share its content with other websites and tools. An example of a website using RSS to syndicate content is CNN. If you open your browser to www.cnn.com/services/rss/, you'll see a complete list of RSS feeds covering different parts of their content (figure 12.1).

Each RSS link goes to an XML file. Different browsers render RSS feeds a bit differently, but many will display an RSS feed pretty nicely (figure 12.2).

Think of RSS as a "content-pure" version of a website. Looking at the CNN "Top Stories" RSS feed in figure 12.2, what you're getting is just the articles. No sidebars and no headers and footers with navigation, but the pure content from CNN.

Title	Copy URLs to RSS Reader		
Top Stories	http://rss.cnn.com/rss/cnn_topstories.rss		MY YAHOO!
World	http://rss.cnn.com/rss/cnn_world.rss		MY YAHOO!
U.S.	http://rss.cnn.com/rss/cnn_us.rss		MY YAHOO!
Business (CNNMoney.com)	http://rss.cnn.com/rss/money_latest.rss		MY YAHOO!
Politics	http://rss.cnn.com/rss/cnn_allpolitics.rss		MY YAHOO!
Technology	http://rss.cnn.com/rss/cnn_tech.rss		MY YAHOO!
Health	http://rss.cnn.com/rss/cnn_health.rss		MY YAHOO!
Entertainment	http://rss.cnn.com/rss/cnn_showbiz.rss		MY YAHOO!
Travel	http://rss.cnn.com/rss/cnn_travel.rss		MY YAHOO!
Living	http://rss.cnn.com/rss/cnn_living.rss		MY YAHOO!
Video	http://rss.cnn.com/rss/cnn_freevideo.rss		MY YAHOO!
CNN Student News	http://rss.cnn.com/services/podcasting/studentnews/rss.xml		MY YAHOO!
Most Recent	http://rss.cnn.com/rss/cnn_latest.rss		MY YAHOO!
iReports on CNN	http://rss.ireport.com/feeds/oncnn.rss		MY YAHOO!

Want more RSS feeds? Try the **CNNMoney.com** feeds

Figure 12.1   CNN's RSS feeds

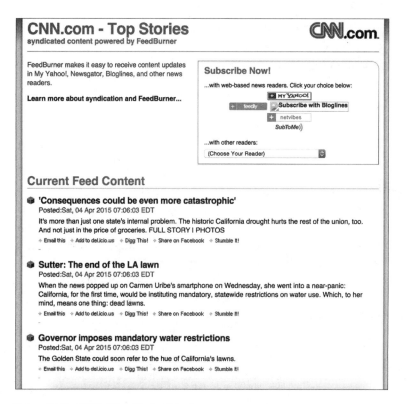

Figure 12.2   CNN's "Top Stories" feed

Because RSS is a known format, many tools exist to parse and render RSS content. Your application will use an RSS feed to drive the content of a hybrid mobile application. Let's look at a simple mockup of the final product. The first screen, shown in figure 12.3, is a list of articles from the RSS feed.

Each item in the list represents an article from the RSS feed. Articles have titles so those titles are used for each particular list item. Clicking on an item should then load the article itself (figure 12.4).

Fairly simple, right? The application has only two screens, so it should be pretty quick to build, but there are a number of things you have to consider:

- What UI framework should you use to make the application work well on mobile?
- What SPA framework should you use to properly architect the application?
- RSS is an XML-based format. How do you get, parse, and use that data?
- This application relies on an external feed for content. What should the strategy be when the application is offline?

Let's begin by addressing the first two questions. Earlier in the book you used jQuery Mobile to both provide a UI and SPA for a Cordova application. jQuery Mobile

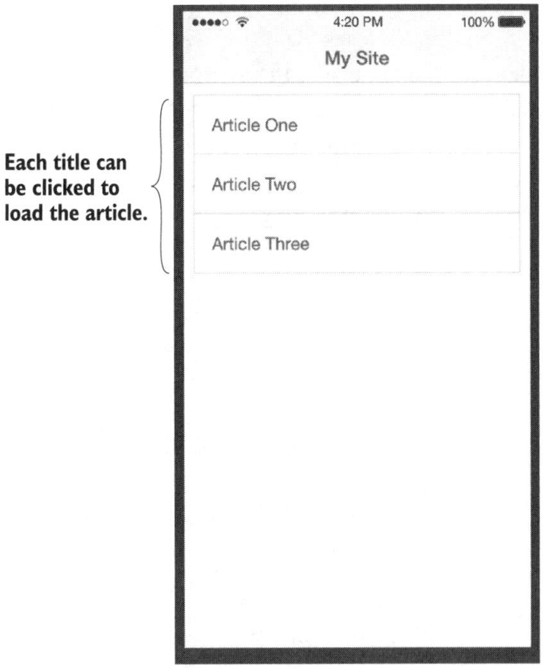

Each title can be clicked to load the article.

Figure 12.3   The app's homepage—a list of articles

This lets the user return to the list of articles.

When the article was created.

Article content.

Figure 12.4   One article view in the app

is simple to use, which is why it was used in the book, but we also discussed the Ionic framework. Ionic is an incredibly powerful framework for building hybrid mobile applications. In my not-so-humble opinion, Ionic is the best thing to happen to Cordova since, well, Cordova was created.

Because it's so powerful, we didn't cover it in this book as it would simply be a bit too much to learn both Cordova *and* Ionic at the same time. Luckily *Ionic in Action* by Jeremy Wilken (Manning Publications, 2015) is available. See details at www.manning .com/wilken/.

We'll use this sample application in this chapter as a way of introducing you to Ionic. Please remember that we're only going to scratch the surface of what Ionic has to offer and I strongly recommend picking up *Ionic in Action* to learn more. Ionic also makes use of the AngularJS, Angular for short, framework. Angular is probably the most popular JavaScript framework available. (Although I'm sure there's room to debate what's the most popular.) Angular can be a bit complex for new users. If this is your introduction to Angular, don't worry, we'll keep it simple. If you want to learn more, you can pick up *AngularJS in Action* (Manning, 2015) by Ford and Ruebbelke (www.manning.com/bford/).

Ionic—briefly

While we won't spend a lot of time talking about Ionic itself here, it may be worthwhile to briefly talk about some of what Ionic provides. When using Ionic, you get a beautiful UI framework—essentially an easy way to make your app look nice. You also get UX features that are common to mobile like pull to refresh. Ionic also adds features to your command line that enhance what you can already do with Cordova. For example, you can send all console.log messages from your application back to the terminal, which provides a simple way to debug your application, on top of the other ways you learned about earlier in the book. Ionic, the company, also provides services that your app can make use of, including Push and Analytics.

12.2   *Using Ionic for Cordova development*

To get started, you need to install the Ionic command line. This is done via the same method you used to install Cordova, npm:

```
npm install -g ionic
```

This gives you access to the Ionic CLI in your terminal. The Ionic CLI is fairly complex, but it also wraps the Cordova CLI so many of the same operations you used there will work within Ionic as well. In other words, the process you've used before (creating a project and sending builds to your device or emulator) is pretty much the same. To get started, you can create a new application. Ionic includes multiple templates to help speed up development, but to keep it simple, we'll use the "blank" template. The template isn't empty, it's just simplified as much as possible:

```
ionic start initial blank
```

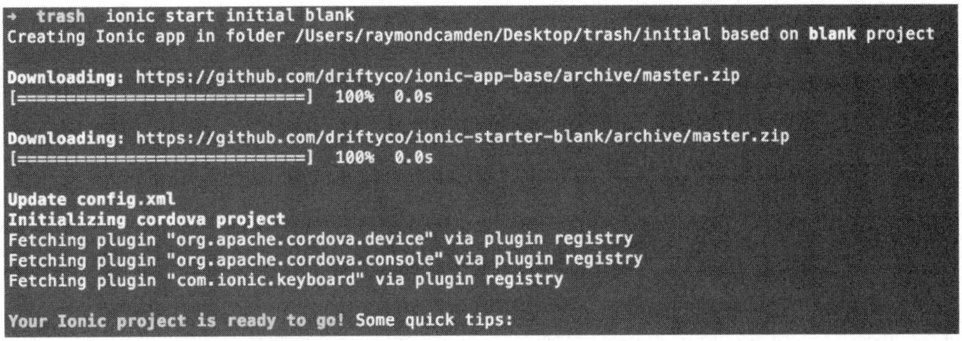

→ trash ionic start initial blank
Creating Ionic app in folder /Users/raymondcamden/Desktop/trash/initial based on blank project
Downloading: https://github.com/driftyco/ionic-app-base/archive/master.zip
[=============================] 100% 0.0s
Downloading: https://github.com/driftyco/ionic-starter-blank/archive/master.zip
[=============================] 100% 0.0s
Update config.xml
Initializing cordova project
Fetching plugin "org.apache.cordova.device" via plugin registry
Fetching plugin "org.apache.cordova.console" via plugin registry
Fetching plugin "com.ionic.keyboard" via plugin registry
Your Ionic project is ready to go! Some quick tips:

Figure 12.5 Creating an application with Ionic

In the preceding command, `start` simply means to create a new project, `initial` is the folder to use, and `blank` is the template (figure 12.5).

At this point, you have a new Ionic application, which is essentially a Cordova project with extras (figure 12.6).

For now, you don't have to worry about any of the additional files, and you can think of this as a regular old Cordova project. Let's test out one of the cooler features that Ionic adds over Cordova.

12.2.1 The ionic serve feature

When you're building a Cordova application, the command line has a built-in web server you can use for testing. We haven't shown this yet as it's a bit limited. If your code waits for the `deviceReady` event, then it will never run unless you manually

initial
XML
JS
bower.json
config.xml
gulpfile.js
hooks
ionic.project
package.json
plugins
scss
www

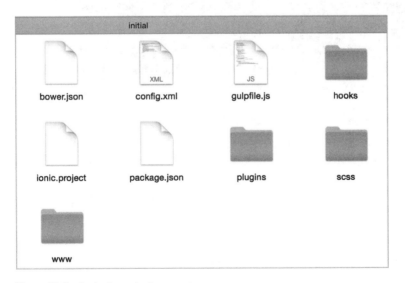

Figure 12.6 An Ionic project

execute it in your browser developer tools. Any plugins your application may use will not work in the desktop. During your initial building of a new application, these limitations may not hinder you too much. You may delay working with plugins until later in your development cycle. Ionic enhances this feature with multiple additions that make it even more worthwhile.

One of the coolest features Ionic adds is Live Reload. What this means is that you can work on your HTML, CSS, and JavaScript, and Ionic will automatically reload your browser (in this case, Chrome) when you save your file. This speeds up development and lets you quickly work on your application. To test this, ensure you've changed directories in your new project and start up the server:

```
ionic serve
```

You'll see output from the terminal confirming that it began and you should see a new tab in your browser, as shown in figure 12.7.

At this point, you can try modifying any of the files under the www folder and you'll see Chrome update automatically.

To see your application on a device, you need to add a platform, just as you'd have done with Cordova. Because this is a Cordova application, you could use `cordova platform add android`. But typically I use Ionic commands only. Ionic passes known Cordova commands directly through to Cordova, so you can do this instead:

```
ionic platform add android
```

Figure 12.7 `ionic serve` **output in the terminal and the browser**

then either emulate or run:

```
ionic emulate android
```

> **NOTE** If you're still running the Ionic server from earlier in the book, you'll need to "kill it" by typing `q`.

Again, we're only going to scratch the surface of what Ionic can do (try the `--lab` option with `ionic serve`, for example) but at this point you can begin working on the RSS reader application.

12.3 RSS reader app: part one

Begin by creating a simple version of the RSS reader application—one that displays a list of entries from the feed and lets you click to read the story (figure 12.8). We're going to enhance this later with powerful new features, but it's always best to start simple.

If you're new to Angular, some of the following code samples may be a bit hard to follow. For now I suggest copying the files from the zip (using the initial folder) to reduce the chance of making mistakes.

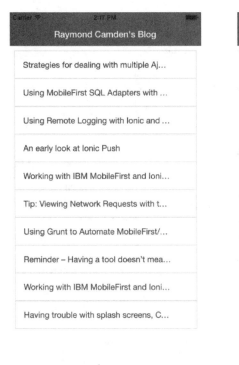

Initial page with all entries   **One particular entry**

Figure 12.8   Two views of the application

12.3.1 *Starting the app*

Begin by creating a new Ionic application based on the blank template. Here you're going to use the folder name initial to match the name of the folder from the zip file, but you could use whatever you like. If you made an application earlier to test the Ionic CLI, you may already have an initial folder. Just move that or delete it. Here's the code:

```
ionic start initial blank
```

Open the www folder in your favorite editor and begin editing the index.html file shown in the following listing.

Listing 12.1   RSS reader application index.html file (initial/www/index.html)

```html
<!DOCTYPE html>
<html>
  <head>
    <meta charset="utf-8">
    <meta name="viewport" content="initial-scale=1, maximum-scale=1,
    ➥ user-scalable=no, width=device-width">
    <title></title>

    <link href="lib/ionic/css/ionic.css" rel="stylesheet">
    <link href="css/style.css" rel="stylesheet">

    <!-- ionic/angularjs js -->
    <script src="lib/ionic/js/ionic.bundle.js"></script>

    <!-- cordova script (this will be a 404 during development) -->
    <script src="cordova.js"></script>

    <!-- your app's js -->
    <script src="js/app.js"></script>
    <script src="js/constants.js"></script>
    <script src="js/controllers.js"></script>
    <script src="js/services.js"></script>
    <script type="text/javascript" src="https://www.google.com/jsapi"></script>

  </head>
  <body ng-app="starter">

    <ion-nav-bar class="bar-positive">
            <ion-nav-back-button></ion-nav-back-button>
    </ion-nav-bar>

    <ion-nav-view>
    </ion-nav-view>

  </body>
</html>
```

❶ Points to files that aren't made by Ionic blank template. You'll be adding them.

Helps parse RSS feeds. ❷

❸ Creates a persistent header.

❹ Defines where pages will be loaded.

The first changes you need to make are to include a few additional `<script>` tags ❶ to support the application. The blank template only uses one JavaScript file (ignoring the files used by Ionic itself), and in theory you could put *everything* in there, but it's a bit cleaner to separate the various aspects of the application into different files to help keep things organized. The last <script> tag ❷ you include is a Google library that you'll use to help parse RSS feeds. You'll see more about that in a moment.

Ionic makes use of multiple Angular directives to build applications. Think of a directive as a custom HTML tag. The tags are incredibly powerful and if you've never seen them before, you may be a bit confused by their use here. In general, when you see these unknown tags in an Ionic application, know that there are both JavaScript and CSS behind the scenes that make these tags work. In this case, you've got one ❸ that creates a persistent header and one ❹ that defines where the main pages of the application will load. Now let's look at the first JavaScript file, app.js.

Listing 12.2   Main application file for the RSS reader (initial/www/js/app.js)

```
angular.module('starter',
  ['ionic','rssappControllers','rssappServices','rssappConfig'])          ←┐ Defines the modules
                                                                              the app will need ❶
.config(['$stateProvider', '$urlRouterProvider', function($stateProvider,
  $urlRouterProvider) {

    $stateProvider
      .state('Entries', {
        url: '/',
        controller: 'EntriesCtrl',
        templateUrl: 'partials/entries.html',
      })
      .state('Entry', {                          ←┐ Defines view for
        url: '/entry/:index',                      ❸ individual entry
        controller: 'EntryCtrl',
        templateUrl: 'partials/entry.html',
      });

    $urlRouterProvider.otherwise("/");

}])

.run(function($ionicPlatform) {
  $ionicPlatform.ready(function() {
    if(window.cordova && window.cordova.plugins.Keyboard) {
      cordova.plugins.Keyboard.hideKeyboardAccessoryBar(true);
    }
    if(window.StatusBar) {
      StatusBar.styleDefault();
    }
  });
})
```

Defines initial view of app, a list of entries ❷

The application will depend on various modules that we're going to discuss in the next section. rssappControllers, rssappServices, and rssappConfig ❶ will be defined in individual files and will come together to create the application. By listing them here ❷ you're telling the application what pieces are required for it to work. This is an example of one of Angular's most powerful features, dependency injection. The application, in this initial version, has two views, a list of entries ❷ and an entry ❸. Angular has a "state" system where it can specify what particular code works with a particular URL, as well as what templates will be loaded. In this way, it acts like a list of possible states the application can be in. Again, this app is simple and only has two states.

12.3.2 *Application modules*

Now let's begin looking at the various modules. The first is the most simple, the configuration module, shown in the following listing.

Listing 12.3   App constants (initial/www/js/constants.js)

```
angular.module("rssappConfig", [])
.constant("settings", {
    RSS_URL: "http://feeds.feedburner.com/raymondcamdensblog",       ◀──  ❶ RSS feed
    TITLE: "Raymond Camden's Blog"                                   ◀──      to use
});                                                                        ❷ Name of site
```

The application uses an Angular module to define constant values, in this case called settings, that the code will make use of. You can see both an RSS URL ❶ and a name ❷. You can, and should, change these values to see how they impact the application. You could, for example, use one of the CNN examples from earlier in the chapter. Any valid RSS URL is fine, and the TITLE value can be whatever makes sense. Now let's look at the controllers.js file.

Listing 12.4   Controllers for the RSS app (/initial/www/js/controllers.js)

```
angular.module('rssappControllers', [])

.controller('EntriesCtrl', ['$ionicPlatform', '$scope', 'RSSService',
    'settings', function($ionicPlatform, $scope, RSSService, settings) {

    $ionicPlatform.ready(function() {

        $scope.title = settings.TITLE;
        RSSService.getEntries(settings.RSS_URL).then(function(entries) {
            $scope.entries = entries;
        }, function(err) {
            console.log("error", err);
        });

    });

}])

.controller('EntryCtrl', ['$scope', 'RSSService', '$stateParams',
    function($scope, RSSService, $stateParams) {

    RSSService.getEntry($stateParams.index).then(function(entry) {
        $scope.entry = entry;
```

Controller used when first view is rendered ❶

Sets app's title to the setting

Asks RSSService to get one particular entry ❺

❷ Event analogous to Cordova's deviceReady

RSSService handles fetching RSS data ❸

❹ Controller used when second view is rendered

```
}, function(err) {
  console.log("error", err);
});
```

```
}]);
```

The previous listing focuses on the controllers for the application. In an MVC-based application like Angular, controllers are responsible for processing data between services and the views that the user interacts with. In this case, you can see two controllers, with EntriesCtrl ❶ being used for the first view (all entries) and EntryCtrl ❹ being used for the detail view. In both cases, the RSSService module (❸, ❺) is used to fetch data.

Make special note of the $ionicPlatform.ready code block ❷. This is an Ionic-specific event that's called after Cordova's deviceReady event fires. In an Ionic application, you'll see this event code block instead of the typical deviceReady code. Let's examine the final bit of JavaScript in the app, services.js, shown in the following listing.

Listing 12.5   Application services (initial/www/js/services.js)

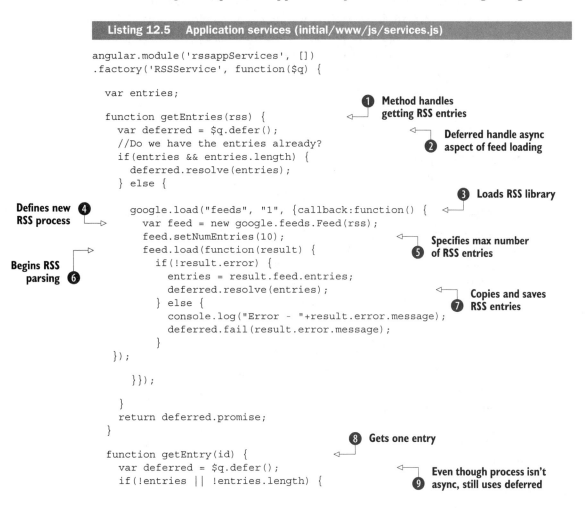

```
angular.module('rssappServices', [])
.factory('RSSService', function($q) {

  var entries;
                                                    ❶ Method handles
  function getEntries(rss) {                          getting RSS entries
    var deferred = $q.defer();
    //Do we have the entries already?               ❷ Deferred handle async
    if(entries && entries.length) {                    aspect of feed loading
      deferred.resolve(entries);
    } else {
                                                    ❸ Loads RSS library
      google.load("feeds", "1", {callback:function() {
        var feed = new google.feeds.Feed(rss);
        feed.setNumEntries(10);                     ❺ Specifies max number
        feed.load(function(result) {                   of RSS entries
          if(!result.error) {
            entries = result.feed.entries;
            deferred.resolve(entries);              ❼ Copies and saves
          } else {                                     RSS entries
            console.log("Error - "+result.error.message);
            deferred.fail(result.error.message);
          }
        });

      }});

    }
    return deferred.promise;
  }
                                                    ❽ Gets one entry
  function getEntry(id) {
    var deferred = $q.defer();                      ❾ Even though process isn't
    if(!entries || !entries.length) {                  async, still uses deferred
```

Defines new RSS process ❹

Begins RSS parsing ❻

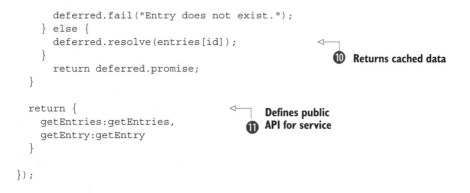

```
            deferred.fail("Entry does not exist.");
        } else {
            deferred.resolve(entries[id]);
        }                                              ⑩ Returns cached data
        return deferred.promise;
    }

    return {                                           ⑪ Defines public
        getEntries:getEntries,                            API for service
        getEntry:getEntry
    }

});
```

The service handles two main things: parsing and returning an RSS feed, and handling getting one particular item from an RSS feed. You can see this API defined ⑪ toward the bottom of the file. The getEntries() ❶ method is what you'll use to both parse the RSS and return the data. As noted earlier, RSS is an XML dialect, and while you can work with XML in JavaScript, working with simple JSON data is much easier. To get your data in this format, you'll make use of the Google Feed API (https://developers.google.com/feed/). As you can guess, this is a service that parses RSS feeds. Not only does it convert XML into JSON, it also handles the various different "flavors" of RSS and returns a consistent set of data. I mentioned that RSS is a specification, and that's true, but multiple versions of this specification can be found in the wild. Google's API simplifies everything for you by giving you a consistent result.

Because RSS parsing involves network calls and network calls are asynchronous, deferred ❷ is used to handle the delayed callbacks. A proper look at deferred objects would be too off-topic for this chapter, but you can consider them as a nice way of handling calls that finish at some point in the future.

To load this API, Google provides a load function ❸. The google variable used here is a global one made available by their library. When this API loads the library you want, you can begin working with the RSS feed ❹. There are a few configuration options available for the API, but all you really care about is specifying a sensible maximum ❺ for the number of entries returned.

You can ask the library to start parsing the RSS feed ❻. Once it's done, you store the results in a local variable ❼. What does this data look like? It's a big JSON string, but once parsed in JavaScript, it's an array. If you dump that to the console (using console.dir), you can see all the data yourself, as shown in figure 12.9. Figure 12.9 shows you how Google returns the RSS data. The parts of the data that the application will make use of are noted, but note that even more data exists.

The final method of the service ❽ returns one particular entry. Even though this will not be asynchronous, you use deferred ❾ again simply to be consistent with the other method. Because you've already stored all the data, you can fetch it ⑩ and return it.

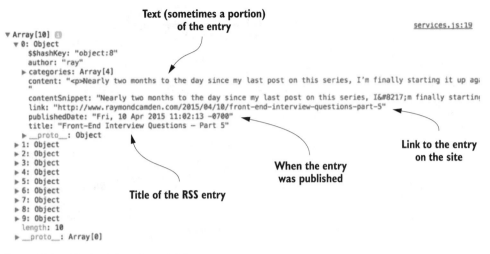

Figure 12.9 A look at the returned data

12.3.3 *Reviewing what you've done*

Let's take stock of what we've looked at so far. In listing 12.2, you saw the core application code, kind of the top-level "director" for the application. Listing 12.3 defined the constants for the application. Listing 12.4 defined a controller. This was responsible for getting the data and making it available to your display. Listing 12.5 demonstrated a service that handled fetching RSS feeds.

So how do you display all of this? The application makes use of templates (see listing 12.2) for each view. Let's look at the first one, the list of feed entries.

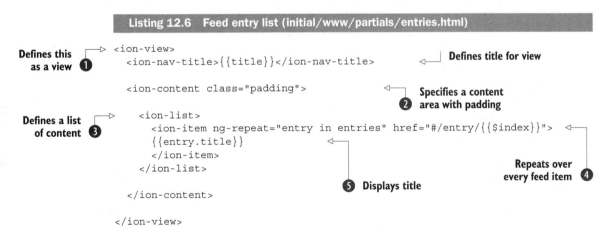

If you've never seen directives in Angular (or web components) before, you may be freaking out a bit now. There isn't one tag in listing 12.6 that looks like regular HTML. This is where the power of Angular, and Ionic, really begin to shine. Angular lets you

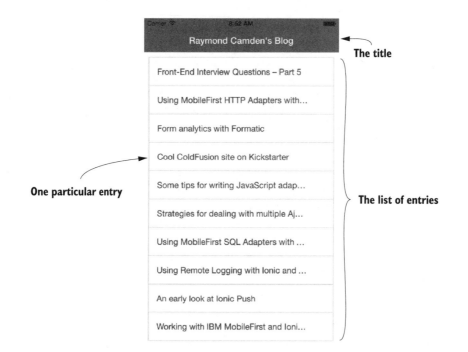

Figure 12.10 Application's homepage

define directives. These may be new attributes to existing tags or even new tags that are controlled behind the scenes with JavaScript, HTML, and CSS. When you see the unknown tags in the listing (❶, ❷, ❸), know that Ionic created code to define what these tags should output. The end result will be regular HTML—div tags, ul tags, and so forth. But the Ionic framework lets you use these shortcuts to create the end result. Angular directives also support logical behavior like looping ❹, which lets you define what to do for each feed entry. In this case, you're going to link to a detail page and show the title ❺. You saw the app in figure 12.8, but let's look at this page again in figure 12.10.

Figure 12.10 shows how the template from the previous listing is rendered by Ionic once the RSS feed is loaded. Now let's look at an individual entry template in the following listing.

Listing 12.7   Feed detail page (initial/www/partials/entry.html)

```
<ion-view>

    <ion-nav-title>{{entry.title}}</ion-nav-title>                ❶ Renders title for entry

    <ion-content class="padding">

            <p><b>Published:</b> {{entry.publishedDate}}</p>      ❷ Renders date
                                                                    for entry
```

```
        <div ng-bind-html="entry.content"></div>      ⟵
    </ion-content>
```
❸ Renders content for entry

```
</ion-view>
```

This template is rather simple as it needs only to display the title ❶, published date
❷, and content ❸ for the entry. The only thing to note here is that Angular doesn't
like to display data that contains HTML content. It considers it a security risk so it
requires you to be explicit about when data is allowed to contain HTML. Hence, the
ng-bind-html attribute ❸ to specifically say that this content will contain HTML. Let's
reacquaint ourselves with how this looks in figure 12.11.

This is a perfect time to try the ionic serve feature mentioned earlier. Type that
in at the command prompt and the application should open in your Chrome browser.
This works because the application isn't doing anything special—yet. You aren't using
any particular plugins or device features so you can run it just fine within a regular
browser. Now it's time to kick it up a notch.

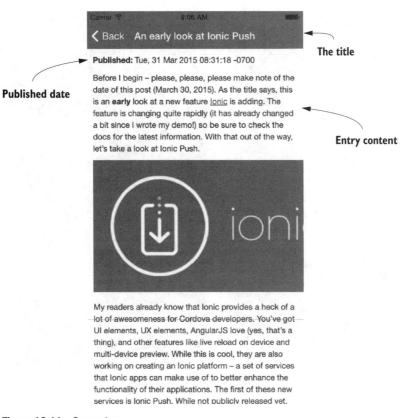

Figure 12.11   One entry

12.4 RSS reader app: part two

In the first iteration of the application, you made use of Ionic and a Google API to create a simple RSS reader application. While this works, it doesn't make use of device-
specific features and probably wouldn't be allowed by Apple on its store. Let's look at
a few things you can add to improve the user experience of the application. Note that
many of the things you'll add here will require you to start testing in the emulator or a
real device as opposed to the web browser.

The first thing you can add to the application is a simple loading indicator. When
the application launches and tries to parse the RSS feed, that may take a second or so.
While that's not a long time, you should let the user know something is going on in
the meantime. Even better, you should use a loading indicator that's specific to a
device and looks familiar to other native applications (figure 12.12).

The next change is to let users read RSS entries on the website itself. Currently you
render the entry within an Ionic template. This is okay but may not look as good as
the content on the website. Also, some RSS feeds only contain partial text. They want

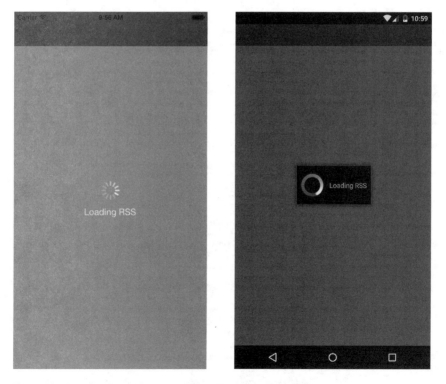

Figure 12.12 A loading indicator for iOS (left) and Android (right)

to "tease" people essentially into coming to the website to read the full entry. Luckily there's a cool way to load HTML content in a Cordova application. You can use the InAppBrowser plugin to create a popup web browser to render a page. This popup will include a simple Close button that then returns the user to the app, as shown in figure 12.13.

While viewing an RSS entry, it may also be cool to let the user share that entry with others. Sharing could be done via multiple ways: Facebook, Twitter, email, SMS, and so on. Luckily there's a simple plugin to add this, SocialSharing. Figure 12.14 demonstrates this plugin in action.

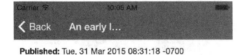

Published: Tue, 31 Mar 2015 08:31:18 -0700

Before I begin – please, please, please make note of the date of this post (March 30, 2015). As the title says, this is an **early** look at a new feature Ionic is adding. The feature is changing quite rapidly (it has already changed a bit since I wrote my demo!) so be sure to check the docs for the latest information. With that out of the way, let's take a look at Ionic Push.

My readers already know that Ionic provides a heck of a lot of awesomeness for Cordova developers. You've got UI elements, UX elements, AngularJS love (yes, that's a thing), and other features like live reload on device and multi-device preview. While this is cool, they are also working on creating an Ionic platform – a set of services that Ionic apps can make use of to better enhance the

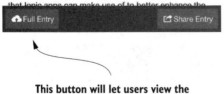

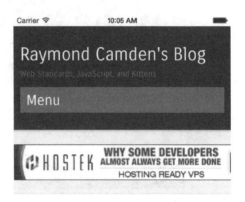

This button will let users view the content on the original site.

This is the content with the InAppBrowser popup. Note the Done button.

Figure 12.13   The app rendering the real entry

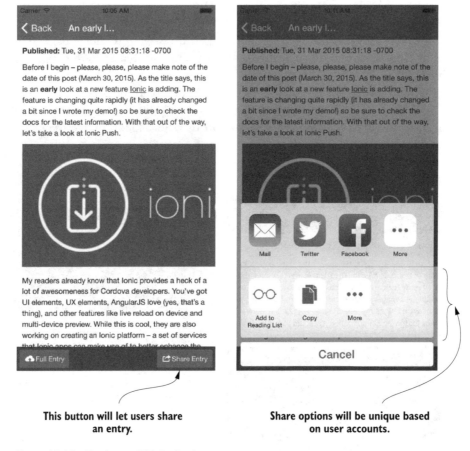

This button will let users share
an entry.

Share options will be unique based
on user accounts.

Figure 12.14   Sharing an RSS feed entry

The final update you'll make is something your initial version should have had—network detection. Obviously the application won't be much use if a user is offline, so at a minimum, you should tell users when they aren't online (figure 12.15).

Before you begin, though, let's look at an alternative place to find Cordova plugins. We've mentioned the main plugin directory at http://plugins.cordova.io. You should bookmark that website and make it one of the first places you look when working with Cordova. But this certainly isn't the only place you can find plugins. Telerik has created what it calls a verified plugin directory. The Verified Plugins Marketplace (http:// plugins.telerik.com/) is a directory of plugins that they have verified work

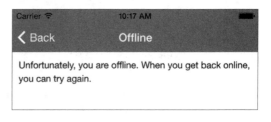

Figure 12.15   Offline status for the app

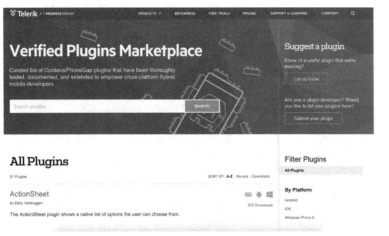

**Figure 12.16
Telerik Verified
Plugin Marketplace**

well and are properly documented. This isn't to say that the core Cordova directory is full of broken, poorly documented plugins. Far from it, but you may encounter plugins there that don't work properly in the current version of the Cordova framework or are a bit buggy. Telerik's verified list gives you more assurance that what you install will work well (figure 12.16).

12.4.1 Adding the loading indicator

The first thing you'll add is the simple loading indicator. Ionic supports one out of the box, but it's rendered with HTML, CSS, and JavaScript. At the Telerik marketplace, you can find a simple plugin called Spinner (http://plugins.telerik.com/plugin/spinner). The Spinner plugin creates a loading widget that's specifically designed to be appropriate for each different platform. If you open the Spinner plugin page in your browser, you'll see instructions telling you how install the plugin via the Cordova CLI, as shown in figure 12.17.

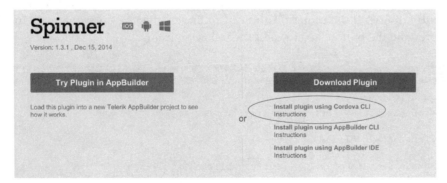

Figure 12.17   Installation instructions for the plugin

Clicking that link opens a dialog with the specific command line call you need:

```
cordova plugin add https://github.com/Telerik-Verified-Plugins/Spinner
```

Do this now for the project. Note that the zip file you downloaded for the chapter includes a final folder where you can find the completely modified version of this project as opposed to updating the initial version. Once the plugin is installed, it's time to make use of it. As you remember, the controller file (controllers.js) called the services file (services.js) to request the parsed RSS. This is where the main delay will come from so let's have you update the code within the `EntriesCtrl` block to make use of the Spinner. See the updated code in the following listing.

Listing 12.8   Modified controller code to show a spinner (final/www/js/controller.js)

```
window.plugins.spinnerDialog.show(null, "Loading RSS", true);      ◁──  Shows spinner

$scope.title = settings.TITLE;
RSSService.getEntries(settings.RSS_URL).then(function(entries) {
  window.plugins.spinnerDialog.hide();            ◁──
  $scope.entries = entries;                             Hides spinner
}, function(err) {
  window.plugins.spinnerDialog.hide();
  console.log("error", err);
});
```

As you can see, the modifications are rather simple. You have one line to show the spinner and one to hide it after the RSS feed is loaded. The Spinner plugin API includes multiple options, but your needs are simple here—just a bit of text.

12.4.2 *Adding the InAppBrowser plugin*

Now let's move on to the next feature, the InAppBrowser plugin. As you saw in figure 12.13, this plugin lets you load a web browser on top of your existing application. To add this plugin, use the following command:

```
cordova plugin add cordova-plugin-inappbrowser
```

To use this feature, you need to do two things. Remember in figure 12.13 there's a button to fire off the request. You need to first modify the entry template to add the footer and the button, as shown in the following listing.

Listing 12.9   Modified entry template (final/www/partials/entry.html)

```
<ion-view>
  <ion-nav-title>{{entry.title}}</ion-nav-title>

  <ion-content class="padding">

    <p><b>Published:</b> {{entry.publishedDate}}</p>

    <div ng-bind-html="entry.content"></div>
```

```
        </ion-content>
```
⬤**1** **Creates footer**
```
        <ion-footer-bar class="bar-dark">
```
Button that ⟶ `<button class="button button-positive icon-left ion-upload"`
loads entry ⬤**2** `ng-click="readEntry(entry)">`
```
            Full Entry
          </button>
          <button class="button button-positive icon-left ion-share"
          ng-click="shareEntry(entry)">
```
SocialSharing
⬤**3** **plugin**
```
            Share Entry
          </button>
        </ion-footer-bar>

      </ion-view>
```

You begin by adding a simple footer to the template ⬤**1**. This footer will be persistent as the user scrolls through the content. Inside the footer are two buttons. The first is the one you care about now—it will fire off a request to use the InAppBrowser plugin ⬤**2**. The second ⬤**3** is for the SocialSharing plugin to be discussed next.

Using the InAppBrowser plugin requires an incredibly small change to the `Entry-Controller`. Add the block from the following listing immediately after the `EntryCtrl` block begins.

Listing 12.10   Snippet from `EntryController` (final/www/js/controllers.js)

```
$scope.readEntry = function(e) {
      window.open(e.link, "_blank");
};
```

The InAppBrowser plugin uses the same API that the desktop browser uses to create a popup window. While most people avoid that on the web (in fact, browsers actively block popups), the API is simple, probably familiar, and works well for your needs here.

12.4.3   Adding the SocialSharing plugin

For the next feature, you'll add the SocialSharing plugin. This is the feature that lets a user share a feed entry with other people via social networks or email. Once again you'll use the Telerik Verified Plugin Marketplace to find the SocialSharing plugin (http://plugins.telerik.com/plugin/socialsharing). Using the instructions, we see we can add the plugin like so:

```
cordova plugin add https://github.com/Telerik-Verified-Plugins/SocialSharing
```

Using the plugin is rather simple. While its API allows for various options (for example, you can support sharing only with Twitter), you'll take the default "anything goes" approach here. In listing 12.9 you saw how to add the button, so now let's look at the code in the controller to make this work. The code from the following listing can be added immediately after the function you added in listing 12.10.

Listing 12.11   Snippet from `EntryController` (final/www/js/controllers.js)

```
$scope.shareEntry = function(e) {
  window.plugins.socialsharing.share("","",null, e.link);
}
```

Yep, one line. The first and second arguments represent a default message and subject. If you wanted to prefill the `share` with text, like "Look at this cool article," then you could do so. As I personally don't like this, I left both blank. The third argument is for sharing a file so you set it to `null` because you aren't doing that here. The final option is for a link and you pass in the link value from the feed entry. As I said, this plugin allows for multiple other ways of using it, but your needs here are rather simple. Now let's get to the final modification.

12.4.4 *Adding offline support*

We discussed offline support in chapter 6. We discussed what it means to build a good hybrid mobile application and detecting network status was one of them. To make this work you need to first add the network plugin:

```
cordova plugin add cordova-plugin-network-information
```

You have a couple of different ways you could handle this feature. You could constantly check and monitor network status, or you could simply check when the application starts. To keep things simple, you'll check when the application starts. This requires a few modifications. To add a new view to the application, you'll modify app.js to give it a new state, as shown in the following listing.

Listing 12.12   Snippet from app.js (final/www/js/app.js)

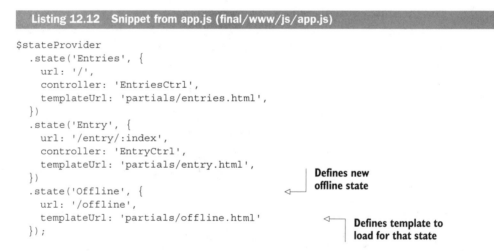

```
$stateProvider
  .state('Entries', {
    url: '/',
    controller: 'EntriesCtrl',
    templateUrl: 'partials/entries.html',
  })
  .state('Entry', {
    url: '/entry/:index',
    controller: 'EntryCtrl',
    templateUrl: 'partials/entry.html',
  })
  .state('Offline', {                         ⟵  Defines new
    url: '/offline',                               offline state
    templateUrl: 'partials/offline.html'      ⟵  Defines template to
  });                                             load for that state
```

In listing 12.12, you can see the new state defined, as well as what template to load when that state is active. Now let's look at how you check to see if the user is offline.

Listing 12.13 Snippet from `EntriesCtrl` (final/www/js/controllers.js)

```
.controller('EntriesCtrl', ['$ionicPlatform', '$location', '$scope',
➡ 'RSSService', 'settings',
function($ionicPlatform, $location, $scope, RSSService, settings) {

  $ionicPlatform.ready(function() {

    var network = navigator.connection.type;
    if(network == Connection.NONE) {
      $location.path('/offline');
    }
```

This snippet from the `EntriesCtrl` block shows all you need to do. You simply ask for the current connection value, see if it equals `Connection.NONE`, and if so, redirect the user to the offline state. The template for this view is pretty simple as you can see in the following listing.

Listing 12.14 Offline template (final/www/partials/offline.html)

```
<ion-view>
  <ion-nav-title>Offline</ion-nav-title>

  <ion-content class="padding">
    Unfortunately, you're offline. When you get
    back online, you can try again.
  </ion-content>

</ion-view>
```

12.5 Summary

Let's review the major topics covered in this chapter.

- The Ionic project provides a great way to build Cordova applications, with a built-in UI, UX, and even command-line enhancements.
- A simple RSS reader can be built using the Google Feeds API to help parse the XML.
- You can easily extend a simple application with a few plugins to add useful improvements.

Welcome to the end of *Apache Cordova in Action*. I hope you've enjoyed this book and have learned to appreciate the power and simplicity of building mobile apps with Cordova. I still remember the first time my "Hello World" application ran on my device and it has been a nonstop source of fun, challenge, and excitement since then. Now go outside in the sun—you'll thank me later.

index